The Well-Crafted Sentence

A Writer's Guide to Style

The Well-Crafted Sentence

A Writer's Guide to Style

Nora Bacon
University of Nebraska at Omaha

Bedford/St. Martin's
Boston ▪ New York

For Bedford / St. Martin's

Executive Editor: Leasa Burton
Developmental Editor: Michelle A. McSweeney
Senior Production Editor: Lori Chong Roncka
Production Associate: Sarah Ulicny
Marketing Manager: Molly Parke
Editorial Assistant: Sarah Guariglia
Production Assistants: Lidia MacDonald-Carr and David Ayers
Copyeditor: Steven Patterson
Indexer: Mary White
Text Design: Lisa Buckley
Cover Design: Sara Gates
Composition: Greg Johnson, Art Directions
Printing and Binding: Haddon Craftsmen, Inc., an RR Donnelley & Sons Company

President: Joan E. Feinberg
Editorial Director: Denise B. Wydra
Editor in Chief: Karen S. Henry
Director of Marketing: Karen R. Soeltz
Director of Editing, Design, and Production: Marcia Cohen
Assistant Director of Editing, Design, and Production: Elise S. Kaiser
Managing Editor: Elizabeth M. Schaaf

Library of Congress Catalog Card Number: 2008933112

Manufactured in the United States of America.

3   2   1   0   9   8
f   e   d   c   b   a

For information, write: Bedford / St. Martin's, 75 Arlington Street, Boston, MA 02116
(617-399-4000)

ISBN-10: 0–312–47155–6
ISBN-13: 978–0–312–47155–2

Acknowledgments

Preface for Instructors

The Well-Crafted Sentence is designed to help undergraduates develop facility in writing smooth, clear, fully developed sentences. It is not a grammar book: it does not focus on avoiding or correcting errors, and it makes no attempt to offer a thorough description of English syntax. Instead, it asks students to examine prose written by accomplished stylists, to note the relationship between syntactic structures and their rhetorical effect, and to practice using specific structures that all adult writers *can*, but only the best writers often *do*, take advantage of in their work. The book invites student writers to take sentences seriously, and it invites you to make room for sentences in your curriculum.

When I started teaching college writing courses in the late 1970s, we paid a great deal of attention to sentences. Some writing programs featured sentence-combining exercises designed to promote students' "syntactic maturity." Other programs were focused on sentence-level error; teachers learned to identify dozens of errors, and they were expected to mark every error in every paper, often using a system of numbers or symbols which students decoded by referring to charts in their handbooks.

By the mid-1980s, the pendulum had swung to the other extreme as writing teachers attended to larger units of discourse. The shift resulted from a new understanding of our mission. If our purpose is to teach the writing process, and if that is understood to be a process of discovering meaning through the activities of writing and revising, then class time is most appropriately spent on brainstorming and workshopping material generated by student writers. If our purpose is to help students find their voices in academic or public discourse communities, then we should spend our time together reading academic or public texts, discussing the issues they raise, analyzing the rhetorical strategies used, and planning written responses. None of these activities is theoretically inconsistent with work on sentences, but they have tended to displace it.

In addition, teachers devoted less time to sentences because research on the effects of grammar instruction was widely misunderstood. When the traditional approach to grammar instruction—parsing sentences, identifying errors, memorizing arcane usage rules—was demonstrated to have no positive effect on students' writing, some concluded that any attention to sentence structure was doomed to be fruitless. No researcher has made or would make such a claim. But the traditional approach to grammar was so ubiquitous and had such power over our imaginations that, as a profession, we were better prepared to abandon work on sentences than to imagine other approaches. The distinction between teaching students to dissect sentences and asking them to create or manipulate sentences fell from view, and pedagogies like sentence-combining lost currency. Many writing teachers made an effort to help their students write stronger sentences, but we tended to do that work privately, in tutorials rather than classrooms, and we seldom used our professional conferences and journals to share ideas about teaching sentence structure or style.

As the profession finds its footing in the new century, I see signs of a resurgence of interest in sentence structure and style. Robert Connors gave the pendulum a nudge in his 2000 article "The Erasure of the Sentence," published in *College Composition and Communication.* Connors chronicles the rise and fall of three sentence pedagogies (Francis Christensen's generative rhetoric, imitation exercises, and sentence-combining), noting the empirical research that documented their effectiveness. Additionally, several scholars interested in the intersection of composition and creative writing, notably Wendy Bishop, have encouraged teachers and students to approach sentences in an experimental, playful spirit. And the growth of our field, especially the development of major programs in writing studies, has cleared curricular space for sentence structure and style.

While writing *The Well-Crafted Sentence,* I have been guided by three pedagogical principles. The first is that writers can improve their style by studying the work of excellent stylists. A distinctive feature of *The Well-Crafted Sentence* is the use of model texts by accomplished writers—Louise Erdrich, Henry Louis Gates Jr., Tim O'Brien, Arundhati Roy, Oliver Sacks, David Sedaris, Jane Smiley, Andrew Sullivan, and Amy Tan. These are engaging texts, and many of the sentences are remarkably beautiful; the passages not only provide a store of authentic examples, but they enliven the chapters. In addition, they motivate student writers. I could simply assert that appositives, for example, are a useful addition to a writer's toolbox, but why should student writers believe me? Why should they care enough to spend their time practicing apposition? When they see what Louise Erdrich or Oliver Sacks can accomplish with appositives, and when they find that in exercises they can successfully imitate the prose of these writers, students are more likely to experiment with appositives in their own work.

Second, the textbook stresses the principle of rhetorical variation. The model texts have been selected to illustrate contemporary prose in a range of genres. If a discussion of sentences is to be truly rhetorical, it is not enough to examine sentences in context to see how they contribute to the overall effect of a paragraph or essay (though that's certainly a good start). Equally important is the imperative to examine sentences from multiple genres. Students need to see published writers making one sort of choice on one occasion and making a *different* choice on a different occasion. These observations sensitize students to the relationship between text and context and protect them against the impulse to seek simple, over-generalized rules for good writing. Although it is possible to understand the chapters and complete most of the exercises in *The Well-Crafted Sentence* without reading the model texts in full, I encourage you to assign them. They're good reading. And the more students know about a text, its writer, and the socio-political context in which it was written, the better prepared they will be to appreciate (or to criticize) the writer's choices.

The third principle is a commonplace of composition pedagogy: People learn to write by writing. After the opening paragraphs in each chapter explain and illustrate a stylistic principle, the exercises give students the chance to push words around on the page. Students are asked to analyze passages from the model texts, to practice particular structures in imitation and sentence-development exercises, to create and compare two versions of a passage. You'll probably want to use the exercises in several ways. Some are easy to do on the spot, so a class can go over them aloud; others are designed as individual writing tasks; those that ask students to evaluate the effects of different rhetorical choices are well suited for small-group discussion. What matters most is that, in the end, students turn from the exercises to their own texts, using their skills in crafting sentences to revise their own essays and stories, pushing their writing ever closer to truth, clarity, and beauty.

With its almost exclusive focus on sentences, *The Well-Crafted Sentence* is not intended to serve as the backbone of a composition course. It is, however, appropriate as a supplement to composition courses. After you've had a chance to read one or two papers from your students, after you have some sense of which syntactic structures they control easily, which they overlook, and which give them trouble, you can select chapters for classroom work or individual practice. The book is also appropriate for upper-division courses on style and/or editing offered through programs in creative writing or writing studies.

Acknowledgments

I am indebted to many people who have helped in the creation of this book. Its approach to sentence pedagogy has roots in the work of theorists and teachers including Francis Christensen, Patrick Hartwell, Joseph M. Williams, and especially William Robinson and Jo Keroes.

The first readers were students at the University of Nebraska at Omaha who enrolled in The Rhetoric of the Sentence in the spring of 2007. Many thanks to Sam Evans, Kim Schwab, Becky Christi, Kjetil Espelid, Evan Freemyer, Sangkyun Danny Kang, James Lee, Kendall Sigmon, Bob Vacanti, and Jeff Wellwood for thoughtful feedback on the first five chapters. I am grateful to Kim, Danny, and Bob for taking time out of their summers to test-drive exercises in the later chapters.

At Bedford/St. Martin's, I have had the pleasure of working with an extraordinary team of editors. Joan Feinberg offered crucial support at an early stage; Leasa Burton, who choreographed the project from beginning to end, was unfailingly helpful and encouraging; Sarah Guariglia provided essential assistance, particularly with the headnotes. Developmental editor Michelle McSweeney pushed every chapter from a rough to a final draft with a blend of critical rigor, tact, and patience that could serve as a model to any editor or writing teacher. My thanks to Lori Chong Roncka, Anna Palchik, Lisa Buckley, and Steven Patterson for effecting the transformation from a manuscript into a book.

I am grateful to the reviewers who offered suggestions in response to early drafts: Charlotte Brammer, Samford University; Marc. C. Conner, Washington & Lee University; Laurie Cubbison, Radford University; Joan Frederick, James Madison University; Susan M. Grant, University of Missouri–St. Louis; Paul Harris, Loyola Marymount University; Joseph C. Holobar, Penn State University; Katherine Kapitan, Buena

Vista University; Jennifer Lee, University of Pittsburgh; Mary Hurley Moran, University of Georgia; David A. Nentwick, Syracuse University; Jill Onega, University of Alabama–Huntsville; Howard Sage, Hunter College; Alf Seegert, University of Utah; Julie Clark Simon, Southern Utah University; Jo Beth Van Arkel, Drury University; and Venise Wagner, San Francisco State University.

Closer to home, I would like to thank my sister Nan Stone Allen and my colleague Anna Monardo for their contributions to the introduction; Kristi Bolstad for her help in tracking down "Shamengwa"; and Hollis Glaser, Mike Carroll, Stu Bernstein, and Mardelle Bacon for their encouragement. Special thanks to Dana Joiner for unconditional and unwavering support.

Nora Bacon

About the Author

NORA BACON is an associate professor of English and writing program administrator at the University of Nebraska at Omaha. She started her career in the late 1970s at San Francisco State University, whose writing program was then heavily influenced by the work of Francis Christensen. The program highlighted sentence structure, encouraging students to experiment with style by joining and developing their sentences.

Nora went on to teach at Stanford University, where she helped to launch a service-learning program called Community Service Writing. As she worked with students writing in multiple settings—English classes, classes in other disciplines, and community organizations—she was intrigued by the variation in the texts they created and by the learning strategies they used to make successful adaptations. Her research, begun at UC Berkeley in the 1990s, has examined service-learning pedagogy, the development of "writing agility," and the relationship between texts and the contexts in which they are written and read. Nora's current research focuses on the stylistic choices preferred in different disciplines, uniting her interest in variation and her abiding fascination with sentences.

Contents

8. Special Effects: Expectations and Exceptions 120

Model Texts for Writers 137

The Well-Crafted Sentence

A Writer's Guide to Style

Introduction

IF YOU'VE GROWN UP speaking English, or if you've been speaking it regularly for several years, then it's likely that you create hundreds of well-formed sentences every day. You open your mouth and words spill out: it doesn't require much effort for you to create sentences or for your listeners to understand them. Maybe the sentences aren't *perfect* — you might make a false start, or interrupt yourself, or mispronounce a word — but they're clear enough, they're easy, and chances are that nobody criticizes your style.

There are, I'm told, people who enjoy a similar fluency when they write. It's said that Shakespeare never blotted a line. But for most of us, writing is far more difficult than speaking: we take on more complicated intellectual tasks (longer stretches of language, more challenging concepts, ideas with more complex relationships), and, aware of the permanence of written texts, we aspire to higher standards of accuracy and eloquence. When we write, we don't have the opportunity to watch our listeners and make repairs if they seem puzzled or resistant; instead, we have to anticipate the reactions of readers who may be complete strangers.

Writing, then, rarely involves the spontaneous production of language; instead, we write and rewrite, revise and edit, arranging and rearranging words. Because writing rests on the page, we have the opportunity to return to it, to tinker with it, to play with it and work on it, before we send it on to a reader. That's why it makes sense to speak of writing as a craft: writers begin with the raw material of language and shape it until it expresses something of ourselves — our experiences, observations, and feelings, our ideas and convictions. This book is designed to help you become more skillful at the craft of writing and editing sentences.

Making Choices About Structure and Style

"Structure" and "style" are related concepts. They have different connotations: we tend to think of "sentence structure" as a mechanical matter, something that can be explained by grammatical rules. By contrast, we associate "style" with creativity, originality, individuality. But, as any experienced writer will attest, style is not the consequence of untamed self-expression. It is, instead, the outcome of deliberate choice-making. To achieve an effective style, a writer needs enough knowledge of sentence structure to be aware of the range of options for expressing an idea, enough understanding of the rhetorical context to predict a sentence's impact on readers, and enough commitment to the idea itself to keep testing options until the sentence rings true.

As an example of the kind of choices I have in mind, I'll show you two successful writers at work, creating and choosing among various ways to arrange their words.

In the spring of 1994, novelist Anna Monardo sat down to write a story exploring the mindset of young people in the late 1960s and early 1970s. She began with this line:

> Natassia was born in Rome, while Mary and Ross were on a junior-year-abroad program.

As she worked on the story, she revised the opening:

> Natassia was conceived in Rome, while Mary and Ross were students in a junior-year-abroad program, when another couple, also students, dared them not to use birth control. "Do it with no birth control. We'll do it if you do it."

This is a significant revision. Monardo moves back nine months, from Natassia's birth to the more telling moment of her conception. As the sentence introduces Mary and Ross, it provides not only their names but a glimpse of their circumstances and their frame of mind at this turning point in their lives. And this opening is more pleasing to the ear. The prose has its own rhythm: if you read it aloud, you'll find that your voice rises and falls. Important information comes in short, dramatic clauses — "Natassia was conceived in Rome," "Do it with no birth control" — while less important information ("also students") is tucked into the middle of the sentence.

The story eventually grew into a novel, *Falling in Love with Natassia*. As the story took shape, Monardo realized that her opening sentence needed to direct readers' attention to Mary, to establish her as the main character. When the novel was published in 2006, the opening sentence appeared as follows:

> Mary and Ross were in Rome on a junior-year-abroad program when they had their baby, Natassia, who was conceived on a dare: "Do it with no birth control," another couple challenged. "We'll do it if you do it."

To signal the importance of the parents, Monardo made "Mary and Ross" the subject of the sentence. By contrast, the phrase "also students" has disappeared so that the other couple, who never reappear in the novel, have little presence as individuals. And Monardo reinforced the idea of a dare, adding the verb "challenged" and setting off the dare with a colon — strong punctuation to say "*here it comes*."

Monardo's choices were guided by her goals as a writer of fiction. A novel is a work of art, so Monardo crafted her opening sentences with an eye to the beauty of the language. And a novel tells a story driven by the actions and interactions of a set of characters, so Monardo very intentionally led readers toward a particular understanding of Mary and Ross.

Other writers, creating different kinds of texts in different circumstances, may respond to a different set of goals. The passage below was crafted by Nan Stone Allen, the director of sales at a large hotel in Dallas, Texas. Allen's most important writing task is an annual report to the hotel's owners describing her sales team's achievements and their plans for the coming year. In a recent report, she put one passage through three variations, beginning with this one:

> The construction of two new hotels in the area is an indication of the success of the hospitality industry in establishing Dallas as a destination city as well as an indication of the challenges to be expected in 2008 due to increased competition.

Allen disliked the sentence for stylistic reasons: it's wordy and repetitive. The sentence doesn't have any grammatical errors, but it's a chore to read because you have to trudge through all those nouns — construction, hotels, area, indication, success, hospitality, industry, blah, blah, blah. She decided to cut through the clutter, producing the sentences below:

> We have enjoyed a good year in 2007 due to Dallas's growing reputation as a destination city. However, we face increased competition in 2008 because of the construction of two new hotels.

That's better, isn't it? The changes illustrate some of the guidelines that editors typically recommend. The average sentence length is now 16 words rather than 44; both sentences begin with personal subjects and active verbs ("we have enjoyed," "we face"); and the passage is admirably cohesive because the sentences are similar in structure, each of them making a claim about the hotel's performance in a particular year and then providing a reason.

Nevertheless, Allen rejected this version for two reasons. The first had to do with the context, the passage's place in the overall document. "We have enjoyed a good year" seemed too general, the sort of sentence that should come at the beginning of a report, not in the middle. The second reason had to do with the rhetorical context of the report, the people who would read it and the effect it was designed to have on them. For the readers of this document, Allen has to maintain just the right tone. She has to be sure the hotel's owners have realistic expectations for next year's revenues, but she has to stay positive and upbeat. The sentence beginning "however" gives too much weight to the bad news. She finally settled on these sentences:

> In 2008, Dallas will see the construction of two new hotels, a mark of our growing reputation as a destination city. This development means that we will face a vibrant—but increasingly competitive—market.

The novelist and the hotel executive were producing different kinds of texts, and their choices were guided by different rhetorical goals. But they had this in common: To craft effective sentences, they had to create a range of options and then evaluate each one. When we say somebody is a good writer, we mean, in part, that he or she is prepared to create and evaluate options like these. A skillful writer has an extensive repertoire of options at his or her command — a large vocabulary of words and a large vocabulary of syntactic structures — and enough sensitivity to the rhetorical situation to make wise choices.

Developing Control over Structure and Style: The Road Ahead

Like other skills, skill in crafting sentences develops through *observation* (reading — especially reading with a writer's eye, attending to the choices that other writers have made), *practice,* and *feedback.* The chapters that follow give you opportunities to observe sentences closely and analytically and to practice crafting sentences of your own.

Chapter 1 provides a bare-bones refresher of grammatical terms and concepts that most people learn in the eighth grade and forget in the ninth. You will make use of these terms and concepts when you read subsequent chapters and any time you wish to carry on a reasonably precise conversation about sentences (with, say, an instructor, classmate, coworker, or editor). Note that all grammatical terms and concepts in the book are highlighted in boldface when they appear for the first time, and they are all included, with definitions, in the glossary at the back of the book. Chapter 2 is also foundational. It examines the heart of any sentence, the subject and verb, and recommends strategies for choosing subjects that will get a sentence off to a strong start.

Chapters 3 through 8 are lessons in sentence development. The lessons focus on specific structures that published writers use frequently but that undergraduate writers tend to overlook. The structures are illustrated in passages drawn from "model texts," essays and stories by distinguished contemporary writers. Along with the sample passages, you'll find commentary drawing your attention to the choices the writer has made and the effects of those choices.

The commentary is followed by exercises in which you will identify the structure of interest and then practice using it yourself. The exercises are intended not only to clarify a concept but, more important, to get you to practice using the structure so that it begins to feel perfectly natural to you. Borrowing a time-honored instructional technique that the ancient Romans called *imitatio,* I've written several exercises that ask you to rework a passage from one of the model texts. These exercises call for imitation and variation. If you retain the ideas of the model passage, you'll vary its structure; if you retain the structure, you'll create content of your own.

It's important that you work through the exercises with some care. Some exercises (especially those early in the book or early in a chapter) have correct answers, but most are open-ended, with a virtually unlimited range of possible responses. Please don't think of the exercises as tests: they're rehearsals, not performances. When you've finished an exercise, you can check your work by comparing your responses to those in the back of the book.

As you're studying each syntactic structure, make it a point to practice it when you write and revise your own prose. Ideally, you should read this book in the context of a writing class where you're always at work on at least one essay or story. Use a draft of your current paper to reinforce what you're learning about sentences, inserting the new structure into three or four sentences to see how it works. Finally, get as much feedback as you can. Show your writing to others to learn how your experiments with sentence structure affect them as they read.

Model Texts

Who are these distinguished contemporary writers whose sentences you will analyze and imitate? They are nine authors whose work is published in highly respected books, journals, and magazines. Louise Erdrich is a short-story writer, David Sedaris a humorist. Tim O'Brien writes fiction inspired by events in his own life, blurring the line between memory and imagination. Jane Smiley and Amy Tan are best known for their novels, though the selections you'll be working with are nonfiction: an essay in literary criticism by Smiley and two pieces that Tan characterizes as "musings." Andrew Sullivan is a journalist and editor, Arundhati Roy a novelist and political essayist. Henry Louis Gates Jr. and Oliver Sacks are scholars who describe developments in their academic fields for a general audience.

The model texts have been selected not just for their excellence but for their variety. A central theme of this book is that what makes a sentence effective depends on the rhetorical context. I can't stress this point enough: If anyone asks what makes a good sentence, the only honest answer is "It depends." Whether a word is right or wrong, whether an idea should be emphasized or subordinated, whether a sentence should be short or long, simple or complex — it all depends on the purpose of the text, the intended audience, and the sentences before and after. Writing involves a continual series of judgment calls, some so minor and easy that they feel automatic, others so important and difficult that a single paragraph can take hours to write. The model texts show how nine skillful writers tune their prose to particular occasions.

You can see that I admire these texts. Still, I hope you won't approach them with undue reverence. You may love a sample sentence and approve of the writer's choices, or you may not. In either case, it is worthwhile to articulate what the sentence does to you and to imagine how a different arrangement of words might change the impact. Please read with an experimental eye, thinking of how any given sentence might have developed in the hands of another writer — like you.

The Writing Process(es)

Just as conventions for good writing vary from one genre to another, so do the processes by which texts come into being. In some settings, writers typically work in teams, and in others they work alone. In some settings, writers work quickly, and in others their labor is slow. I often find myself sending one document off with hardly a second look while another sits on my desk in its ninth or tenth draft. So it's a mistake to speak of "the writing process" as if it were one thing. We move back and forth among a surprisingly complex set of activities — cooking up ideas, writing them down, revising the language, discovering new ideas, revising again — and no single path will make sense for all occasions.

Most of the time, as we write, our attention is fixed on what we want to say. We think about the *meaning* that we're pushing into existence, and the words arrange themselves accordingly. But then we pause to look back — to reread, to reflect, to revise — and that's when we see that no, it's not quite right: this sentence doesn't quite capture what I meant to say, or that one doesn't deserve so much space; this sentence contradicts itself, or that one is hopelessly tangled; this sentence could be misinterpreted and that one doesn't even sound like me.

At those points in the writing process, it is useful to be able to draw upon a rich store of linguistic resources. The principal goal of this book is to expand the repertoire of syntactic structures available to you when you write and revise. As you work through the following chapters, you will examine structures that most undergraduate writers understand but seldom use, and if you practice, you will make them your own.

1

The Sentence's Working Parts

AS A WRITING TEACHER, I occasionally find myself in conversation with people — students, neighbors, strangers at parties — who reveal peculiar beliefs about grammar. "I'm not a good writer," they tell me. "I don't know anything about grammar." Depending on when and where they went to school, they may once have been able to diagram a sentence or define "predicate nominative," but if they can't do it today, they despair of ever improving their writing. They believe that a thorough understanding of grammar is essential for writers.

By contrast, there are people who dismiss grammar altogether. Observing that every five-year-old can generate sentences without having learned a single grammatical term, they conclude that studying sentence structure is a waste of time. People develop language skills effortlessly just by being part of a human community; this intuitive knowledge, they believe, is all they need.

I'd like to suggest an alternative view of the relationship between writing and grammar. I'd prefer not to ask "Do writers need to know grammar?" and then answer "yes" or "no." Instead, we might ask "How much grammar do writers need to know?" and then answer "It depends."

Perhaps the most useful way to think about grammatical knowledge is to consider the many fields of human activity in which technical knowledge lies on a continuum, with different levels of activity corresponding to different levels of expertise. Take cooking as an example. If you fix your meals by zapping frozen dinners in the microwave, you don't need to know much about cookery. But if you want to improve as a cook, you'll need some technical knowledge: in order to follow recipes and talk to other cooks, you have to learn the difference between *broil* and *braise*. You will acquire the words for *chives* and *chervil* about the time you learn to identify them by taste, and that's how you'll know which one to put in the soup. Professional chefs typically have a very discriminating palate; a wide vocabulary of terms for ingredients, tools, and techniques; and even some understanding of the chemistry underlying food preparation. A cook's analytical knowledge informs his or her hands-on practice in the kitchen.

You can probably think of many other activities — playing basketball, drawing portraits, playing the piano — that people can participate in with varying levels of technical knowledge. Beginners can jump right in, and with practice, they will improve. As their proficiency develops, they acquire a vocabulary for talking about the activity, and they learn to observe other athletes, artists, or musicians with an appreciation of their technique.

How much grammar do you need to know? For everyday speech, your intuitive knowledge is adequate. For everyday writing at school and work, you need to know enough terminology to comprehend a handbook and to understand editing suggestions from your classmates, teachers, coworkers, or boss. To gain still more control over written language, you'll want to read the work of other writers with a discriminating eye; this requires the ability to look at sentences analytically, seeing what the parts are and how they fit together.

In this chapter, our mission is to break the English sentence into pieces and take a look at each piece, reviewing the terminology used to describe sentences.[1] When a grammatical term appears for the first time, it is printed in boldface and is followed by a definition, which appears again in the glossary (p. 272). If you need a refresher on the parts of speech — *noun, verb, adjective, adverb, preposition, conjunction, pronoun, determiner* — or any other grammatical terms or concepts used in this text, consult the glossary.

Since every sentence has at least one clause, we'll begin with the clause. Later in the chapter, we'll consider some of the options writers use to expand on clauses or join them together.

Clause Structure

Oliver Sacks's article, "The Case of the Colorblind Painter," opens by quoting a letter that Sacks, an eminent neurologist, received from a man who later became his patient and research subject. To protect the man's privacy, Sacks refers to him as "Mr. I." Mr. I. has an alarming story to tell:

> I am a rather successful artist just past 65 years of age. On January 2nd of this year I was driving my car and was hit by a small truck on the passenger side of my vehicle. When visiting the emergency room of a local hospital, I was told I had a concussion. While taking an eye examination, it was discovered that I was unable to distinguish letters or colors. The letters appeared to be Greek letters. My vision was such that everything appeared to me as viewing a black and white television screen. Within days, I could distinguish letters and my vision became that of an eagle—I can see a worm wriggling a block away. The sharpness of focus is incredible. BUT—I AM ABSOLUTELY COLOR BLIND. I have visited ophthalmologists who know nothing about this color-blind business. I have visited neurologists, to no avail. Under hypnosis I still can't distinguish colors. I have been involved in all kinds of tests. You name it. My brown dog is dark grey. Tomato juice is black. Color TV is a hodge-podge. . . .

This paragraph comes from a letter. Unlike the paragraphs that follow it — paragraphs by Oliver Sacks himself, carefully crafted for publication — these were probably written quite spontaneously. Still, I think they're fine sentences, admirably clear and direct, and I like the drama that Mr. I. achieves by using very short sentences at the end of the paragraph. Beginning with "I AM ABSOLUTELY COLOR BLIND," read the passage aloud. The prose starts and stops, starts and stops, starts and stops. You can almost hear the frustration in Mr. I.'s voice as he visits experts, one after another "to no avail," and as he finds that objects, one after another, look colorless and ugly.

Whatever you may think of their rhetorical effect, the short sentences are convenient as relatively uncomplicated examples of clause structure. A **clause** is a group of words containing a **subject** and a **predicate**. Here are Mr. I.'s simplest sentences, divided into subject and predicate:

SUBJECT	PREDICATE
You	name it
My brown dog	is dark grey
Tomato juice	is black
Color TV	is a hodge-podge

A subject is a **noun phrase** — that is, a noun (or pronoun) or a group of words headed by a noun. A predicate consists of a verb or a group of words headed by a verb. In each of the previous sentences, the subject names the actor or topic and the predicate says what the subject is or does.

The verb may be a single word or it may include an **auxiliary** such as *could* or *have*. An auxiliary precedes a main verb to establish the time, duration, or certainty of its action. In "I was driving my car," the verb is "was driving" — the auxiliary "was" and the main verb "driving."

In any clause, the verb will be one of three types: transitive, intransitive, or linking. If the verb takes an object, it's a **transitive verb**:

SUBJECT	TRANSITIVE VERB	OBJECT
You	name	it
I	could distinguish	letters
I	can see	a worm
I	have visited	ophthalmologists
I	have visited	neurologists

In all of the sentences above, the subject names the actor, the verb names the action, and the **object** is a noun phrase naming the person or thing that receives the action. What should you name? It. What could I distinguish? Letters. What can I see? A worm.

If the verb has no object, it's an **intransitive verb**:

SUBJECT	INTRANSITIVE VERB	
Mr. I.	smoked	constantly
He	talked	with animation

What did Mr. I. smoke? Probably cigarettes — but "cigarettes" doesn't appear in the sentence, so the verb has no object. In this sentence, the verb "smoked" is intransitive. What did he talk? The question doesn't even make sense; "talk" has no object in this sentence (it rarely does, except in special cases like "he talked nonsense"). So, again, the verb is intransitive.

Perhaps you're wondering why "constantly" is not an object. Notice the meaning: it does not say *what* Mr. I. smoked. Also, it can't be an object because "constantly" is not a noun phrase.

A third type of verb is called a **linking verb** because it links the subject to a word or phrase that appears after the verb, called the **complement**. Mr. I.'s letter provides many examples of linking verbs, particularly forms of "be" — *is, are, was, were,* and so on — by far the most common of linking verbs.

SUBJECT	LINKING VERB	COMPLEMENT
My brown dog	is	dark grey
Tomato juice	is	black
Color TV	is	a hodge-podge
My vision	became	that [the vision] of an eagle

In the first two sentences above, the verb links the subject to an adjective which describes the subject. In the last two, the subject is linked to a noun phrase.

One last point about subjects and predicates. The subject of a clause is, as I've said, a noun phrase — sometimes a single word (a noun or pronoun) and sometimes a cluster of words headed by a noun or pronoun. The predicate consists of a verb or a cluster of words headed by a verb. When we divide a clause into its subject and predicate, it's a simple matter of splitting the clause into parts:

My brown dog   is dark grey.

Often, it's useful to identify the **headword** in each part of the clause — the key noun in the noun phrase, the verb itself in the predicate.

My brown <u>dog</u>   <u>is</u> dark grey.

In this sentence, the headwords "dog is" constitute the **subject-verb pair**. The subject-verb pair is the beating heart of an English sentence; readers intuitively focus their attention on these words, expecting them to name the sentence's key actor and action. For a more detailed discussion of the stylistic importance of the subject-verb pair, see Chapter 2.

EXERCISE 1A

The following clauses are split into subject and predicate. The subject is a noun phrase: underline just the headword once. The predicate includes a

verb: underline it twice. When you identify verbs, include auxiliaries like
have, *should*, or *will*.

Examples

I̲ <u>can see</u> a worm wriggling a block away.

The <u>sharpness</u> of focus <u>is</u> incredible.

1. Oliver Sacks — is a neurologist.
2. Sacks — studies patients with unusual neurological disorders.
3. He — sometimes publishes his case studies in *The New Yorker*.
4. His description of Mr. I. — also appears in the book *An Anthropologist on Mars*.
5. Mr. I.'s world — changed profoundly.
6. As an artist, he — could speak of his colorblindness with special insight.
7. Sacks — conveys Mr. I.'s dismay at the loss of color vision.
8. As a clinician, Sacks — has developed empathy for his patients.
9. His compassion — enriches his work as a doctor and as a writer.
10. Sacks's readers — glimpse the complexity of the human mind.

EXERCISE 1B

Examine the verbs you've underlined in Exercise 1A. Identify each of them as a transitive, intransitive, or linking verb. For transitive verbs, circle the object.

Examples

I can see (a worm) wriggling a block away.

transitive

The sharpness of focus <u>is</u> incredible.

linking

Transformations Within the Clause

While all verbs can be described as transitive, intransitive, or linking, the sentence patterns are not always so easy to recognize. Speakers and writers often use sentences in which the core elements have been rearranged. Beginning with the sentence "He drove his car through two red lights," we could generate variations such as these:

NEGATION	He didn't drive his car through two red lights.
QUESTION	Did he drive his car through two red lights?
PASSIVE VOICE	His car was driven through two red lights.
"IT" IN SUBJECT POSITION	It was he who drove his car through two red lights.

These transformations change the meaning of the sentence in significant ways. The structural changes are significant, too; for example, the subject of the passive voice sentence is no longer "he" but rather "his car." Nevertheless, beyond observing that these transformations are possible, we will take little notice of them because every English-speaking adult creates sentences like these with no trouble.

Extending the Clause

We've been focusing on the last part of Mr. I.'s letter, where the series of very short sentences communicates his frustration with having lost his color vision. A series of very short sentences is unusual: when we read such a passage, it gets our attention. But, fortunately, most of us aren't in the business of communicating frustration, nor do we have any other compelling reason to use such short sentences. Instead, we seek variety in sentence lengths, mixing long and short sentences so that the prose moves smoothly.

Just listen to how choppy Mr. I.'s letter would sound if he had used short sentences from beginning to end, limiting each sentence to a single clause:

I am a rather successful artist just past 65 years of age. On January 2nd of this year I was driving my car. I was hit by a small truck on the passenger side of my vehicle. I visited the emergency room of a local hospital. I had a concussion. I took an eye examination. I was unable to distinguish letters or colors. The letters appeared to be Greek letters. My vision was damaged. Everything appeared to me as viewing a black and white television screen. Within days, I could distinguish letters. My vision became that of an eagle. I can see a worm wriggling a block away. The sharpness of focus is incredible. BUT—I AM ABSOLUTELY COLOR BLIND. I have visited ophthalmologists. They know nothing about this color-blind business. I have visited

> neurologists, to no avail. Under hypnosis I still can't distinguish colors.
> I have been involved in all kinds of tests. You name it. My brown dog is
> dark grey. Tomato juice is black. Color TV is a hodge-podge. . . .

It sounds like the work of a child, doesn't it? The point is that very short
sentences are a special effect and, if they're to have the desired effect,
they have to be used sparingly.

When Mr. I. wrote his letter, he began with longer, more complicated — and more typical — sentences. As a general rule, an English
sentence will have at least one **independent clause**, one clause that can
stand alone to constitute a complete sentence. A wide range of structures may be added to that base.

Each of the sample sentences shown on pages 11–13 is composed
of a single independent clause. You can identify them as clauses because
they have a subject and predicate; you can identify them as independent because, when you read them aloud, they sound complete.

The next sections review three ways that independent clauses can be
extended. First, one independent clause can be joined to another. Second,
a clause can be extended by means of words or phrases used as modifiers.
Third, dependent clauses — structures that contain a subject and predicate but can't stand alone — can be added to the independent clause.

Joining Independent Clauses

When two independent clauses are closely related in meaning, it makes
sense to join them with a conjunction such as *and* or *but*. Each of the
sentences below contains two independent clauses describing the difficulties Mr. I. faced after losing his color vision:

> His wife had to pick out his clothes, **and** this dependency he found
> hard to bear.

> He had always loved flowers, **but** now he could only distinguish them
> by shape or smell.

English has seven **coordinating conjunctions**: *and, or, nor, but, for,
yet, so*. When two independent clauses are joined with a coordinating conjunction, they have roughly equal emphasis. A more detailed
discussion of coordination appears in Chapter 3.

Like many published writers, Oliver Sacks frequently links independent clauses without the conjunction. Instead, he does the job with
punctuation — specifically, with the semicolon, colon, or dash.

If two independent clauses are coordinate to each other — that is, if they are about equal in importance, and they function the same way in the overall passage — a semicolon is a good choice.

He constantly smoked as he talked; his fingers, restless, were stained with nicotine.

These first weeks were a time of agitation, even desperation; he was constantly hoping that he would wake up one fine morning and find the world of color miraculously restored.

If the first sentence sets the stage for the second, a colon works well.

Locke, in the seventeenth century, had held to a "sensationalist" philosophy (which paralleled Newton's physicalist one): our senses are measuring instruments, recording the external world for us in terms of sensation.

For Helmholtz, as for Young, color was a direct expression of the wavelengths of light absorbed by each receptor, the nervous system just translating one into the other: "Red light stimulates the red-sensitive fibres strongly, and the other two weakly, giving the sensation red."

In the first sentence above, the independent clause sets the stage by making a promise: you know that you'll be finding out how Locke's philosophy was "sensationalist." The second sentence illustrates a very common use of the colon: the independent clause sets up a quotation.

A dash can also appear between independent clauses, as in this sentence from Mr. I.'s letter:

Within days, I could distinguish letters and my vision became that of an eagle—I can see a worm wriggling a block away.

The dash suggests spontaneity, and it's usually used to set off brief phrases inserted into sentences or added to the end. The punctuation illustrated above, with the dash appearing between independent clauses, is most likely to be found in fiction and in informal genres like letters, but you'll see it in business and academic writing, too.

In short, the options for joining independent clauses are these:

- Coordinating conjunction (preceded by a comma)
- Semicolon, colon, or dash

EDITOR'S NOTE: Notice that a comma alone is not among the options for linking independent clauses. Published writers do sometimes use a comma in this way, but the choice is infrequent and appears only when both sentences are short. Pasting two independent clauses together with a comma is usually viewed as an error — a "comma splice" — and it's one worth watching for as you edit because it is highly stigmatized.

Modifiers

A **modifier** is a word, phrase, or clause that elaborates upon some other element in the sentence, describing it, limiting it, or providing extra information. For example, in "My brown dog is dark grey," "brown" modifies "dog" and "dark" modifies "grey."

When a modifier is longer and more complex, it becomes more interesting from a stylistic point of view: writers can make choices about where to place a modifier, and we manipulate emphasis by deciding whether an idea should be presented in a modifier or allowed to occupy a sentence of its own. Chapters 4 through 7 discuss various kinds of clauses and phrases used as modifiers.

The most common modifier is the prepositional phrase. You won't find a chapter on prepositional phrases because you don't need one: virtually all writers use prepositional phrases effortlessly from an early age. However, we should take a moment to observe their structure.

We first saw him in April 1986.

He was a tall, gaunt man, with a sharp, intelligent face.

A **prepositional phrase** is made up of a preposition and a noun phrase. The noun phrase is called the object of the preposition. For example, "in" is a preposition with "April 1986" as its object, and "with" is a preposition with "a sharp, intelligent face" as its object.

Prepositional phrases can modify verbs or nouns. "In April 1986" modifies the verb "saw," telling when Sacks and his colleague first *saw* Mr. I. "With a sharp, intelligent face" modifies the noun "man."

Dependent Clauses

Examine these clauses:

He talked.   As he talked.

| He knew it to be a bright | Even though he knew it to be a bright |
| and sunny morning. | and sunny morning. |

Your ear will immediately tell you that the clauses on the right are not complete sentences. They sound unfinished, as if they are waiting to be attached to something else. While the clauses on the left are independent, those on the right are dependent. A **dependent clause** (also called a **subordinate clause**) is a group of words that contains a subject-verb pair but that cannot stand alone as a complete sentence.

EDITOR'S NOTE: If you write a phrase or a dependent clause and leave it standing alone, you've created a fragment. Fragments are common in advertising, and some fiction writers like to use them as well. In formal writing such as academic essays, fragments are usually regarded as errors, so don't leave a dependent clause standing alone in a formal paper unless you have a truly compelling reason to do so — unless it sounds so *right* that your reader will respond with "ahh" rather than "oops." Fragments are discussed in more detail in Chapter 8.

Dependent clauses come in three varieties: adverb clauses, adjective clauses, and noun clauses.

Adverb Clauses

Adverb clauses are introduced by subordinating conjunctions like the "as" in "as he talked" and "even though" in "even though he knew it to be a bright and sunny morning." English has dozens of these **subordinating conjunctions** (sometimes called **subordinators**). Here's a partial list:

as	if	provided that	just as
because	as if	in order that	inasmuch as
since	as though	now that	while
unless	in case	so that	whereas
though	before	as soon as	where
although	after	as long as	whenever
even though	until	when	wherever

An **adverb clause** can be recognized by the presence of a subject-verb pair (this makes it a clause) and by the subordinating conjunction at the beginning. Adverb clauses do the characteristic work of an adverb, telling when, where, why, or how some action takes place.

Subordination with adverb clauses permits a writer to manipulate emphasis. For example, compare these sentences:

> Even though I want a piece of cherry pie, I'm committed to my diet.
>
> Even though I'm committed to my diet, I want a piece of cherry pie.

You can tell that the writer of the first sentence will stick to that diet, while the writer of the second is already reaching for a fork. The sentences read differently because in both cases we see the independent clause — "I'm committed to my diet" in the first, "I want a piece of cherry pie" in the second — as having more weight. Information tucked into the adverb clause is de-emphasized.

Adverb clauses can be appended before or after an independent clause, or they can be embedded in the middle:

> As soon as he entered, he found his entire studio now utterly grey and void of color.
>
> Fixed and ritualistic practices and positions had to be adopted at the table; otherwise he might mistake the mustard for the mayonnaise, or, if he could bring himself to use the blackish stuff, ketchup for jam.
>
> Although his brown dog would stand out sharply in silhouette against a light road, it might get lost to sight when it moved into soft, dappled undergrowth.
>
> He felt his perception of black-and-white images to be relatively normal, whereas something bizarre and intolerable occurred whenever he looked at colored images.

EXERCISE 1C

An adverb clause can be recognized by the presence of a subject and verb and by the subordinator at the beginning. Mark each of the following adverb clauses to highlight the defining elements. First, identify the subject-verb pair: in the noun phrase that serves as subject, underline just the headword (the key noun) once, and underline the verb (including any auxiliaries) twice. Then, draw a circle around the subordinator.

Example

(As soon as) he entered

1. if he could bring himself to use the blackish stuff

2. although his brown dog would stand out sharply in silhouette against a light road

3. when it moved into soft, dappled undergrowth
4. whereas something bizarre and intolerable occurred
5. whenever he looked at colored images

Adjective Clauses

Adjective clauses are discussed at length in Chapter 5. For now, it is enough to say that an **adjective clause** (also called a **relative clause**) is a dependent clause used to modify a noun. Most adjective clauses are introduced by these words:

who	which	when
whom	that	where
whose		

I have visited ophthalmologists who know nothing about this color-blind business.

As soon as he entered, he found his entire studio, which was hung with brilliantly colored paintings, now utterly grey and void of color.

It was not "grey" that he experienced, he said, but perceptual

qualities for which ordinary experience, ordinary language, had no equivalent.

These sentences illustrate the usual placement of adjective clauses, immediately following the noun they modify.

Noun Clauses

Noun clauses are dependent clauses that perform the function of nouns. Unlike adverb and adjective clauses, noun clauses are not modifiers. Instead, they perform an essential grammatical function within an independent clause, serving as a subject or an object. In these sentences, the noun clauses are objects:

We learned that his accident had been accompanied by a transient amnesia.

These first weeks were a time of agitation, even desperation; he was constantly hoping <u>that he would wake up one fine morning and find the world of color miraculously restored</u>.

He would dream <u>that he was *about* to see in color</u>, but then he would wake and find <u>that nothing had changed</u>.

What did we learn? "That his accident had been accompanied by a transient amnesia." What was he hoping? "That he would wake up one fine morning and find the world of color miraculously restored."

Noun clauses can also serve as subjects, as in this sentence:

<u>What he did see</u> had a distasteful, "dirty" look, the whites glaring, yet discolored and off-white, the blacks cavernous—everything wrong, unnatural, stained, and impure.

EXERCISE 1D

The sentences below are copied or adapted from "Housecalls," a chapter in Oliver Sacks's memoir in which he recalls his boyhood impressions of his father. The sentences have been broken up into clauses. First, identify the subject-verb pair: in the noun phrase that serves as the subject, underline just the headword (the key noun) once, and underline the verb (including any auxiliaries) twice. Then, identify each clause as independent or dependent. Finally, identify each dependent clause more specifically as an adverb clause, an adjective clause, or a noun clause.

Example

If there were no housecalls to do in the evening, my father would settle down after dinner with a torpedo-shaped cigar. He would palpate it gently, then hold it to his nose to test its aroma and freshness, and if it was satisfactory he would make a V-shaped incision in its tip with his cutter.

If <u>there</u> <u>were</u> no housecalls to do in the evening,

dependent (adverb) clause

my <u>father</u> <u>would settle down</u> after dinner with a torpedo-shaped cigar.

independent clause

He <u>would palpate</u> it gently, then <u>hold</u> it to his nose to test its aroma and freshness,

independent clause

and . . . he would make a V-shaped incision in its tip with his cutter.

independent clause

if it was satisfactory

dependent (adverb) clause

I sometimes went along with my father on housecalls on Sunday mornings. He loved doing housecalls more than anything else, for they were social and sociable as well as medical.

1. I sometimes went along with my father on housecalls on Sunday mornings.
2. He loved doing housecalls more than anything else,
3. for they were social and sociable as well as medical.

He would have a typed list of a dozen patients and their addresses, and I would sit next to him in the front seat of the car while he told me, in very human terms, what each patient had. When he arrived, I would get out with him, allowed, usually, to carry his medical bag.

4. He would have a typed list of a dozen patients and their addresses,
5. and I would sit next to him in the front seat of the car
6. while he told me, in very human terms,
7. what each patient had.
8. When he arrived,
9. I would get out with him, allowed, usually, to carry his medical bag.

He also had a motorcycle, a Scott Flying Squirrel, with a two-stroke, 600 cc, watercooled engine, and a high-pitched exhaust like a scream. He loved to take off on this if he had a free Sunday morning. Sometimes I had dreams in which I was riding or flying the bike myself, and I determined to get one when I was grown up.

10. He also had a motorcycle, a Scott Flying Squirrel, with a two-stroke, 600 cc, watercooled engine, and a high-pitched exhaust like a scream.
11. He loved to take off on this
12. if he had a free Sunday morning.
13. Sometimes I had dreams
14. in which I was riding or flying the bike myself,
15. and I determined to get one
16. when I was grown up.

CHAPTER 1 NOTE

[1]Analyzing sentences would be simpler if everybody used the same terminology. In fact, however, analysts with different objectives use different sets of terms. The most thorough and precise terminology is used by linguists, who sometimes explain their project as an effort to spell out the thousands of rules that a native speaker knows intuitively. Why do you say *the big blue truck* rather than *the blue big truck?* You have the intuitive knowledge to place *big* before *blue* when you speak or write, but you probably can't articulate the rule you're following. A linguist can. To do the work of linguistic science, linguists have developed an extensive technical vocabulary.

Writers and editors need to talk about sentences in clear and consistent ways, but we don't need to account for every conceivable grammatical expression. We rely on a simpler vocabulary with broader categories. For writers and editors, the most important reference book is a good handbook — the sort of volume you consult with questions about grammatical correctness (Is this a fragment? Is that a dangling modifier?), about usage (*affect* or *effect? less* or *fewer?*), and about mechanics (colon or semicolon? italics or underlining?). With any luck, the terms you'll encounter throughout this book will match those in your handbook.

2

Well-Focused Sentences

The Subject-Verb Pair

WHEN LINGUISTS DESCRIBE languages, they categorize them according to the typical order of a sentence's key components. English is said to be an SVO language. The core of an English clause is made up of a Subject, Verb, and Object, most often in that order: *Cats eat mice; Matthew caught the ball; Elizabeth assumed the throne; Calculus teachers assign problem sets; I love you.*

We pick up the SVO pattern at an early age. When babies are learning to speak, they begin with one-word utterances — "ball," "Mama," "peekaboo," "hot," — but soon graduate to two-word and three-word strings. By the age of two, toddlers demonstrate an understanding of the SVO order: with remarkable consistency, they say "baby eat," "eat cereal," or "baby eat cereal," never mixing up the word order (never, for example, saying "cereal baby eat"). In English-speaking communities, we hear and produce hundreds of SVO sentences every day.

For writers, the SVO order has particular significance because it represents the norm. Without really thinking about it, readers develop an expectation that, as they approach a new sentence, they'll encounter first the subject, then the verb, and then an object. Of course, many English sentences are more complex than *Cats eat mice*, many are cast in other patterns (with, for example, an intransitive or linking verb — see pp. 12–13), and some use alternative word order. Still, the SVO norm has a great deal of power in shaping readers' expectations and in determining how easily they process sentences.

In this chapter, I want to make a case for choosing subjects carefully, taking full advantage of the subject position. Because readers intuitively expect the first noun phrase in a clause to be the subject, they pay attention to that noun phrase. A wise writer will direct the reader's attention to the key player, using the subject position to name the person or thing that the clause is really *about*. A sentence is well focused when the most important actor and action appear as the subject and verb.

Populated Prose

We'll begin with some examples of well-focused sentences from Tim O'Brien's book *The Things They Carried*. In a chapter titled "On the Rainy River" (reprinted on p. 171), the narrator describes a turning point in his life. In 1968, just out of college, he had to decide whether to comply with the military draft, virtually ensuring a tour in Vietnam, or flee to Canada. He spent a few days at a fishing lodge near the Canadian border, where his moral crisis was witnessed by the lodge's owner, Elroy Berdahl.

Note the subject of each clause:

For ten or fifteen minutes Elroy held a course upstream, the river choppy and silver-gray, then he turned straight north and put the engine on full throttle. I felt the bow lift beneath me. I remember the wind in my ears, the sound of the old outboard Evinrude. For a time I didn't pay attention to anything, just feeling the cold spray against my face, but then it occurred to me that at some point we must've passed into Canadian waters, across that dotted line between two different worlds, and I remember a sudden tightness in my chest as I looked up and watched the far shore come at me. This wasn't a daydream. It was tangible and real. As we came in toward land, Elroy cut the engine, letting the boat fishtail lightly about twenty yards off shore. The old man didn't look at me or speak. Bending down, he opened up his tackle box and busied himself with a bobber and a piece of wire leader, humming to himself, his eyes down.

This paragraph is about two men. If you do a quick count, you'll find that twelve of the fifteen clauses have **human subjects**, nouns or pronouns referring to people. The narrator (*I*) appears as the subject of five clauses, Elroy Berdahl is the subject of five more, and *we*, referring to the pair of them, is the subject of two. By consistently placing the narrator and Elroy Berdahl in the subject position, O'Brien ensures that even as we're visualizing a fishing boat or a shoreline, the human beings have a presence. The consistent focus unifies the paragraph as a whole.

The same consistent focus appears in this passage where, in a striking move, O'Brien has the narrator address the reader directly:

Twenty yards. I could've done it. I could've jumped and started swimming for my life. Inside me, in my chest, I felt a terrible squeezing pressure. Even now, as I write this, I can still feel that tightness. And I want you to feel it—the wind coming off the river, the waves, the silence, the wooded frontier. You're at the bow of a boat on the Rainy River. You're twenty-one years old, you're scared, and there's a hard squeezing pressure in your chest.

Again, the subjects capture the essential relationship, the interaction between the narrator and the reader: until the final clause, every subject is *I* or *you*.

What would happen if the prose weren't so tightly focused? In the passage below, I've tried to retain as much of O'Brien's meaning as possible without using so many human subjects.

Twenty yards. It was do-able. It would have been possible to jump and start swimming for my life. Inside me, in my chest, there was a terrible squeezing pressure. Even now, as these words are being written, there is still that feeling of tightness. And it is important to me to share this feeling with you—the wind coming off the river, the waves, the silence, the wooded frontier. Imagine yourself at the bow of a boat on the Rainy River, twenty-one years old, scared, and there's a hard squeezing pressure in your chest.

To my ear, the altered passage is less effective — less cohesive, less vivid, with a slower pace. Words like *it* and *there* are just about meaning-free; as subjects, they have little power to focus a reader's attention or to steer a sentence in a clear direction. It's easy to understand O'Brien's preference for human subjects.

| EXERCISE 2A |

In the passages below, I've altered sentences from "On the Rainy River" by removing words referring to people from the subject position. Repopulate these passages to improve their focus. Ask who the passage is really about—who is doing something in the sentences—and whenever possible, use a noun or pronoun referring to that person as the subject.

Example
In the mornings it was sometimes our routine to go on long hikes into the woods, and at night there were usually Scrabble games or record-playing or reading in front of his big stone fireplace.

Restored to Original
In the mornings we sometimes went out on long hikes into the woods, and at night we played Scrabble or listened to records or sat reading in front of his big stone fireplace.

1. Even after two decades it is possible for me to close my eyes and return to that porch at the Tip Top Lodge. There is an image in my mind of the old guy staring at me. Elroy Berdahl: eighty-one years old, skinny and shrunken and mostly bald. His outfit was a flannel shirt and brown work pants. In one hand, if memory serves, was a green apple, a small paring knife in the other.

2. His fishing continued. His line was worked with the tips of his fingers, patiently, his eyes squinting out at his red and white bobber on the Rainy River. His eyes were flat and impassive. There was no speech. There was simply his presence, like the river and the late-summer sun.

Sentences with human subjects stand a good chance of having strong verbs. Compare, for example, the two versions of the example sentence in Exercise 2A:

In the mornings it was sometimes our routine to go on long hikes into the woods, and at night there were usually Scrabble games or record-playing or reading in front of his big stone fireplace.

In the mornings we sometimes went out on long hikes into the woods, and at night we played Scrabble or listened to records or sat reading in front of his big stone fireplace.

In the first sentence, the verbs are forms of *be*, the most colorless verb in our language. In the second sentence, the verbs are varied, and they name actions. This is a typical pattern in English prose: the writer who chooses a human subject has a wide range of verbs to choose from, and his or her sentences have life and energy. You can see the contrast again in the passages in which the narrator contemplates a swim to the Canadian shore:

> Twenty yards. It <u>was</u> do-able. It <u>would have been</u> possible to jump and start swimming for my life. Inside me, in my chest, <u>there</u> <u>was</u> a terrible squeezing pressure. Even now, as these <u>words</u> <u>are being written</u>, <u>there</u> <u>is</u> still that feeling of tightness. And <u>it</u> <u>is</u> important to me to share this feeling with you—the wind coming off the river, the waves, the silence, the wooded frontier.

> Twenty yards. I <u>could've done</u> it. I <u>could've jumped</u> and <u>started</u> swimming for my life. Inside me, in my chest, <u>I</u> <u>felt</u> a terrible squeezing pressure. Even now, as <u>I</u> <u>write</u> this, <u>I</u> <u>can</u> still <u>feel</u> that tightness. And <u>I</u> <u>want</u> you to feel it—the wind coming off the river, the waves, the silence, the wooded frontier.

In the first version, five of the six verbs are forms of *be* (and the sixth, *are being written*, is in the passive voice, a topic discussed below). A subject like *it* or *there* can't be paired with very interesting verbs — *there* isn't capable of doing much. By contrast, people can do many things, so human subjects license a wide variety of verbs.

EXERCISE 2B

Observe the stylistic effects of choosing human subjects.

1. Return to Exercise 2A, underlining the subject-verb pairs in each passage before and after your revisions. When you shifted to human subjects, did your verbs shift as well? Do the revised passages rely less heavily on forms of *be*?

2. It often happens that the choice of a human subject makes a sentence more concise. Examine the passages in Exercise 2A, counting the words before and after revision. When you revised, were you able to capture the meaning in fewer words?

3. A paragraph containing well-focused sentences often gains cohesion from the repeated appearance of a key person in the subject position. Examine the passages from Exercise 2A as Tim O'Brien wrote them (see "On the Rainy River," p. 171, paras. 19 and 75). How many different words has O'Brien used in the subject position?

It's simple enough to populate the prose if you're writing about a person or group of people sharing an experience, but what happens when you're operating in the realm of ideas?

The paragraph below comes from "Say It Ain't So, Huck," Jane Smiley's 1996 article comparing *The Adventures of Huckleberry Finn* to *Uncle Tom's Cabin* (reprinted on p. 237). The paragraph illustrates a common pattern in academic writing: the main point — which is an idea, requiring abstract language — is spelled out at the beginning, and the writer continues by illustrating the point with specific examples. In the first few sentences, the writer uses (mostly) abstract nouns and relies heavily on *be* as the verb; in the examples, she uses (mostly) human or concrete nouns and verbs other than *be*.

> The power of *Uncle Tom's Cabin* is the power of brilliant analysis married to great wisdom of feeling. Stowe never forgets the logical end of any relationship in which one person is the subject and the other is the object. No matter how the two people feel, or what their intentions are, the logic of the relationship is inherently tragic and traps both parties until the false subject/object relationship is ended. Stowe's most oft-repeated and potent representation of this inexorable logic is the forcible separation of family members, especially of mothers from children. Eliza, faced with the sale of her child, Harry, escapes across the breaking ice of the Ohio River. Lucy, whose ten-month-old is sold behind her back, kills herself. Prue, who has been used for breeding, must listen to her last child cry itself to death because her mistress won't let her save it; she falls into alcoholism and thievery and is finally whipped to death. Cassy, prefiguring a choice made by one of the characters in Toni Morrison's *Beloved*, kills her last child so that it won't grow up in slavery. All of these women have been promised something by their owners — love, education, the privilege and joy of raising their children — but, owing to slavery, all of these promises have been broken. . . .

If we isolate the subject-verb pairs in the opening sentences, where Smiley is explaining her point, we can easily see the reliance on abstract nouns and *be*:

power is

Stowe forgets

person is

other (person) is

people <u>feel</u>
intentions <u>are</u>
logic <u>is</u> . . . <u>traps</u>
relationship <u>is ended</u>
representation <u>is</u>

Five of the subjects (*power, intentions, logic, relationship, representation*) are abstractions, and six of the verbs are *is* or *are*. By contrast, note the subject-verb pairs in Smiley's examples:

<u>Eliza</u> <u>escapes</u>
<u>Lucy</u> <u>kills</u>
<u>ten-month-old</u> <u>is sold</u>
<u>Prue</u> <u>must listen</u>
<u>who</u> <u>has been used</u>
<u>mistress</u> <u>won't let</u>
<u>she falls</u> . . . <u>is whipped</u>
<u>Cassy</u> <u>kills</u>
<u>it</u> <u>won't grow up</u>
<u>women</u> <u>have been promised</u>
<u>promises</u> <u>have been broken</u>

In these sentences, all of the clauses except the last have human subjects, and none has *be* as its main verb.[1]

The passage below illustrates the same movement from stating an abstract point to supporting it with specific examples.

<u>Stowe</u> also <u>understands</u> that the real <u>root</u> of slavery <u>is</u> that <u>it</u> <u>is</u> profitable as well as customary. <u>Augustine</u> and his <u>brother</u> <u>live</u> with slavery because <u>it</u> <u>is</u> the system <u>they</u> <u>know</u> and because <u>they</u> <u>have</u>n't the imagination to live without it. <u>Simon Legree</u> <u>embraces</u> slavery because <u>he</u> <u>can make</u> money from it and because <u>it</u> <u>gives</u> him even more absolute power over his workers than <u>he</u> <u>could find</u> in the North or in England.

The first sentence explains Stowe's understanding about slavery. The sentence contains two clauses with abstract words as subjects (*root* and *it*, referring to slavery itself) and *is* as the verb. The subsequent sentences describe specific characters in the novel to show how Smiley has inferred Stowe's insight. Of the eight clauses in these sentences, six have human subjects:

Augustine . . . brother live
they know
they haven't
Simon Legree embraces
he can make
he could find

Harriet Beecher Stowe made the case against slavery come alive for a generation of readers by creating characters that touched their hearts. Her "brilliant analysis" of the institution reaches readers in the shape of men and women whose names we still recognize — Uncle Tom, Little Eva, Simon Legree — awakening our natural interest in human beings engaged in significant action. When Jane Smiley structures her paragraph by moving from analysis to specific examples, from "power is" to "Eliza escapes," she capitalizes on that same interest in human activity.

EXERCISE 2C

Choose one of the following as an opening sentence and write a short paragraph that develops the statement with specific examples. The opening sentence has an abstract subject. Use human subjects in most or all of the subsequent clauses.

1. The legacy of slavery still haunts America.
2. The local economy has experienced some unexpected reversals.
3. Communication is the key to employer-employee relationships.
4. Religious differences can cause friction in family life.

When the topic under discussion does not include any humans, the best subjects are concrete nouns — nouns naming something tangible, something a reader can visualize. Compare these sentences:

In the last thirty years, there has been a decline in the quality of produce in freshness and flavor.

In the last thirty years, a decline in the quality of produce in freshness and flavor has occurred.

In the last thirty years, produce has declined in freshness and flavor.

Of the three sentences, the third is the leanest and strongest. Vegetables will never have much dramatic power, but a concrete subject is a step in the right direction, focusing the reader's attention on what the sentence is about.

Active Voice and Passive Voice

The distinction between active voice and passive voice is useful to know, especially if your writing handbook is one of the many that advises writers to prefer the active to the passive voice. I'd like to take a minute to explain these terms, and then I'll echo the conventional advice, with the caveat that the preference for the active voice is stronger on some occasions than others.

In an **active-voice** construction, the subject names the actor, performing the action described by the verb. In a **passive-voice** construction, the subject does not name the actor; instead, it names the person or thing that receives the action of the verb, the person or thing being acted upon. Compare the sentences below:

ACTIVE VOICE	PASSIVE VOICE
Jane Smiley admires *Uncle Tom's Cabin*.	*Uncle Tom's Cabin* is admired by Jane Smiley.
Stowe exposed the abuses of slavery to a wide audience.	The abuses of slavery were exposed to a wide audience by Stowe.
Early in the twentieth century, critics elevated *The Adventures of Huckleberry Finn* to the pantheon of great novels.	Early in the twentieth century, *The Adventures of Huckleberry Finn* was elevated to the pantheon of great novels by critics.
Our seminar will discuss both novels.	Both novels will be discussed by our seminar.

Because each of the sentences on the left has a transitive verb — which is to say, the verb has an object — these sentences can be transformed into the passive voice. The transformation moves the object into the subject position, and the verb is adjusted accordingly.

To forestall any confusion, let me point out immediately that voice is unrelated to tense. Whether a sentence is active or passive depends on whether the subject performs or receives the action, not on whether the action takes place in the past, present, or future. *The seminar discusses, the seminar discussed,* and *the seminar will discuss* are all active; *both novels are discussed, both novels were discussed,* and *both novels will be discussed* are all passive.

How do the passive-voice sentences on page 33 strike you? To my ear, the first three sound a bit odd. While the active-voice "Jane Smiley admires *Uncle Tom's Cabin*" sounds easy and natural, the passive-voice "*Uncle Tom's Cabin* is admired by Jane Smiley" sounds forced. Probably because ours is an SVO language, because the subject-verb-object order of the active voice is so very common, readers may pause or stumble over a passive-voice sentence. So, given a choice, most good writers on most occasions will place the actor in the subject position, generating an active-voice sentence.

Under some circumstances, however, the passive voice is more effective.

First, the passive voice is used when the actor is unimportant or unknown. Consider these sentences, for example:

> Early in the twentieth century, <u>critics</u> <u>elevated</u> *The Adventures of Huckleberry Finn* to the pantheon of great novels.

> Early in the twentieth century, *The Adventures of Huckleberry Finn* <u>was elevated</u> to the pantheon of great novels.

The actor in both sentences is *critics*: it is literary critics who have the power to elevate books to the pantheon of great novels. The active-voice construction *critics elevated* makes perfect sense. But perhaps your reader isn't likely to know much or care much about critics; perhaps he or she is more interested in *Huckleberry Finn*. In that case, it makes equally good sense to move the novel itself into the subject position. Similarly, when the actor is unknown, speakers and writers often choose the passive voice, so that we might say "My car was stolen" or "The lights were left on all night."

The passive voice may also be a good choice if you want to use the subject position to name a thing or idea carried over from an earlier sentence. In the cluster of passive-voice sentences on page 33, the last one is the least jarring.

> Both <u>novels</u> <u>will be discussed</u> by our seminar.

Because the previous sentences discuss *Uncle Tom's Cabin* and *The Adventures of Huckleberry Finn, novels* keeps the focus on the current topic, so it makes a fine subject. If you return to the Smiley passage on page 30, you can see why the passive voice works so well in her final sentence: "All of these women have been promised something by their owners — love, education, the privilege and joy of raising their children — but, owing to slavery, all of these promises have been broken. . . ." *All of these women* refers to Eliza, Lucy, Prue, and Cassy, the characters who have just been discussed, so the paragraph coheres better for having *all of these women* in the subject position. In the second clause, *all of these promises* refers to the just-mentioned promises of love, education, and the privilege and joy of raising one's own children, so this phrase as subject lends coherence to the sentence.

Finally, the passive voice can emphasize the absence of agency and power in a person or thing that is acted upon. Smiley provides a good example in the sentence "Prue, who has been used for breeding, must listen to her last child cry itself to death because her mistress won't let her save it; she falls into alcoholism and thievery and is finally whipped to death."

In short, while writers usually prefer the active voice because of what we know about readers' expectations and their response as they process language, it is important to remember that the passive voice is available, too, as a stylistic option.

EXERCISE 2D

Rewrite the boldface clauses below to restore O'Brien's active-voice sentences. When you've rewritten each clause, underline the subject once and the verb twice to confirm that the subject performs the action.

Example

I was never confronted about it by the old man.

Restored to Active Voice

The old <u>man</u> never <u>confronted</u> me about it.

1. **Most graduate school deferments had been ended by the government.**
2. **Fight songs were played by a marching band.**
3. **Cartwheels were done along the banks of the Rainy River by a squad of cheerleaders.**

4. It seemed to me that when a nation goes to war it must have reasonable confidence in the justice and imperative of its cause. **Your mistakes can't be fixed.**

5. If you support a war, if you think it's worth the price, that's fine, but **your own precious fluids have to be put on the line.**

EXERCISE 2E

In the passage below, Jane Smiley opts to use the passive voice. Identify instances of the passive voice and underline the subject-verb pair to confirm that the subject names not the actor but a person or thing being acted upon. (I've underlined the first pair; there are four more.) Why might Smiley have chosen to cast these sentences in the passive voice?

The story, familiar to most nineteenth-century Americans, . . . may be sketched briefly. A Kentucky slave, Tom, is sold to pay off a debt to a slave trader, who takes him to New Orleans. On the boat trip downriver, Tom is purchased by the wealthy Augustine St. Clare at the behest of his daughter, Eva. After Eva's death, and then St. Clare's, Tom is sold again, this time to Simon Legree, whose remote plantation is the site of every form of cruelty and degradation. The novel was immediately read and acclaimed by any number of excellent judges: Charles Dickens, George Eliot, Leo Tolstoy, George Sand—the whole roster of nineteenth-century liberals. . . .

Variation in Sentence Focus

A general rule—even a fine, time-tested, oft-cited general rule like "prefer human or concrete subjects and active verbs"—is just a starting point. In the end, writing doesn't work by rules: it's a matter of judgment. And a writer's judgment will depend on his or her individual style and on what seems appropriate for the occasion—for the audience, purpose, and genre (memoir, editorial, short story, report).

To see how sentence focus varies, let's consider some of the model texts. Stories and memoirs describe people's experiences as they interact with one another, so you'd expect these texts to have a high frequency of human subjects and active verbs. By contrast, academic writing typically reports the findings of research, with the findings themselves—which may or may not have to do with human behavior—taking center stage. So you'd expect academic writing to have more abstract or non-human words as subjects and more verbs that can be paired with non-human subjects (*be*, passive-voice verbs). And sure enough, when I analyzed the model texts, these expectations were confirmed. This table describes the subject-verb pairs in four texts.

	% of clauses with human subject	% of clauses with *I* as subject	% of clauses with passive-voice verb
Story O'Brien, "On the Rainy River" (p. 171)	67	43	2
Memoir Gates, "Sin Boldly" (p. 155)	77	23	4
Case study (academic topic and genre, general audience) Sacks, "Colorblind Painter" (p. 199)	47	2	30
Literary criticism (academic topic and genre, general audience) Smiley, "Say It Ain't So, Huck" (p. 237)	54	3	14

The numbers demonstrate several points:

- Taken together, the four texts illustrate writers' strong preference for human subjects and active verbs.
- The preference for human subjects and active verbs is stronger in some genres than in others. (The patterns visible in this small sample have been observed in larger studies as well.[2])
- There is no law against using *I*! Teachers sometimes encourage young writers to avoid *I* to push them toward more worldly topics or more formal prose. But the choice to use *I* — like other choices writers make — depends on a number of factors including the writer's personal style, the topic, the audience, the purpose, and the genre.

EXERCISE 2F

Write two brief texts, just a few paragraphs each, about a past or present job.

First, write a narrative about yourself in relationship with a coworker, capturing a moment of interaction. Choose an incident that reveals the dynamics of the relationship; feel free to use dialogue.

Second, explain the purpose of your workplace, describing the product or service it provides and the processes that employees engage in to achieve the overriding purpose.

When you've finished writing, identify the subject-verb pair in each clause. Are all of your sentences well focused? That is, do the subjects keep the reader's attention focused where it ought to be? Is the frequency of *I* or other human subjects about the same in the two texts, or does it differ? Is the frequency of active verbs, passive verbs, and *be* about the same, or does it differ? Might the similarities and/or differences be explained by the topics, by your rhetorical purposes, by your personal stylistic preferences?

Sharpening the Focus

In my experience, the concept of focus is useful at two points in the writing process. First, there's that moment early in a sentence's life, when it's not even a sentence yet but a thought waiting to be articulated. "Who is doing something?" I ask. "What is he or she doing?" When I can name the actor and action, when I can piece them together as the subject and verb of a clause, the sentence is on its way.

More frequently, I think about the subject-verb pair late in the writing process, when I read through a draft and find myself snagged by a clumsy, wordy, or confusing sentence. "Who is doing something? What is he or she doing?" These simple questions can be remarkably powerful in guiding a writer toward leaner, clearer sentences.

This section presents a series of exercises organized around five editing tips, all designed to keep the actor and action in focus:

- Double-check sentences that begin with an abstract subject.
- Double-check sentences with *there* in the subject position.
- In general, keep subject phrases short.
- When a sentence seems badly focused, see whether its subject is buried in an introductory phrase.
- When a sentence seems badly focused, see whether its verb is masquerading as a noun.

The tips overlap; for example, when an abstract word occupies the subject position (a problem you'll work on in Exercise 2G), it may have landed there because the sentence's natural subject is buried in an introductory phrase (see Exercise 2J). Please use the tips not to label faulty sentences but to guide your editing.

Double-Check Sentences with Abstract Subjects

When a sentence begins with an abstract subject, see whether you can streamline it by finding a human or concrete noun somewhere in the sentence and relocating that noun to the subject position.

ABSTRACT SUBJECT

The <u>phenomenon</u> of "boomerang children," young adults who return to live with their parents after graduating from college, is an occurrence faced by many families today.

<u>Disagreement</u> about financial matters such as the expectation of paying rent for the young adult's "own" room may be a point of difference between parents and children.

The first sentence links the abstract subject *phenomenon* to the equally abstract complement *occurrence,* so the heart of the sentence, "the phenomenon is an occurrence," says almost nothing. The second sentence similarly links two abstractions: "Disagreement may be a point of difference." To revise, find a human or concrete noun somewhere else in the sentence — find the actor — and move that noun to the front.

BETTER

"<u>Boomerang children</u>" are young adults who return to live with their parents after graduating from college; many families face this phenomenon today.

Many <u>families</u> face the phenomenon of "boomerang children," young adults who return to live with their parents after graduating from college.

<u>Parents and children</u> may disagree about financial matters such as rent for the young adult's "own" room.

<u>Parents</u> may expect payment for a room that the young adult considers his or her own room.

Sentences beginning *the next way, the second reason,* or *another aspect* are especially likely to appear as paragraph starters in academic papers. Yes, you have to make a transition — but you can do better than that!

ABSTRACT SUBJECT

A second <u>way</u> that families can address the ambiguities of their new situation is to establish ground rules.

Another <u>reason</u> that the U.S. invasion of Iraq was a mistake is that it caused the stature of the United States as a world leader to plummet.

BETTER

Second, families can address the ambiguities of their new situation by establishing ground rules.

Furthermore, when the United States invaded Iraq, its stature as a world leader plummeted.

EXERCISE 2G

In the sentences below, underline the abstract noun that occupies the subject position. Then circle the actor, the person who is *doing* something. Revise the sentence to place the actor in the subject position, once again underlining your subject.

Example

Compared with a generation ago, relationships between parents and children seem to be much better.

Suggested Revision

Parents and children get along better than they did a generation ago.

1. The incidence of moonlighting among schoolteachers is high.
2. The reason for Maybelle's desire to leave Minneapolis was her desire to avoid the harsh winter weather.
3. Similarities exist in the strategies Jackson and LeGuin use to portray the conflict between individual conscience and the influence of the social group.
4. The reason the characters in the stories are willing to victimize their neighbors is because they think their own comfort depends on somebody's sacrifice.
5. With the growing use of PowerPoint in academic and business settings, the advantages and disadvantages of the technology should be considered by speakers.

Double-Check Sentences with *There* in the Subject Position

In a sentence whose purpose is to assert that something exists, *there* may be just the right subject. Often, however, *there* just takes up space, delaying the appearance of a sentence's true subject. Since *there* is almost invariably followed by a form of *be*, it displaces not only the subject but the whole subject-verb pair.

THERE AS SUBJECT

There are some television news programs that tell only one side of the story.

BETTER

Some television news programs tell only one side of the story.

EXERCISE 2H

Revise the sentences below to eliminate *there* from the subject position. In the new sentence, underline the subject-verb pair.

Example

There are many young mothers who want to work.

Suggested Revision

Many young mothers want to work.

1. Consequently there are far too many children who are spending their days in underfunded daycare centers.

2. To comply with the new laws, there are too many extra expenses that a family daycare provider must contend with.

3. Outside, there was an ice cream truck ringing its bell, but the children were all indoors watching television.

4. In the story "The Ones Who Walk Away from Omelas," there is a single boy who is chosen to suffer in order for the rest of the town to prosper.

5. There are three points in the story where the author uses foreshadowing.

Keep Subject Phrases Short

Readers expect a subject-verb pair. If the subject is a lengthy phrase, the reader is held in suspense waiting for the verb, and the sentence feels awkward.

LONG SUBJECT PHRASE

Many hours of labor, several meetings, including an emergency meeting of the whole committee, and several revisions of the contract were the result of one hasty e-mail.

BETTER

One hasty e-mail resulted in many hours of labor, several meetings, including an emergency meeting of the whole committee, and several revisions of the contract.

As in the previous example, sometimes the best revision strategy is to see whether the sentence can be inverted.

EXERCISE 21

In the sentences below, underline the long subject phrase. Then find a noun or noun phrase elsewhere in the sentence that would make a more concise subject. Rewrite the sentence, underlining the new subject.

Example
"Short-term temporary employment, or, in some cases, contract labor paid daily" describes the only promise the company will make.

Suggested Revision
The company will promise only "short-term temporary employment or, in some cases, contract labor paid daily."

1. Commitment to ethical behavior, respect for the rules of confidentiality, courtesy to coworkers and customers, and fully professional behavior on all occasions should be demonstrated by every employee.
2. Disorderly conduct, horseplay in the work area, fighting, threatening behavior, and profane or insulting remarks are strictly prohibited by company policy.
3. An unprecedented number of layoffs, a reduction of earnings, profits, and stock values, and a steadily worsening competitive position vis-à-vis the other high-tech companies in the area were among the factors being responded to by the CEO's decision to resign.
4. Accounting irregularities in both the purchasing office and the president's operating accounts were discovered by the auditors.
5. Planning your whole trip, from searching for the lowest airfare to finding an affordable rental car to locating a convenient hotel and even making restaurant reservations, can now be done using the Internet.

Uncover Subjects Buried in Introductory Phrases

The sentence below illustrates a trap into which many hapless subjects have fallen:

To the people of Minnesota, they develop a tolerance for freezing temperatures.

The writer has something to say about the people of Minnesota; the people are the sentence's natural subject. But because the sentence begins with *to*, the people of Minnesota appear as the object of a preposition, and the writer is forced to cast about for a substitute (*they*) to use as a subject.

An editor's task is simply to move the key noun phrase to the front of the sentence:

The <u>people</u> of Minnesota develop a tolerance for freezing temperatures.

EXERCISE 2J

In the sentences below, identify the key noun phrase and move it to the subject position. Underline the new subject.

Example
By having a large selection of organic vegetables, this appeals to the high-end buyer.

Suggested Revision
A large <u>selection</u> of organic vegetables appeals to the high-end buyer.

1. At the health food store, there are good bargains featured every weekend.
2. According to the store manager, he said he would be happy to stock more locally produced produce if he saw evidence of customer demand.
3. Because of the desk clerk at the hotel not knowing, it was unclear whether the rooms would be available both nights.
4. On San Francisco's beaches, it is beautiful but too cold for sunning or swimming.
5. After a visit to Chinatown, it made her nostalgic for her childhood in Shanghai.

Transform Nouns to Verbs

When a sentence seems badly focused, see whether its verb is masquerading as a noun.

An <u>emphasis</u> is placed on the development of research skills in our graduate program.

Emphasis makes a poor subject for reasons we've considered: as an abstraction, it can't do anything, so it leads to a passive-voice verb. But an alert editor will note that *emphasis* has a sister verb, *emphasize*, which names exactly the action that the writer wants to highlight:

Our graduate program <u>emphasizes</u> the development of research skills.

EXERCISE 2K

Each of the boldface nouns below has a sister verb. Refocus the sentence, pairing a well-chosen subject with the verb form of the word. Underline the subject-verb pair.

Example

As graduate students work on their dissertation projects, the **development** of sophisticated research skills is achieved.

Suggested Revision

As graduate students work on their dissertation projects, <u>they</u> <u>develop</u> sophisticated research skills.

1. The candidate's **decision** to drop out of the race occurred when she fell to sixth place in the polls.

2. There is a **tendency** in the main character to damage relationships with everyone she meets.

3. Every Saturday morning, the **distribution** of fresh, organic produce happens when local truck farmers bring organic produce to the farmer's market.

4. The **establishment** of a more equitable tax policy won't happen on the city council until council members have to answer to voters in district elections.

5. The **success** of the project will be achieved only if the **contribution** of every team member is a 100% effort.

These tips should help you produce tighter, more clearly focused sentences. But editing, like other aspects of writing, depends above all on your good judgment. If, as you work on your own prose, you follow these tips only to find that a sentence sounds worse, or that it suffers a loss of clarity, substance, or precision, then set the tip aside for another day.

CHAPTER 2 NOTES

[1] Reader, beware: if you don't love grammar, you don't want to read this footnote. But if you like grammatical puzzles, you may already have noticed that the noun phrases *all of these women* and *all of these promises* raise an interesting question: Which is the headword? A case can be made for *all*: in *all of these women*, *all* must be the headword because *women* is part of a prepositional phrase; the structure of the noun phrase is a simple and familiar one, with a headword followed by a prepositional phrase that modifies it. By contrast, a case can be made for *women*: *all of these* is a determiner introducing the noun *women*.

Here's why, of the two analyses — both of which are defensible and might be persuasive to a reasonable grammarian or linguist — I've selected the second.

All of these strikes me as equivalent to *all these*, which we recognize as a determiner:

All these <u>women</u> . . . all these <u>promises</u>.

Moreover, there's the fact that in English, we make our verbs agree with their subjects. Compare these sentences:

All of the <u>money</u> <u>was</u> gone.

All of the <u>coins</u> <u>were</u> gone.

We choose *was* to agree with the singular *money* and *were* to agree with the plural *coins*, suggesting that we interpret the subject of the sentence as *money* or *coins*. In these sentences, *all of the* functions as a determiner, and *all of these* functions the same way in the Smiley sentences.

[2] If you're interested in learning about how language use varies across contexts, look for the *Longman Student Grammar of Spoken and Written English* by Douglas Biber, Susan Conrad, and Geoffrey Leech (Essex, England: Pearson Education Limited, 2002). The Longman grammar is a descriptive grammar; its purpose is not to offer advice but to describe what English speakers and writers actually do. Because its description is based on a large corpus — over 40 million words — the Longman grammar can make well-documented claims about patterns within and across contexts. Biber, Conrad, and Leech present the frequency of passive-voice clauses in four contexts: about 1% in speech, 4% in fiction, 15% in news reports, and 25% in academic prose (167–168).

3

Well-Balanced Sentences

Coordination and Parallel Structure

IN *COLORED PEOPLE: A MEMOIR*, Henry Louis Gates Jr. describes his first year of college in a chapter titled "Sin Boldly" (reprinted on p. 155). The theme of bold sins is introduced in the chapter's first paragraph. Delivering his high school valedictory address, the young Gates rejected the "traditional prepared speech" he had practiced with his English teacher, instead writing a speech of his own about topics of the day:

> My speech was about Vietnam, abortion, and civil rights, about the sense of community our class shared, since so many of us had been together for twelve years, about the individual's rights and responsibilities in his or her community, and about the necessity to defy norms out of love.

Look carefully at that sentence. It's long — 49 words — but its structure is quite simple. The main clause begins with the subject-verb pair *speech was* and then describes the content of the speech in four prepositional phrases:

> about Vietnam, abortion, and civil rights

> about the sense of community our class shared, since so many of us had been together for twelve years

about the individual's rights and responsibilities in his or her
community

about the necessity to defy norms out of love

The prepositional phrases are joined by a kind of glue you can buy for a
penny at any sentence-structure shop: the coordinating conjunction *and*.
This chapter begins with some observations about Gates's work in
"Sin Boldly" and goes on to examine other texts in which coordinating conjunctions join pairs or series, exploring the stylistic options that
coordination makes available to writers.

Coordination

Let's take a moment to review the concept of coordination. English has
seven coordinating conjunctions — *and, or, nor, but, for, yet, so* — which
are used to join two or more independent clauses or smaller units
within a clause. Almost always, the units joined by the coordinator will
be similar in structure.

In the sentence about his valedictory speech, Gates has used coordinators not only to link a series of four prepositional phrases but also to
connect some smaller units.

Vietnam, abortion, **and** civil rights,
The coordinator and *joins three noun phrases.*

the individual's rights **and** responsibilities
The coordinator and *joins two nouns.*

in his **or** her community
The coordinator or *joins two determiners. Since the phrase "his or her" is automatic for most writers and processed by readers as a single unit, it is of little
stylistic interest.*

As noted in Chapter 1, coordinators can also link independent clauses.

Certainly Maura and I had been no strangers to controversy, **but** we
usually took pains not to invite it.

We were apparently the first interracial couple in Mineral County, **and**
there was hell to pay.

The Potomac Valley Hospital was called the meat factory because one
of the doctors was reputed to be such a butcher, **so** we drove on past it
and headed for my house.

| EXERCISE 3A |

The sentences below are by Henry Louis Gates Jr. ("Sin Boldly," p. 155) and Louise Erdrich ("Shamengwa," p. 139). Circle every coordinating conjunction and identify the units being joined. Some sentences have more than one coordinator; identify them clearly using single and double underlining.

Examples

My one year at Potomac State College of West Virginia University, in Keyser, all of five miles away, was memorable for two reasons: because of <u>my English classes with Duke Anthony Whitmore</u> (and) <u>my first real love affair, with Maura Gibson</u>.

It was he who showed me, by his example, <u>that ideas had a life of their own</u> (and) <u>that there were other professions as stimulating</u> (and) <u>as rewarding as being a doctor</u>.

1. Once we were at college, Maura and I started having long talks on the phone, first about nothing at all and then about everything.

2. In his own redneck way, 'Bama Gibson was a perfectly nice man, but he was not exactly mayoral material.

3. My grandfather was colored, my father was Negro, and I am black.

4. Geraldine, a dedicated, headstrong woman who six years back had borne a baby, dumped its father, and earned a degree in education, sometimes drove Shamengwa to fiddling contests.

5. He treated this instrument with the reverence we accord our drums, which are considered living beings and require from us food, water, shelter, and love.

6. I am a tribal judge, and things come to me through the grapevine of the court system or the tribal police.

7. I took my bedroll, a scrap of jerky, and a loaf of bannock, and sat myself down on the crackling lichen of the southern rock.

8. There were rivers flowing in and flowing out, secret currents, six kinds of weather working on its surface and a hidden terrain beneath.

9. Each wave washed in from somewhere unseen and washed out again to somewhere unknown.

10. He had taken the old man's fiddle because he needed money, but he hadn't thought much about where he would sell it or who would buy it.

Combine each group into a single sentence by creating a coordinate pair or series, joining the units with *and*.

Example

I made my way to Mr. Whitmore's table. I introduced myself tentatively. I stated my case, telling him my cousin Greg had said that he was a great teacher.

Suggested Revision

I made my way to Mr. Whitmore's table, introduced myself tentatively, and stated my case, telling him my cousin Greg had said that he was a great teacher.

1. I wrote to Harvard. I wrote to Yale. I wrote to Princeton.
2. Horse Lowe put his big red face into Maura's window. He beat on the windshield with his fist. He told me to get the hell off his property.
3. Geraldine was not surprised to see the lock of the cupboard smashed. She was not surprised to see the violin gone.
4. As the days passed, Corwin lay low. He picked up his job at the deep fryer.
5. He straightened out. He stayed sober. He used his best manners. When questioned, he was convincingly hopeful about his prospects. He was affable about his failures.
6. A surge of unfamiliar zeal filled him. He took up the instrument again. He threw back his hair. He began to play a swift, silent passage of music.
7. I remember my father playing chansons on his fiddle. He played reels. He played jigs.
8. He smiled. He shook his fine head. He spoke softly.

Parallel Structure

As a general rule, units in a series should have **parallel structure**; that is, they should be the same kind of grammatical unit, and they should fit into the same "slot" in the sentence. As I've noted, the series in Gates's sentence about his valedictory speech comprises four prepositional phrases, and any one of the phrases fits naturally after the subject and verb:

My speech was	about Vietnam, abortion, and civil rights
My speech was	about the sense of community our class shared, since so many of us had been together for twelve years

My speech was	about the individual's rights and responsibilities in his or her community
My speech was	about the necessity to defy norms out of love

In this sentence, the second prepositional phrase is longer and more complex than the others. Nevertheless, because all four units are prepositional phrases that fit naturally into the slot after *my speech was*, the series is parallel and the sentence is easy to read.

Sometimes the units in a well-crafted series match very closely:

My one year at Potomac State College of West Virginia University, in Keyser, all of five miles away, was memorable for two reasons: because of my English classes with Duke Anthony Whitmore **and** my first real love affair, with Maura Gibson.

Here, the noun phrases are about the same length, the nouns are signaled by the same determiner ("*my* English classes," "*my* first real love affair") and each noun is modified by a prepositional phrase beginning with *with* and ending with a person's name.

If a writer fails to use parallel structure in a series, the sentence will be awkward and potentially confusing. It's a good idea to check the parallelism in any series by applying two tests. First, are the units grammatically similar? Second, do they fit into the same slot in the sentence?

Somehow, for reasons having to do with nudity and sensuality, blacks were not allowed to walk along most beachfronts **or** attend resorts.

PARALLELISM TEST 1
Are the units grammatically similar?

walk along most beachfronts	*verb phrase*
attend resorts	*verb phrase*

PARALLELISM TEST 2
Do the units fit into the same slot in the sentence?

blacks were not allowed to	walk along most beachfronts
blacks were not allowed to	attend resorts

The sentence above passes both tests, so the most particular editor can be at peace. By contrast, note the faulty parallel structure in this sentence:

I was used to being stared at and somewhat used to being the only black person on the beach, **or** in a restaurant, **or** a motel.

PARALLELISM TEST 1
Are the units grammatically similar?

on the beach	*prepositional phrase*
in a restaurant	*prepositional phrase*
a motel	*noun phrase*

PARALLELISM TEST 2
Do the units fit into the same slot in the sentence?

the only black person	on the beach
the only black person	in a restaurant
the only black person	a motel

This sentence fails both tests, so it requires revision. The simplest revision is to restore the preposition that Gates used in his original sentence:

I was used to being stared at and somewhat used to being the only black person on the beach, or in a restaurant, or **at** a motel.

EXERCISE 3C

Each of these sentences contains a series in which the parallelism has gone awry. If you hear the problem immediately, revise the sentence. If you don't hear the problem right away, first identify the units in the series and test for parallel structure; then you'll be prepared to revise.

Example
He will probably be admitted to Officer Candidate School because he is young, strong, he can work hard, and has a good education.

The series is mixed, with two adjectives, then a clause, then a verb phrase.

Suggested Revisions
He will probably be admitted to Officer Candidate School because he is young, strong, hardworking, and well educated.

Four adjectives fit into the slot after "he is."

He will probably be admitted to Officer Candidate School because he is young and strong, he can work hard, and he has a good education.

Three clauses fit into the slot after "because."

1. He was always looking for money—scamming, betting, shooting pool, even now and then a job.
2. My mother out of grief became strict with my father, my older sister, and hard on me.
3. The U.S. government has, in a rush of publicity and embarrassing rhetoric, cobbled together an "international coalition against terror," mobilized its army, its air force, its navy and its media, and committing them to battle.
4. In fact, the problem for an invading army is that Afghanistan has no conventional coordinates or signposts to plot on a military map—no big cities, no highways, no industrial complexes, it doesn't have any water treatment plants.
5. Dropping more bombs on Afghanistan will only shuffle the rubble, scramble some old graves, and the dead will be disturbed.
6. During her first two years, Lucienne declared four majors: French, history, philosophy, and her favorite subject was still computer science.
7. The function of a university is to develop analytical skills of students and a place where they should learn to express themselves.
8. He argued for financial aid for the children of immigrants in order to ensure the equal right to study the liberal arts, an equal chance at higher-paying jobs, and to learn the communication skills that prepare young adults for full participation in a democracy.

Correlative Conjunctions

If you've heard a child describe his or her day ("We went to the playground and Jeremy fell off the high bar and there was blood all over his face and the teacher called his grandma . . ."), you get a sense of how heavily we depend on *and* (and, to a lesser extent, *but*) in our everyday speech. Naturally, then, all of us, from elementary school children to published authors, use coordination frequently when we write.

By contrast, coordinators' first cousins, the correlative conjunctions, are quite rare in spoken English, and you seldom see them in the work of young writers. It is experienced writers who use correlatives, exploiting their ability to join syntactic units and to manipulate emphasis.

Correlative conjunctions come in pairs:

both/and   not/but
either/or   not only/but (also)
neither/nor

In living sentences, they sound like this:

> She shook her head as if she were **both** annoyed with me **and** exasperated with her father.

> The speck seemed to **both** advance **and** retreat.

> It was a canoe. But **either** the paddler was asleep in the bottom **or** the canoe was drifting.

The correlatives *not/but* and *not only/but (also)* give greater weight to the second unit in the pair. Consider the sentences below, from Arundhati Roy's "The Algebra of Infinite Justice" (p. 188).

> American people ought to know that it is **not** them **but** their government's policies that are so hated.

> Could it be that the stygian anger that led to the attacks has its taproot **not** in American freedom and democracy, **but** in the U.S. government's record of commitment and support to exactly the opposite things—to military and economic terrorism, insurgency, military dictatorship, religious bigotry, and unimaginable genocide (outside America)?

Roy's use of the correlative backgrounds the material following *not* while emphasizing the material following *but*.

Like other coordinators, correlatives call for parallel structure. The editor's task is to be sure that the two parts of the correlative conjunction are followed by similar grammatical units that fit into the same slot in the sentence:

> She shook her head as if she were **both** <u>annoyed with me</u> **and** <u>exasperated with her father</u>.

PARALLELISM TEST 1
Are the units grammatically similar?

| annoyed with me | *adjective phrase* |
| exasperated with her father | *adjective phrase* |

PARALLELISM TEST 2
Do the units fit into the same slot in the sentence?

| She shook her head as if she were | <u>annoyed with me</u> |
| She shook her head as if she were | <u>exasperated with her father</u> |

The sentence passes both tests. Now examine a sentence with faulty parallelism:

I pretended to sleep, **not** because I wanted to keep up the appearance of being sick **but** I could not bear to return to the way things had been.

PARALLELISM TEST 1
Are the units grammatically similar?

because I wanted to keep up the appearance of being sick	*subordinate clause*
I could not bear to return to the way things had been	*independent clause*

PARALLELISM TEST 2
Do the units fit into the same slot in the sentence?

I pretended to sleep	because I wanted to keep up the appearance of being sick
I pretended to sleep	I could not bear to return to the way things had been

This sentence fails both tests, so it requires revision. In Erdrich's actual sentence, the subordinator *because* is repeated at the beginning of the second clause so that both clauses joined by *not/but* are subordinate:

I pretended to sleep, **not** because I wanted to keep up the appearance of being sick **but** because I could not bear to return to the way things had been.

I sometimes like to experiment with the placement of correlative conjunctions, placing them early in the sentence to create some repetition or late in the sentence for maximum efficiency:

The old woman knew enough **not** to trust her vision **but** to trust her touch.

The old woman knew enough to trust **not** her vision **but** her touch.

The purpose of dialogue is **not** to help participants reach agreement **but** to help them achieve mutual understanding.

The purpose of dialogue is to help participants achieve **not** agreement **but** mutual understanding.

EXERCISE 3D

Join the following sentences, using the correlative conjunctions indicated.

Example
both/and
When my father died he left the fiddle to my brother Edwin. He also left it to me.

Joined
When my father died he left the fiddle both to my brother Edwin and to me.

1. *both/and*
   Shamengwa loved the fiddle. Shamengwa's father loved the fiddle.
2. *both/and*
   His mother lost her capacity for joy. Ultimately, his father lost his capacity for joy.
3. *not/but*
   The narrator does not give Corwin a break because he believes he is innocent. He gives Corwin a break because he hopes he can be redeemed.
4. *either/or*
   He would learn to play the violin. Otherwise, he would do time.
5. *neither/nor*
   Billy Peace did not play fair in the race for the violin. His brother Edwin did not play fair in the race.
6. *both/and*
   Shamengwa can face the past without blinking. Billy Peace, who owned the violin before him, can face the past without blinking.
7. *both/and*
   The violin brings great heartache. It brings great joy.
8. *not only/but also*
   The violin brings great heartache. It brings great joy.
   The violin brings great joy. It brings great heartache.

Variation in Coordinate Series

Length

The number of units in a series has a strong influence on its rhetorical effect. In general, a series with two or three units is unmarked — that is, the length of the series doesn't call attention to itself — so it simply suggests completeness.

I wrote to Harvard, Yale, and Princeton.

A series with four units begins to feel long, and one with five or more conveys a sense of abundance, perhaps excess, perhaps exhaustion. This effect is even stronger when the writer omits the conjunction. In the sentence below, Gates describes his drives from Virginia to Delaware to meet Maura, stringing one prepositional phrase after another to create a long series and using no conjunction. By the end of the sentence, it's surprising to learn that he has any energy left:

> I'd leave work on Friday at about four o'clock, then drive all the way to Delaware, through Washington and the Beltway, past Baltimore and Annapolis, over the Chesapeake Bridge, past Ocean City, arriving at Rehoboth before midnight, with as much energy as if I had just awakened.

In the following passage, Arundhati Roy places several long series in a row.

> The September 11 attacks were a monstrous calling card from a world gone horribly wrong. The message may have been written by Bin Laden (who knows?) and delivered by his couriers, but it could well have been signed by the ghosts of the victims of America's old wars. The millions killed in Korea, Vietnam, and Cambodia; the 17,500 killed when Israel—backed by the U.S.—invaded Lebanon in 1982; the 200,000 Iraqis killed in Operation Desert Storm; the thousands of Palestinians who have died fighting Israel's occupation of the West Bank. And the millions who died, in Yugoslavia, Somalia, Haiti, Chile, Nicaragua, El Salvador, the Dominican Republic, Panama, at the hands of all the terrorists, dictators, and genocidists whom the American government supported, trained, bankrolled, and supplied with arms. And this is far from being a comprehensive list.

The power of the numbers Roy cites — millions, tens and hundreds of thousands, millions more — is heightened by the long series of military actions and the longer list of embattled countries. As readers, we perceive those lists as potentially continuing because of the number of units and, in the list of countries, the absence of a conjunction. Roy's closing assertion that the list could go on is already implicit in the structure of her sentences.

EXERCISE 3E

Analyze the effect of a long coordinate series. Choose a passage from a text you admire, or use one of the model texts—Roy's paragraph 33 (p. 197),

O'Brien's paragraph 11 (p. 176), a few sentences from O'Brien's paragraph 65 (p. 184).

1. Spend some time with the passage: read it aloud and type it.

2. Make the structure of the series visible, identifying the units being joined and any coordinating conjunctions, as you did in Exercise 3A.

3. For each series, count the number of units. I've claimed that a series of three feels complete, a series of four feels longish, and a series of five or more suggests abundance or excess. Do these generalizations apply to the passage you've selected?

4. For each series, consider the writer's choice of a conjunction. Are the units joined by *and*? another coordinator? no conjunction at all? What is the effect of adding, deleting, or changing the conjunction?

5. Describe the role of the passage you've selected in the text as a whole. Is this an important moment in the development of the story or argument? Why? How does the use of coordinate series serve the writer's rhetorical purpose?

Repetition

One reason that coordinate series are so widely used is that they make sentences more concise: it is more efficient to write "I remember my father playing chansons, reels, and jigs on his fiddle" than to name the songs in three separate sentences. However, conciseness isn't the only virtue writers seek, and we sometimes opt to repeat a few words in a coordinate series. Compare these sentences:

I wrote to Harvard, Yale, and Princeton.

I wrote to Harvard, to Yale, and to Princeton.

One way to think about the difference in this pair is that they indicate different ways of defining the slot into which coordinate units fit. For example, in the first sentence, the slot begins after *to*, and it is filled with three nouns:

I wrote to	Harvard
	Yale
	Princeton

In the second sentence, the slot begins after *wrote*, and it is filled with three prepositional phrases:

I wrote	to Harvard
	to Yale
	to Princeton

Both versions of the sentence are perfectly correct, and both are concise and easy to read. In this case, Gates chose the first version, using the preposition *to* just once.

In the sentence below, Gates chose to repeat a preposition. Compare these sentences:

My speech was about Vietnam, abortion, and civil rights, the sense of community our class shared, since so many of us had been together for twelve years, the individual's rights and responsibilities in his or her community, and the necessity to defy norms out of love.

My speech was about Vietnam, abortion, and civil rights, about the sense of community our class shared, since so many of us had been together for twelve years, about the individual's rights and responsibilities in his or her community, and about the necessity to defy norms out of love.

In the sentences above, the slots have been defined like this:

My speech was about	Vietnam, abortion, and civil rights
	the sense of community our class shared . . .
	the individual's rights and responsibilities . . .
	the necessity to defy norms out of love.
My speech was	about Vietnam, abortion, and civil rights
	about the sense of community our class shared . . .
	about the individual's rights and responsibilities . . .
	about the necessity to defy norms out of love.

Gates had a strong incentive to go with the second option, repeating the preposition *about* to make the four units match. The preposition functions like a bullet or a number, indicating that we're moving on to the next unit. It helps the reader piece the sentence together.

Finally, consider this pair:

Each wave washed in from somewhere unseen and out again to somewhere unknown.

Each wave washed in from somewhere unseen and washed out again to somewhere unknown.

Louise Erdrich wrote the second sentence, repeating the verb *washed*. It seems to me that the choice is easily explained on esthetic grounds. The repetition of *washed* makes the image more vivid, and it creates a rhythm in the sentence that captures the movement of the waves, washing in, washing out.

In short, a coordinate series creates the option of repeating words or phrases. Most writers strive for conciseness, so the default position may be to avoid repetition — but in the interest of clarity, emphasis, or beauty, repetition is sometimes a wise choice.

In "Shamengwa," Erdrich plays with repetition not just within sentences but from one sentence to the next. Shamengwa's story of finding his violin on the lake closes like this:

> "That is how my fiddle came to me," Shamengwa said, raising his head to look steadily at me. He smiled, shook his fine head, and spoke softly. "And that is why no other fiddle will I play."

And, as the story of the violin's previous owner comes to a close, we again hear a repeated structure echoing over the lake:

> The uncles have returned to their houses, pastures, children, wives. I am alone on the shore. As the night goes black, I sing for you. As the sun comes up, I call across the water. White gulls answer. As the time goes on, I begin to accept what I have done. I begin to know the truth of things.

EXERCISE 3F

In "Sin Boldly" (p. 155), Gates presents a memorable scene in which he and his friends forcibly integrate the Swordfish nightclub. At the entrance of the four black men, Gates reports, everybody froze—and he breaks "everybody" into four sets of people.

> Everybody froze: the kids from Piedmont and Keyser who had grown up with us; the students from Potomac State; the rednecks and crackers from up the hollers, the ones who came to town once a week all dressed up in their Sears, Roebuck perma-pressed drawers, their Thom McAn semi-leather shoes, their ultimately *white* sox, and their hair slicked back and wet-looking. The kids of rednecks, who liked to drink gallons of 3.2 beer, threaten everybody within earshot, and puke all over themselves—they froze too, their worst nightmare staring them in the face.

A quick analysis of the passage shows that the four sets of people are presented in a coordinate series, with three groups in one sentence ("the kids from Piedmont and Keyser," "the students from Potomac State," "the rednecks and crackers from up the hollers") and the fourth group ("the kids of rednecks") in a separate sentence. Another coordinate series describes how the "rednecks and crackers" dressed, and another describes how their children liked to behave.

1. Rewrite the passage without using any series, instead breaking the passage into shorter sentences.
2. Consider the effect of the change. What is gained and what is lost?

EXERCISE 3G

Imitate this passage from Tim O'Brien's story, "On the Rainy River." Begin by reading the whole passage in its original context (paragraph 11, p. 176). Then think of some set of people who have inconvenienced or irritated you because of their failure to understand something you care about. Write four sentences structured just like O'Brien's: copy the first few words of each sentence, and let your imagination take it from there.

1. All of them—I held them personally and individually responsible—the polyestered Kiwanis boys, the merchants and farmers, the pious churchgoers, the chatty housewives, the PTA and the Lions club and the Veterans of Foreign Wars and the fine upstanding gentry out at the country club.
2. They didn't know Bao Dai from the man on the moon.
3. They didn't know history.
4. They didn't know the first thing about Diem's history, or the nature of Vietnamese nationalism, or the long colonialism of the French.

4

Well-Developed Sentences

Modification

IN THE LAST CHAPTER, we considered several examples of coordination, examining sentences in which the parts are lined up one after another, like beads on a string. This chapter turns to a different kind of relationship, modification, whereby one part of a sentence extends, clarifies, or qualifies another part.

In the opening paragraph of his article, "Marriage or Bust: Why Civil Unions Aren't Enough" (p. 249), the journalist Andrew Sullivan writes two long sentences, underlined below. In one, the parts are organized in a simple coordinate series. The other is developed by means of modification.

Perhaps the current moment was inevitable. Around one-third of Americans support civil marriage for gay men and lesbians; another third are strongly opposed; the final third are sympathetic to the difficulties gay couples face but do not approve of gay marriage as such. In the last ten years or so, there has been some movement in these numbers, but not much. The conditions, in short, were ripe for a compromise: a pseudomarital institution, designed specifically for gay couples, that would include most, even all, of the rights and responsibilities of civil marriage but avoid the word itself. And last

week, in a historic decision, Vermont gave it to us: a new institution
called "civil union."

In the first underlined sentence, Sullivan describes the range of attitudes toward gay marriage with a series of independent clauses. His
sentence, like the American population, is divided into thirds, with the
final clause, describing the fence-sitters, balancing two predicates. The
three clauses line up in a simple, coordinate list:

Around one-third of Americans support civil marriage for gay men and
lesbians;
independent clause

another third are strongly opposed;
independent clause

the final third are sympathetic to the difficulties gay couples face but
do not approve of gay marriage as such.
independent clause

The other long sentence has just one independent clause: "The conditions were ripe for a compromise." Everything else in the sentence modifies the main clause, modifies some part of it, or modifies a modifier:

The conditions . . . were ripe for a compromise
independent clause

in short
transitional modifier, linking this sentence to the previous material

a pseudomarital institution
modifies "compromise," naming it more specifically

designed specifically for gay couples
modifies "pseudomarital institution"

that would include most . . . of the rights and
responsibilities of civil marriage but avoid the word
itself
*modifies "pseudomarital institution," highlighting its
two-sided character as a compromise*

even all
modifies "most," indicating an alternative

A modifier is a structure — a word, a phrase, or a dependent
clause — that is added to a sentence at the beginning, where it paves the

way for the independent clause, or at the end, where it elaborates on the clause. To examine the effects of modifiers, we'll analyze passages from "Marriage or Bust" (p. 249), David Sedaris's story "Genetic Engineering" (p. 231), and Oliver Sacks's "The Case of the Colorblind Painter" (p. 199).

Early Modifiers and the Pleasures of the Periodic Sentence

Early modifier is a shorthand way of referring to initial modifiers, which open their sentences, and medial modifiers like Sullivan's *in short*, which are embedded within the main clause.

In "Genetic Engineering," David Sedaris describes the relationship between an engineer and his children.[1] "The greatest mystery of science," he writes, "continues to be that a man could father six children who shared absolutely none of his interests." In the passages below, Sedaris uses early modifiers to establish the time and circumstances of the action:

> As children, we placed a great deal of faith in his ability but learned to steer clear while he was working. The experience of watching was ruined, time and time again, by an interminable explanation of how things were put together. Faced with an exciting question, science tended to provide the dullest possible answer. . . .
>
> Once, while rifling through the toolshed, I came across a poster advertising an IBM computer the size of a refrigerator. Sitting at the control board was my dad the engineer, years younger, examining a printout no larger than a grocery receipt. When I asked about it, he explained that he had worked with a team devising a memory chip capable of storing up to fifteen pages' worth of information.

Later in the story, the narrator explains that his father's tiresome explanations of scientific phenomena affected the children's enjoyment of their annual trip to the beach. ("We enjoyed swimming," he writes, "until the mystery of tides was explained in such a way that the ocean seemed nothing more than an enormous saltwater toilet, flushing itself on a sad and predictable basis.") The next sentences begin with early modifiers:

> By the time we reached our teens, we were exhausted. No longer interested in the water, we joined our mother on the beach blanket and dedicated ourselves to the higher art of tanning. Under her guidance,

we learned which lotions to start off with, and what worked best for various weather conditions and times of day.

By the time we reached our teens establishes the time of the action. The next modifiers make a link from old information to the content of the coming sentence. *No longer interested in the water* recalls that dispiriting image of the ocean as "an enormous saltwater toilet" and prepares us to learn what the children did instead of playing in the water. *Under her guidance* is also transitional, referring to the mother mentioned in the previous sentence and setting up the specific lessons that constituted her instruction in the "higher art of tanning."

In Andrew Sullivan's opening paragraph, early modifiers such as *In the last ten years or so* and *And last week* also establish the time of the action. For the most part, however, the structure of Sullivan's piece is quite different from Sedaris's. He is not telling a story, not narrating events that have happened over a period of time. Instead, he is offering a complex and carefully structured argument, so the essential movement is from premises to conclusions: If we grant X, then we must conclude Y. Consequently, many of Sullivan's sentences begin with modifiers that remind us of a condition that he has asserted or that his readers will accept as true.

> So, if we accept that religion doesn't govern civil marriage and that civil marriage changes over time, we are left with a more nebulous worry.

> When civil law already permits the delinquent, the divorced, the imprisoned, the sterile, and the insane to marry, it seems—how should I put this?—revealing that it draws the line at homosexuals.

> When an extremely basic civil right is involved, it seems to me the burden of proof should lie with those who seek to deny it to a small minority of citizens, not with those who seek to extend it.

In both the Sedaris and the Sullivan texts, then, early modifiers work to move the prose along, carrying readers from one point to the next.

By placing some material — information that's already been established, or stage-setting background information — in early modifiers, writers can delay the independent clause, creating suspense as the sentence climbs toward a dramatic closing. A sentence in which the modifiers come at the beginning, building toward the main clause, is called a **periodic sentence**.

Watch how Sullivan builds these sentences:

And last week, in a historic decision, Vermont gave it to us: a new institution called "civil union."

In Denmark, in the decade since Vermont-style partnerships have been legal, gays have had a lower divorce rate than straights.

If the modifiers were moved to the end, the rhythm and the drama of the sentences would fizzle. Compare:

Vermont gave us a new institution called "civil union" last week in a historic decision.

Gays have had a lower divorce rate than straights in Denmark in the decade since Vermont-style partnerships have been legal.

You can see the same principle at work (though not in modifiers) in these sentences:

"That's all very well," she [my mother] told me in my first discussion with her on the subject, "but can't you call it something other than 'marriage'?" The answer to that question is no.

To concede that gay adults are responsible citizens, to concede that there will be no tangible damage to the institution of marriage by their inclusion within it, and then to offer gay men and women a second-class institution called civil union makes no sense.

In the first example above, Sullivan builds toward the climactic "no." In the second, he builds toward his judgment of the contradiction: that it "makes no sense." Compare:

"That's all very well," she told me in my first discussion with her on the subject, "but can't you call it something other than 'marriage'?" No is the answer to that question.

It makes no sense to offer gay men and women a second-class institution called civil union if you concede that gay adults are responsible citizens and you concede that there will be no tangible damage to the institution of marriage by their inclusion within it.

In short, writers can add punch to a sentence by placing the key point at the end. One way to accomplish that is to begin the sentence with early modifiers.

EDITOR'S NOTE: Early modifiers are usually set off by commas.

EXERCISE 4A

Each of the numbered sentences below is a single independent clause. Develop each sentence by adding at least two modifiers before the independent clause, setting up the independent clause so that it has a strong impact.

These sentences do not appear in the model texts, but they make statements about characters in "Genetic Engineering" and ideas in "Marriage or Bust." If you haven't already done so, read those texts for information to use in developing the sentences.

Example
Gretchen deserves to win the annual Miss Emollient pageant.

Suggested Revisions
Again this year, to the dismay of her sisters and her brother, Gretchen deserves to win the annual Miss Emollient pageant.

Because she has faithfully followed her mother's advice, seeking just the right balance of oils and lotions, lying outside when the sun was high, and using aluminum foil to reflect the sun's rays to those hard-to-reach spots, Gretchen deserves to win the annual Miss Emollient pageant.

1. The engineer is isolated from his family.
2. The fishermen have sold their homes near the ocean.
3. Many gay rights groups have avoided a discussion of marriage.
4. Social policy is not driven by religious doctrine.

EXERCISE 4B

Rewrite the sentences you created in Exercise 4A, moving the independent clause to the beginning of the sentence. Do you read the new sentence differently? Is there a change in its meaning, emphasis, or effect? Explain.

Example
Gretchen deserves to win the annual Miss Emollient pageant again this year, to the dismay of her sisters and her brother.

Sample Explanation
It seems less important that Gretchen deserves to win—that's treated like a given—so I as a reader focus more on the effect on her siblings.

Example
Gretchen deserves to win the annual Miss Emollient pageant again this year because she has faithfully followed her mother's advice, seeking just

the right balance of oils and lotions, lying outside when the sun was high, and using aluminum foil to reflect the sun's rays to those hard-to-reach spots.

Sample Explanation
In the earlier version, the purpose of the sentence seems to be to announce that Gretchen deserves to win; the reasons are a drumroll leading up to the announcement. In this version, the purpose seems to be to explain the principles of successful tanning.

End Modifiers and the Pleasures of the Cumulative Sentence

Look once more at the long sentence from Andrew Sullivan's opening paragraph:

The conditions, in short, were ripe for a compromise: a pseudomarital institution, designed specifically for gay couples, that would include most, even all, of the rights and responsibilities of civil marriage but avoid the word itself.

This is a good example of a cumulative sentence, a term coined many years ago by the rhetorician Francis Christensen.

A **cumulative sentence** begins with the main clause, then extends the sentence with one or more end modifiers. Christensen offers a sentence of his own as both a definition and an example of the cumulative sentence:

The main clause, which may or may not have a sentence modifier before it, advances the discussion; but the additions move backward, as in this clause, to modify the statement of the main clause or more often to explicate or exemplify it, so that the sentence has a flowing and ebbing movement, advancing to a new position and then pausing to consolidate it, leaping and lingering as the popular ballad does."[2]

Christensen claims that the cumulative sentence is the mainstay of contemporary style because it serves both the writer, pushing him or her toward specificity, and the reader, who can follow the play of the writer's mind as it tests, expands, qualifies, and otherwise modifies ideas.

Of the writers represented by the model texts, none makes more frequent use of the cumulative sentence than Oliver Sacks. One reason that his case studies are so engaging is that they are richly detailed, so that we care about the people being described and feel that we understand their experience. In the sentences below, Sacks explains that the colorblind painter, Mr. I., perceived color differently if the light source changed.[3]

This phenomenon was very marked
independent clause

    if the quality of illumination suddenly changed,
    modifies the main clause, describing the conditions under which the
    phenomenon was marked

        as . . . when a fluorescent light was turned on,
        modifies the previous clause, giving an example of a sudden
        change

            for example
            transitional modifier

            which would cause an immediate change in
            the brightness of objects around the room.
            modifies the previous clause, describing the
            consequence of a light's turning on

Mr. I. commented that he now found himself in an inconstant world,
independent clause

    a world whose lights and darks fluctuated with the wavelength of
    illumination,
    modifies "an inconstant world"

        in striking contrast to the relative stability . . . of the
        color world he had previously known.
        modifies "a world whose lights and darks fluctuated . . ."

            the constancy
            modifies "stability," clarifying it by restating

EXERCISE 4C

Outline these sentences by David Sedaris and Oliver Sacks. Place the independent clause farthest to the left, and indent the other clauses or phrases to show how they relate to the main clause or to each other. Add notes to explain what each modifier is doing.

How many pieces should you break the sentence into? For the purposes of this exercise, let the punctuation be your guide: place each unit set off by commas or dashes on its own line.

Example

During the first week of September, it was my family's habit to rent a beach house on Ocean Isle, a thin strip of land off the coast of North Carolina.

Suggested Outline

    During the first week of September,
    modifies independent clause below, setting the time

it was my family's habit to rent a beach house on Ocean Isle,
independent clause

        a thin strip of land off the coast of North Carolina.
        modifies "Ocean Isle"

1. As youngsters, we participated in all the usual seaside activities—which were fun, until my father got involved and systematically chipped away at our pleasure.

2. We enjoyed swimming, until the mystery of the tides was explained in such a way that the ocean seemed nothing more than an enormous saltwater toilet, flushing itself on a sad and predictable basis.

3. He had *become* colorblind, after sixty-five years of seeing colors normally— *totally* colorblind, as if "viewing a black and white television screen."

4. Black and white for him was a *reality*, all around him, 360 degrees, solid and three-dimensional, twenty-four hours a day.

5. Helmholtz was very conscious of "color constancy"—the way in which the colors of objects are preserved, so that we can categorize them and always know what we are looking at, despite great fluctuations in the wavelength of the light illuminating them.

On the following pages are passages by Sullivan, Sacks, and Sedaris printed twice — first pared down to the independent clauses, then with the modifiers restored. If you compare the two versions, you can see the degree to which these writers depend on modifiers to communicate the content of their sentences.

ANDREW SULLIVAN

Pared down: Perhaps the current moment was inevitable. Around one-third of Americans support civil marriage for gay men and lesbians; another third are strongly opposed; the final third are sympathetic to the difficulties gay couples face but do not approve of gay marriage as such. There has been some movement in these numbers. The conditions were ripe for a compromise. And Vermont gave it to us.

Restored: Perhaps the current moment was inevitable. Around one-third of Americans support civil marriage for gay men and lesbians; another third are strongly opposed; the final third are sympathetic to the difficulties gay couples face but do not approve of gay marriage as such. In the last ten years or so, there has been some movement in these numbers, but not much. The conditions, in short, were ripe for a compromise: a pseudomarital institution, designed specifically for gay couples, that would include most, even all, of the rights and responsibilities of civil marriage but avoid the word itself. And last week, in a historic decision, Vermont gave it to us: a new institution called "civil union."

OLIVER SACKS

Pared down: This phenomenon was very marked. Mr. I. commented that he now found himself in an inconstant world.

Restored: This phenomenon was very marked if the quality of illumination suddenly changed, as, for example, when a fluorescent light was turned on, which would cause an immediate change in the brightnesses of objects around the room. Mr. I. commented that he now found himself in an inconstant world, a world whose lights and darks fluctuated with the wavelength of illumination, in striking contrast to the relative stability, the constancy, of the color world he had previously known.

DAVID SEDARIS

Pared down: It was my family's habit to rent a beach house on Ocean Isle. We participated in all the usual seaside activities. Miniature golf was ruined with a lengthy dissertation on impact, trajectory, and wind velocity, and our sand castles were critiqued with stifling lectures on the dynamics of the vaulted ceiling. We enjoyed swimming.

Restored: During the first week of September, it was my family's habit to rent a beach house on Ocean Isle, a thin strip of land off the coast of North Carolina. As youngsters, we participated in all the usual seaside activities—which were fun, until my father got involved and systematically chipped away at our pleasure. Miniature golf was ruined with a lengthy dissertation on impact, trajectory, and wind velocity, and our sand castles were critiqued with stifling lectures on the dynamics of the vaulted ceiling. We enjoyed swimming, until the mystery of the tides was explained in such a way that the ocean seemed nothing more than an enormous saltwater toilet, flushing itself on a sad and predictable basis.

But in the end, the point is not to analyze another writer's sentences. The point is to generate material of your own — to know that, before and after an independent clause, there are spaces where you can elaborate, and when you've elaborated, there are spaces where you can elaborate some more. Christensen called his model *generative* in the hope that it would help writers see the possibilities for pushing sentences toward further levels of precision, clarity, and specificity.

EXERCISE 4D

Think about a place you've visited more than once, perhaps a family vacation spot or a relative's house. Spend a few minutes remembering: think about what the place looked like, the buildings, the landscape, the people you met there, what those people did at work and at play. Then, using David Sedaris's sentences as models, imitating their structure as closely as possible, create well-developed sentences about the place and/or the people.

Example

> During the first week of September,

> it was my family's habit to rent a beach house on Ocean Isle,

>> a thin strip of land off the coast of North Carolina.

Sample Response

> Every other year in the summertime,
> *In a modifier, establish the time.*

it was my family's habit to bunk up in a condo in the Ozarks,
independent clause

>> a resort area surrounding an S-shaped lake in Missouri.

1.   On one of those walks,

     I came across my father

         standing not far from a group of fishermen

                 who were untangling knots in a net the size of a circus tent

_____

In a modifier, establish the time.

_____

independent clause

_____

_____

2.   The men drank from quart bottles of Mountain Dew

         as they paused from their work to regard my father,

             who stood at the water's edge,

             staring at the shoreline with a stick in hand.

_____

independent clause

_____

_____

_____

3.   My father answered their questions in detail

    and they listened intently—

         this group of men with nets,

             blowing their smoke into the wind.

_____

independent clause

_____

independent clause

_____

_____

4. Stooped and toothless,

they hung upon his every word

while I stood in the lazy surf,

thinking of the upcoming pageant

and wondering if the light reflecting off the water might tan the underside of my nose and chin.

In a modifier, provide a detail about the subject of the main clause.

---

independent clause

The next three chapters continue the discussion of modification, each treating a particular kind of modifier. Chapter 5 focuses on adjective clauses, Chapter 6 on verbal phrases, and Chapter 7 on my personal favorites, appositives and absolutes.

CHAPTER 4 NOTES

[1] Sedaris writes in the first person, so it's very tempting to write as if the story were a true account of the Sedaris family. In struggling to distinguish between the writer and the narrator, I am inspired by this scene from "The Learning Curve"— another story in *Me Talk Pretty One Day*, one beloved by writing teachers. Sedaris the writer gives us "Mr. Sedaris," the narrator and main character in a story about a writing workshop:

> ... The way I saw it, if my students were willing to pretend I was a teacher, the least I could do was return the favor and pretend that they were writers. Even if someone had used his real name and recounted, say, a recent appointment with an oral surgeon, I would accept the story as pure fiction, saying, "So tell us, Dean, how did you come up with this person?"

The student might mumble, pointing to the bloodied cotton wad packed against his swollen gum, and I'd ask, "When did you decide that your character should seek treatment for his impacted molar?" This line of questioning allowed the authors to feel creative and protected anyone who held an unpopular political opinion.

"Let me get this straight," one student said. "You're telling me that if I say something out loud, it's me saying it, but if I write the exact same thing on paper, it's somebody else, right?"

"Yes," I said. "And we're calling that fiction."

The student pulled out his notebook, wrote something down, and handed me a sheet of paper that read, "That's the stupidest fucking thing I ever heard in my life."

They were a smart bunch.

[2] Francis Christensen, *Notes Toward a New Rhetoric* (New York: Harper & Row, 1967), 6.

[3] The outlines used in this and subsequent chapters are adapted from Francis Christensen's work in "A Generative Rhetoric of the Sentence." The outlines are convenient because they make a sentence's structure visible, showing how each piece relates to the pieces before it. But don't try this at home — at least not unless you're pretty sure you're working with a cumulative sentence. While the technique is illuminating for the sentences Christensen loves best, those with an ebbing and flowing, "leaping and lingering" sequence of modifiers, it is difficult to adapt to sentences organized by any other plan.

Modifiers Following the Noun

Adjective Clauses and Adjective Phrases

ONE OF THE MOST STRIKING DIFFERENCES between spoken and written language is the frequency of **adjectivals** — words, phrases, and clauses that modify nouns — in written texts. Listen to these sentences:

In this essay, Amy Tan writes about her mother's "broken" English.

In this engaging essay, Amy Tan, who is best known for her novel *The Joy Luck Club*, writes about her mother's "broken" English.

The first sentence sounds like something anyone might say, but the second one is clearly *written*. In everyday conversation, it would strike us as odd and pretentious.

In conversation, we generally interact with people we know, so they share our background knowledge, and we often talk about people and things that are easy to recall, perhaps even present in the room. In those circumstances, detailed description is unnecessary, so most of our nouns stand bare. In writing, when we can't be sure of what our readers know or what mental images they might be forming, we seek specificity by adding modifiers before or after noun phrases.

When asked to develop their sentences — to make them more specific, more vivid — many writers think immediately about adding adjectives. "My grandmother had a cat" grows into "My 85-year-old grandmother had a sleek, black cat," and "The Chevrolet sat in the parking lot" becomes

"The dented, rusty, blue Chevrolet sat in the dark, empty parking lot." This sort of addition comes easily to any adult writer. However, there's a limit to the number of adjectives you can pack in before a noun, and they don't do much for a sentence's rhythm. Modifiers that follow the noun represent an important extension of the writer's range of options.

This chapter examines adjective clauses and adjective phrases in two essays by Amy Tan (pp. 257 and 267) as well as Oliver Sacks's memoir "Housecalls" (p. 223) and Andrew Sullivan's article "Marriage or Bust" (p. 249).

The Structure of Adjective Clauses

An **adjective clause**, as you might imagine, is a clause — that is, a group of words containing a subject-verb pair — that functions adjectivally, supplying information about a noun. Adjective clauses, sometimes called relative clauses, are usually introduced by relative pronouns — *who, whom, whose, which, that* — and occasionally by *where* or *when.*

In the sentences below, the adjective clauses are underlined, and an arrow points to the noun being modified:

> The talk was going along well enough, until I remembered one major
>
> difference that made the whole talk sound wrong. My mother was in the room.

> I'll quote what my mother said during a recent conversation which I videotaped and then transcribed.

> My mother was talking about a political gangster in Shanghai who had the same last name as her family's, Du, and how the gangster in
>
> his early years wanted to be adopted by her family, which was rich by comparison.

> My mother told us about a wedding in Shanghai, where she grew up.

Writers frequently omit the relative pronoun, as in this sentence:

> Just last week, I was walking down the street with my mother, and I
>
> again found myself conscious of the English I was using.

You can recognize *I was using* as a clause by the presence of a subject-verb pair and as an adjective clause by its function, modifying the noun *English*. While the clause could have begun with a relative pronoun — *the English that I was using* — the pronoun is not essential.

The best way to understand the structure of an adjective clause is to think of it as a sentence that has been embedded after a significant noun. So you could write two separate sentences: "*The Joy Luck Club* was written by Amy Tan. She lives in San Francisco." Or you could transform the second sentence into an adjective clause: "*The Joy Luck Club* was written by Amy Tan, who lives in San Francisco." The transformation is effected by changing the pronoun *she* to the relative pronoun *who*.

The following examples illustrate similar transformations:

Amy Tan has written several novels. They explore mother-daughter relationships.

Amy Tan has written several novels that explore mother-daughter relationships.

Amy Tan has written several novels. Critics praise them.

Amy Tan has written several novels that critics praise.

The hospital staff ignored Mrs. Tan. She was deeply worried about her CAT scan results.

The hospital staff ignored Mrs. Tan, who was deeply worried about her CAT scan results.

The hospital staff ignored Mrs. Tan. Her English was imperfect.

The hospital staff ignored Mrs. Tan, whose English was imperfect.

The hospital staff ignored Mrs. Tan. They found her difficult to understand.

The hospital staff ignored Mrs. Tan, whom they found difficult to understand.

EXERCISE 5A

The following passages, from Amy Tan's "Mother Tongue" (p. 259), contain a total of twelve adjective clauses. Underline each adjective clause and draw an arrow to the noun being modified. The first two have been done for you.

Fortunately, for reasons I won't get into here, I later decided I should

envision a reader for the stories I would write. And the reader I decided on was my mother, because these were stories about mothers. So with this reader in mind—and in fact she did read my early drafts—I began to write stories using all the Englishes I grew up with: the English I spoke to my mother, which for lack of a better term might be described as "simple"; the English she used with me, which for lack of a better term might be described as "broken"; my translation of her Chinese, which could certainly be described as "watered down." . . .

Why are there few Asian Americans enrolled in creative writing programs? Why do so many Chinese students go into engineering? Well, these are broad sociological questions I can't begin to answer. But I have noticed in surveys—in fact, just last week—that Asian-American students, as a whole, do significantly better on math achievement tests than on English tests. And this makes me think that there are other Asian-American students whose English spoken in the home might also be described as "broken" or "limited." And perhaps they also have teachers who are steering them away from writing and into math and science. . . .

EXERCISE 5B

The following sentences are based on the selection "Housecalls" by Oliver Sacks (p. 223). In each set, transform the indented sentences into adjective clauses that modify the noun in boldface. (If this exercise takes you more than five minutes to complete, you're over-thinking it. Just change the underlined word to *who, whom, whose, which, that, when,* or *where.*)

Example

In "Housecalls," Oliver Sacks cherishes memories of his **father**.

He was a physician in New York City.

He had studied to be a neurologist.

His patients often invited him to stay for a meal.

Sample Responses

In "Housecalls," Oliver Sacks cherishes memories of his father, who was a physician in New York City.

In "Housecalls," Oliver Sacks cherishes memories of his father, who had studied to be a neurologist.

In "Housecalls," Oliver Sacks cherishes memories of his father, <u>whose</u> patients often invited him to stay for a meal.

The young Oliver liked to swim with his **father**.

1. <u>He</u>, as a young man, had been a champion swimmer.
2. <u>His</u> strokes were slow and smooth.
3. <u>He</u> became graceful in the water though he was huge and cumbersome on land.

They swam in the **Welsh Harp pond**.

4. <u>It</u> was a small lake not far from their house.
5. They also enjoyed fishing <u>there</u>.
6. Sacks's father once kept a boat <u>there</u>.

Sacks went with his father to visit his **patients**.

7. <u>They</u> knew that Dr. Sacks loved to eat.
8. <u>Their</u> refrigerators were stocked with Dr. Sacks's favorite foods.
9. Dr. Sacks examined <u>them</u> in their own living rooms.
10. Dr. Sacks expertly diagnosed <u>them</u> by means of chest percussion.

EXERCISE 5C

In this paragraph, Sacks describes the East End restaurants where he and his father stopped for a bite after making housecalls. Note the underlined adjective clauses:

> There were a dozen superb kosher restaurants within a few blocks, each with its own incomparable specialties. Should it be Bloom's on Aldgate, or Ostwind's, <u>where one could enjoy the marvelous smells of the basement bakery wafting upstairs</u>? Or Strongwater's, <u>where there was a particular sort of kreplach, vernikas, to which my father was dangerously addicted</u>? Usually, however, we would end up at Silberstein's, <u>where, in addition to the meat restaurant downstairs, there was a dairy restaurant, with wonderful milky soups and fish, upstairs</u>.

Imitating the structure of Sacks's sentences as closely as possible, write a brief paragraph with a topic sentence about restaurants in your area followed by three sentences about specific restaurants you might want to visit. Like Sacks, modify each restaurant name with information in a *where* clause describing the treats to be found there.

Choices in Crafting Adjective Clauses

While adjective clauses are quite common and easy to create, they can present some puzzles to writers and editors. Three questions are frequently asked about adjective clauses.

Who or Whom?

The *who/whom* distinction is rarely observed in speech or informal writing. However, the distinction hasn't disappeared entirely. Here's the rule: When the relative pronoun is a subject, replacing a word like *he, she,* or *they,* choose *who.* When the relative pronoun is an object, replacing a word like *him, her,* or *them,* choose *whom.*

These sentences illustrate the rule:

She was the widow of a poor scholar. He died of influenza.

She was the widow of a poor scholar, who died of influenza.

She was the widow of a poor scholar. The doctors were unable to save him.

She was the widow of a poor scholar, whom the doctors were unable to save.

A rich man spotted the young widow. He liked to collect pretty women.

A rich man who liked to collect pretty women spotted the young widow.

A rich man spotted the young widow. She believed him to be trustworthy.

A rich man whom she believed to be trustworthy spotted the young widow.

In speech, most of us would choose *who* every time, violating the rule in the second and fourth sentences. When writing, then, we have to choose whether to comply with the rule or to follow the everyday practice of speakers. Choices like this are governed by the formality of the context: you're safest following the rule in academic papers and choosing whatever sounds natural in less formal genres.

If the relative pronoun follows a preposition, you'll use *whom,* and you won't face any question about it because *who* would sound truly peculiar. (For example, you'd write "an American with whom she'd fallen in love" rather than "an American with who she'd fallen in love.") If you place the preposition at the end of the sentence — which, by the way, you have every right to do when you please — then the range of choices expands. Arranged from most to least formal, the options are these:

> She briefly took the name of an American with whom she'd fallen in love.

> She briefly took the name of an American whom she'd fallen in love with.

> She briefly took the name of an American who she'd fallen in love with.

Most writers prefer *who* or *whom* to *that* when referring to people. But if *whom* sounds overly formal and *who* sounds like an error, *that* offers yet another option, and sometimes it's possible to omit the relative pronoun altogether:

> She briefly took the name of an American that she'd fallen in love with.

> She briefly took the name of an American she'd fallen in love with.

Should an Adjective Clause Be Set Off with Punctuation?

Adjective clauses come in two varieties: restrictive and nonrestrictive. If an adjective clause is essential to the meaning of a noun — if it makes it possible for the reader to pick out the person or thing, of all people and things in the world, that the noun is intended to name — then it's restrictive. If an adjective clause simply supplies extra information about the noun, then it's nonrestrictive.

In speech, we signal whether an adjective clause is restrictive or nonrestrictive by means of intonation, and in writing we signal with punctuation. Nonrestrictive adjective clauses and other nonrestrictive modifiers are set apart, usually by commas but sometimes by dashes or parentheses.

Read these sentences aloud:

> The little girl who appears in this photograph is Tan's mother.

> Du Ching, who appears in this photograph, is Tan's mother.

In the first sentence, the adjective clause is restrictive; it limits the reference of *girl* to the single girl who is under discussion, the girl in the photograph. In the second sentence, the adjective clause is nonrestrictive. It's already clear which girl is under discussion — there's only one Du Ching — so the adjective clause simply provides additional information.

The use of punctuation can determine how a reader understands an adjective clause. Consider these sentences:

> The women in the photo who were unfortunate in their marriages suffered terrible fates.

> The women in the photo, who were unfortunate in their marriages, suffered terrible fates.

Because the first sentence, in the absence of punctuation, presents the adjective clause as restrictive, we understand that it identifies particular women from a larger group. Of all the women in the photo, it is the subset who were unfortunate in marriage that suffered terrible fates. By contrast, the adjective clause in the second sentence is punctuated, so we read it as nonrestrictive. The statement is about all of the women in the photo.

Notice that the presence of punctuation has the same effect with other modifiers. In the sentences below, the modifier is a prepositional phrase:

> Her aunts from the big city went to dance halls and wore stylish clothes.

> Her aunts, from the big city, went to dance halls and wore stylish clothes.

In the first sentence, the prepositional phrase is punctuated as a restrictive modifier, so we understand that it limits the meaning of *her aunts* to those who came from the big city. The second sentence, with a nonrestrictive modifier, makes its assertion about all of her aunts.

While the punctuation mark usually used to set off a nonrestrictive modifier is the comma, writers do have other options. A modifier set off by a dash is highlighted, while one enclosed in parentheses is pushed into the background. Compare:

> Jyou Ma married my great uncle—who complained that his family had chosen an ugly woman for his wife.

> Jyou Ma married my great uncle (who complained that his family had chosen an ugly woman for his wife).

Which or *That*—or Not?

Restrictive adjective clauses can be introduced by *which* or *that*, and often the relative pronoun can be omitted. In general, the prose sounds more formal with *which*, more conversational with *that* or with the pronoun omitted.

Read these sentences aloud:

Lately, I've been giving more thought to the kind of English which my mother speaks.

Lately, I've been giving more thought to the kind of English that my mother speaks.

Lately, I've been giving more thought to the kind of English my mother speaks.

Not surprisingly, in an essay that honors her mother's spoken language ("vivid, direct, full of observation and imagery . . . the language that helped shape the way I saw things, expressed things, made sense of the world"), Tan prefers the third version, achieving an informal tone by omitting the pronoun.

In "Housecalls," Sacks writes of his aunt Lina's generosity, saying that she sometimes provided his family with "certain special items *which* she herself cooked — fish cakes (Marcus and David called her Fishcake, or sometimes Fishface, after these), rich crumbly cheesecakes, and, at Passover, matzoh balls of an incredible tellurian density, which would sink like little planetismals below the surface of the soup." To begin the first adjective clause, he could have chosen *which*, *that*, or no pronoun:

certain special items which she herself cooked

certain special items that she herself cooked

certain special items she herself cooked

To my ear, all of these sound natural and appropriate. Like Sacks, I might choose the first or second version simply because, in such a complex sentence, a function word like *which* or *that* helps to show how the parts fit together.

Like the *who/whom* choice, the *which/that* choice becomes easy if the relative pronoun follows a preposition. You will use *which* — and you won't have to stop to think about it because *that* would sound unacceptable. (For example, you'd write "the neighborhood *in which* Sacks lived" rather than "the neighborhood *in that* Sacks lived.") If you place the preposition at the end of the sentence, then either *which* or *that* will do. Arranged from most to least formal, the options are these:

the neighborhood in which Sacks lived

the neighborhood which Sacks lived in

the neighborhood that Sacks lived in

the neighborhood Sacks lived in

Reducing Adjective Clauses

Adjective clauses are by no means the only structure that can appear after a noun to modify it. In fact, editors striving for conciseness often reduce adjective clauses, removing the subject and/or the verb to create other kinds of modifiers. Look, for example, at this pair:

> In this engaging essay, Amy Tan, who is best known for her novel *The Joy Luck Club*, writes about her mother's "broken" English.

> In this engaging essay, Amy Tan, best known for her novel *The Joy Luck Club*, writes about her mother's "broken" English.

Whether you want to reduce the clause will depend on the rhythm of the surrounding language and your judgment about the smoothness and clarity of the sentence. In general, I reduce adjective clauses if *who is* or *which is* seems entirely superfluous, if I hear a string of adjective clauses, or if a profusion of *that*'s becomes distracting.

The sentences below, adapted from Andrew Sullivan's article "Marriage or Bust," include adjective clauses that could be reduced. (Reducing them restores Sullivan's original sentences.)

> The people ~~who are~~ heralding civil unions are generally sympathetic to homosexual rights.

> They need to see that supporting civil union while opposing marriage is an incoherent position ~~that is~~ based more on sentiment than on reason, more on prejudice than principle.

> The Human Rights Campaign, ~~which is~~ the largest homosexual lobbying group, avoids the m-word in almost all its literature.

> One wonders, for example, what Bill Clinton or Newt Gingrich, both ~~of whom were~~ conducting or about to conduct extramarital affairs at the time, thought they were achieving by passing the DOMA [Defense of Marriage Act].

Reducing adjective clauses produces other kinds of modifiers. In the first and second sentences above, the reduction creates verbal phrases headed by the verbals *heralding* and *based*. In the third sentence, the reduction creates *the largest homosexual lobbying group,* — a noun phrase like those we'll examine in a discussion of appositives. In the fourth sentence, the modifier is an absolute. We'll return to these structures in the next two chapters.

EXERCISE 5D

The sentences below contain a lot of adjective clauses—too many, in my opinion. Reduce some (not all!) of the clauses to phrases. Then, compare your sentences to the originals as they were written by Amy Tan, Oliver Sacks, and Andrew Sullivan.

Example

They are in mourning for my mother's grandmother Divong, who was known as the "replacement wife." The women have come to this place, which is a Buddhist retreat, to perform yet another ceremony for her. Monks who were hired for the occasion have chanted the proper words. *(See Tan, "My Grandmother's Choice," para. 4.)*

Sample Response

They are in mourning for my mother's grandmother Divong, known as the "replacement wife." The women have come to this place, a Buddhist retreat, to perform yet another ceremony for her. Monks hired for the occasion have chanted the proper words.

1. The dark-jacketed woman who is next to her is a servant, who is remembered by my mother only as someone who cleaned but did not cook. *(See Tan, "My Grandmother's Choice," para. 8.)*

2. I do think that the language that is spoken in the family, especially in immigrant families which are more insular, plays a large role in shaping the language of the child. *(See Tan, "Mother Tongue," para. 15.)*

3. I never did well . . . with word analogies, which were pairs of words in which you were supposed to find some sort of logical, semantic relationship. *(See Tan, "Mother Tongue," para. 17.)*

4. At this point he engaged his sister Alida—who was a young widow with two children who had returned to London from South Africa three years before—to work as his assistant in the dispensary. *(See Sacks, "Housecalls," para. 17.)*

5. Lina, who was eighteen or nineteen at the time, had vivid and fascinating memories of Joniski, which was the shtetl near Vilna where they had all been born. *(See Sacks, "Housecalls," para. 24.)*

6. In the Court's view, which was expressed by Chief Justice Earl Warren in Loving *v.* Virginia in 1967, "the freedom to marry has long been recognized as one of the vital personal rights which is essential to the orderly pursuit of happiness by free men." It is one of the most fundamental rights that is accorded under the Constitution. *(See Sullivan, para. 20.)*

7. Friends mention their marriages with ease and pleasure without it even occurring to them that they are flaunting a privilege that was constructed specifically to stigmatize the person they are talking to. *(See Sullivan, para. 22.)*

8. The media will congratulate George W. Bush merely for conceding that the gay people that are supporting his campaign are human beings. *(See Sullivan, para. 24.)*

Adjective Phrases

An adjective or cluster of adjectives that stands outside the noun phrase is called an **adjective phrase**.

> My grandmother's cat, <u>sleek and black</u>, peers at the world through narrow yellow eyes.

> <u>Sleek and black</u>, my grandmother's cat peers at the world through narrow yellow eyes.

> I could see how my old man, <u>huge and cumbersome on land</u>, became transformed in the water.

> I, <u>self-conscious, nervous, and also rather clumsy</u>, found the same delicious transformation in myself.

When an adjective is simple — like *sleek* or *black* — it can reside happily either within the noun phrase or outside it:

> My grandmother's <u>sleek</u>, <u>black</u> cat . . .
> *The adjectives are embedded in a noun phrase.*

> My grandmother's cat, <u>sleek and black</u> . . .
> *An adjective phrase follows the noun phrase.*

Sleek and black, my grandmother's cat . . .
An adjective phrase precedes the noun phrase.

For a long string of adjectives, or for a description that can't be expressed in a single word, the adjective phrase is likely to be more graceful:

The <u>self-conscious, nervous, rather clumsy on his feet</u> boy moved more easily in the water.
A string of adjectives is embedded within the noun phrase — and talk about clumsy!

The boy, <u>self-conscious, nervous, and rather clumsy on his feet</u>, moved more easily in the water.
An adjective phrase follows the noun phrase.

<u>Self-conscious, nervous, and rather clumsy on his feet</u>, the boy moved more easily in the water.
An adjective phrase precedes the noun phrase.

EXERCISE 5E

Modify the noun phrase in boldface with two or three adjectives. First, place the adjectives within the noun phrase, immediately before the noun. Then craft an adjective phrase and experiment with its location in the sentence.

Example
My parents asked me to translate the doctor's questions.

Sample Responses
My <u>exhausted, frustrated, embarrassed</u> parents asked me to translate the doctor's questions.

adjectives before the noun

My parents, <u>exhausted, frustrated, and embarrassed</u>, asked me to translate the doctor's questions.

adjective phrase after the noun phrase

<u>Exhausted, frustrated, and embarrassed</u>, my parents asked me to translate the doctor's questions.

adjective phrase before the noun phrase

1. **The nurse** could not locate the CAT scan.
2. **My mother** asked me to call her stockbroker.

3. **The stockbroker's office** was in a brick building on Wall Street.

4. **The streets of Chinatown** still feel like home to me.

5. **The fog** hovers over the Golden Gate Bridge.

6

Modifiers Built from Verbs

Verbal Phrases

WATCH HOW HENRY LOUIS GATES manages the action in this episode from his memoir ("Sin Boldly," p. 155). The scene is the Swordfish, a nightclub where students from Potomac State enjoy dancing to a live band on weekend nights. The year is 1969; the Swordfish does not admit African Americans. The Fearsome Foursome — Gates and three of his friends — decide that it's time to integrate the club.

We parked the car and strolled up the stairs to the Swordfish. Since there was no cover charge, we walked straight into the middle of the dance floor. That's when the slo-mo started, an effect exacerbated by the strobe lights. Everybody froze: the kids from Piedmont and Keyser who had grown up with us; the students from Potomac State; the rednecks and crackers from up the hollers, the ones who came to town once a week all dressed up in their Sears, Roebuck perma-pressed drawers, their Thom McAn semi-leather shoes, their ultimately *white* sox, and their hair slicked back and wet-looking. The kids of rednecks, who liked to drink gallons of 3.2 beer, threaten everybody within earshot, and puke all over themselves—they froze, too, their worst nightmare staring them in the face.

After what seemed like hours but was probably less than a minute, a homely white boy with extra-greasy blond hair recovered and began to shout "Niggers" as his face assumed the ugly mask of hillbilly racism.

I stared at this white boy's face, which turned redder and redder as *he* turned into the Devil, calling on his boys to kick our asses: calling us niggers and niggers and niggers to help them summon up their courage. White boys started moving around us, forming a circle around ours. Our good friends from Keyser and Potomac State were still frozen, embarrassed that we were *in* there, that we had violated their space, dared to cross the line. No help from them. (I lost lots of friends that night.) Then, breaking through the circle of rednecks, came the owner, who started screaming: Get out of here! Get out of here! and picked up Fisher and slammed his head against the wall.

There is much to be said about this passage, and the important things have to do with race relations. But for now, I'd like to call your attention to the pacing — specifically, to the way Gates stops the action in the first paragraph, as "everybody froze," then starts it up in the second paragraph as the club's patrons begin to circle around the foursome.

Here are three key sentences from the first paragraph again, outlined so that you can see the clauses and modifiers:

That's when the slo-mo started,

an **effect** exacerbated by the strobe lights.

Everybody froze:

the **kids** from Piedmont and Keyser who had grown up with us;

the **students** from Potomac State;

the **rednecks and crackers** from up the hollers,

the **ones** who came to town once a week all dressed up in their Sears, Roebuck perma-pressed drawers, their Thom McAn semi-leather shoes, their ultimately *white* sox, and their hair slicked back and wet-looking.

The **kids** of rednecks,

who liked to drink gallons of 3.2 beer, threaten everybody within earshot, and puke all over themselves —

they froze too,

their worst **nightmare** staring them in the face.

Beginning with the first sentence above, when time slips off its track, Gates relies on noun phrases as modifiers. The sentences present us with a series of still shots, one picture after another, first this group of people, then the next group.

It's in the next paragraph that the action begins. Notice the modifiers here:

I stared at this white boy's face,

    which turned redder and redder

    as *he* turned into the Devil,

        calling on his boys to kick our asses:

        calling us niggers and niggers and niggers to help them summon up their courage.

White boys started moving around us,

    forming a circle around ours. . . .

Then,

    breaking through the circle of rednecks,

came the owner,

    who started screaming: Get out of here! Get out of here!

In this paragraph, many of the modifiers are **verbal phrases** headed by the *-ing* form of verbs. Gates could have described these actions in clauses of their own (for example, "As the white boys started moving around us, they formed a circle around ours" or "Then came the owner, who broke through the circle of rednecks"), but by presenting them in phrases, he creates a dense cluster of simultaneous actions. To me, the paragraph feels tense, almost dizzying, as violence threatens and finally erupts.

Functions of Verbal Phrases

Verbals come in three varieties: the present participle (*-ing*), past participle (*-ed* or irregular form), and infinitive (*to*) forms:

attending college

enrolled in the university; **hidden** from view

to earn a college degree

Verbals with these forms can be used in many ways — some so common and easy that you could write them in your sleep, others worthy of some attention and practice.

Among the common, easy uses of verbals are these:

SUBJECT

Attending Potomac State College was a big step for the young Gates.

At one time, to earn a college degree was to secure a ticket to professional, middle-class employment.

OBJECT OF A VERB

Gates loved studying literature with Professor Duke Whitmore.

At Yale, he and his classmates wanted to understand their obligation to the Black community.

OBJECT OF A PREPOSITION

During the break, students will have lots of time for playing Frisbee.

COMPLEMENT

At one time, to earn a college degree was to secure a ticket to professional, middle-class employment.

ONE-WORD ADJECTIVES

Most students prefer to take challenging classes.

Only enrolled students with stamped identification cards are permitted to use the university library.

For the remainder of this chapter, we'll be concentrating on verbal phrases like those in Gates's second paragraph — more complex phrases that function as modifiers, attached to but not grammatically integrated into a clause.

Phrases beginning with an *-ing* verbal usually describe an action, often one occurring simultaneously with the action described by the attached clause.

We dragged Fisher to the car, ducking the bottles and cans as we sped away.

Back home, we had sneaked around at first, hiding in cemeteries and in a crowd of friends, almost never being seen together in public alone.

"Sin boldly," he would tell me later, citing Martin Luther.

Phrases beginning with an *-ed* verbal usually function as adjectives.

> Our good friends from Keyser and Potomac State were still frozen, embarrassed that we were *in* there.

> And that is why the Swordfish nightclub is now Samson's Family Restaurant, run by a very nice Filipino family.

> I stayed out of Keyser on the day of the election, terrified that I'd already caused Maura's father to lose.

Verbal phrases in the *to* form describe a purpose. *To* verbals sometimes begin *in order to.*

> I searched the audience for Miss Twigg's face, just to see her expression when I read the speech!

> I would attend [Potomac State] too, then go off to "the university" — in Morgantown — to become a doctor.

> I started parking my car on red lines and in front of fire hydrants, just to test her assertion.

Verbal phrases can appear early in the sentence as well. Any of these variations would sound perfectly natural:

> Citing Martin Luther, he told me to "sin boldly."

> Terrified that I'd already caused Maura's father to lose, I stayed out of Keyser.

> Just to test her assertion, I started parking my car on red lines and in front of fire hydrants.

EXERCISE 6A

Read the passages below, adapted from "Sin Boldly." Underline the verbal phrases used as modifiers. I count seven: five with an *-ing* verbal, one with an *-ed* verbal, and one with a *to* verbal.

> On weekends during the summer of 1969, I'd drive over to Rehoboth Beach, in Delaware, to see Maura, who was working as a waitress at the Crab Pot. I'd leave work on Friday at about four o'clock, then drive all the way to Delaware, arriving at Rehoboth before midnight, with as much

energy as if I had just awakened. We'd get a motel room after her shift ended, and she'd bring a bushel of crabs, steamed in hot spice. We'd get lots of ice-cold Budweiser and we'd have a feast, listening to Junior Walker play "What Does It Take" over and over and over again.

It was because of 'Bama's new office that I learned that the West Virginia State Police had opened a file on me in Mineral County, identifying me for possible custodial detention if and when race riots started. Maura gave me the news late one night, whispering it over the phone. Old 'Bama, feeling magnanimous after his victory, had wanted me to know and to be warned.

EXERCISE 6B

Combine the sentences in each group by transforming the sentences in boldface into -*ing* verbal phrases. When you've completed the exercise, compare your sentences to the originals by David Sedaris ("Genetic Engineering," p. 231) and Amy Tan ("My Grandmother's Choice," p. 267).

Example
I'd heard once that if a single bird were to transport all the sand, grain by grain, from the eastern seaboard to the coast of Africa, it would take . . . I didn't catch the number of years. **I preferred to concentrate on the single bird chosen to perform this thankless task.** *(See Sedaris, para. 10.)*

Sample Response
I'd heard once that if a single bird were to transport all the sand, grain by grain, from the eastern seaboard to the coast of Africa, it would take . . . I didn't catch the number of years, preferring to concentrate on the single bird chosen to perform this thankless task.

1. I tried to creep by unnoticed, but he stopped me. **He claimed that I was just the fellow he'd been looking for.** *(See Sedaris, para. 9.)*

2. "Let me ask a little something," one of the men said. **He spat his spent cigarette butt into the surf.** *(See Sedaris, para. 13.)*

3. He moved several yards down the beach and began a new equation. **He captivated his audience with a lengthy explanation of each new and complex symbol.** *(See Sedaris, para. 15.)*

4. In my room, on my desk, sits an old family photo in a plain black frame. **It depicts five women and a girl at a temple pavilion by a lake.** *(See Tan, para. 1.)*

5. **She found no means to support herself or her young daughter.** Nunu Aiyi eventually accepted the lawyer's second proposal—this time, to become his number-two concubine. *(See Tan, para. 6.)*

6. Later Dooma killed herself. **She used some mysterious means that made her die slowly over three days.** *(See Tan, para. 8.)*

7. In my writing room, I go back into the past, to that moment when my grandmother told my mother not to follow her footsteps. My grandmother and I are walking side by side. **We imagine the past differently. We remember it another way.** *(See Tan, para. 19.)*

EXERCISE 6C

Write sentences using each of the three kinds of verbal phrases based on the verbs *force* and *write*. Remember, you're not being asked to use the given verb in the independent clause; instead, create verbal phrases as in the example.

Example

Discover

-ing: Discovering that the nightclub owner is stubborn, the human rights commissioner threatens to shut down the club.

-ed: Her manuscript, discovered beneath the floorboards of the college library, is now being auctioned on eBay.

to: The main character had to travel across Nigeria to discover the truth her family had hidden from her for so many years.

Force

-ing:

-ed:

to:

Write

-ing:

-en:

to:

Managing Emphasis with Verbal Phrases

Verbal phrases, like other modifiers, create an opportunity for writers to manipulate emphasis. Compare these sentences:

> I gave the valedictory address at graduation, defying convention by writing my own speech.

> Giving the valedictory address at graduation, I defied convention by writing my own speech.

In the first sentence, the main point is that Gates gave the valedictory address. The sentence informs us that he was defying convention, but because that information appears in a modifier, we read it as an elaboration. In the second sentence, the defiance of convention has earned a promotion. When it occupies the independent clause, we read Gates's claim to have defied convention as the main point.

The order of information affects emphasis, too. As a general rule, you can highlight material by placing it at the end of the sentence.

> Just to see her expression when I read the speech, I searched the audience for Miss Twigg's face.

> I searched the audience for Miss Twigg's face, just to see her expression when I read the speech!

In both sentences, *just to see her expression* is a modifier, and in the first one it is, as you would expect, de-emphasized, setting the stage for the independent clause about looking for Miss Twigg. But in the second sentence, the emphasis is reversed simply because the modifier comes at the end. Verbal phrases, like other modifiers, tend to be read as background information in periodic sentences and to get more attention in cumulative sentences.

Because there are so many ways to emphasize one element in a sentence — using strong language, rephrasing or repeating, adjusting sentence length, playing with punctuation — no single principle can predict which part of a sentence will be stressed. Still, these are useful generalizations: you can stress material by placing it in an independent clause (reducing other material to modifiers like verbal phrases) or by placing it at the end of the sentence.

Notice how Gates highlights the main clause in this sentence from "The Two Nations of Black America" (p. 164). After describing the disappearance of industrial jobs in the cities, he describes developments in the 1980s:

> Thenceforth, in one of the most curious social transformations in the class structure in recent American history, two tributaries began

to flow, running steadily into two distinct rivers of aspiration and achievement.

The main clause, *two tributaries began to flow,* encapsulates the central idea of the sentence — in fact, the central idea of the essay. Gates builds up to it with a chain of prepositional phrases, preparing readers for an event of great historical significance. At the end of the sentence, the verbal phrase elaborates on the main clause, echoing *two tributaries* with the phrase *two distinct rivers.*

EXERCISE 6D

Combine the material into a single sentence, using one sentence as the independent clause and transforming the others to -*ing* verbal phrases. Then, try a different combination, placing different material in the independent clause. (Feel free to switch the order of the information, too.)

Example
Maura and I sneaked around.
Maura and I hid in cemeteries and in a crowd of friends.
Maura and I were almost never seen together in public alone.

Sample Responses
Maura and I sneaked around, hiding in cemeteries and in a crowd of friends, almost never being seen together in public alone.

Sneaking around, hiding in cemeteries and in a crowd of friends, Maura and I were almost never seen together in public alone.

1. Her father had hidden behind a tree.
   Her father had watched her climb into my car.

2. The police followed us around town.
   The police dared us to go even one mile over the speed limit.

3. Eugene would make up words as he went along.
   Eugene used sounds similar to those he could not remember.
   Eugene made no sense.

4. We spruced up the Soul Mobile for the occasion.
   We replaced the old masking tape over the holes in the roof.

5. Maura's father had lived in Keyser all his life.
   Maura's father worked for the post office.
   Maura's father visited with just about everyone in town.

In general, material in a sentence is stressed when it appears in a clause rather than a phrase or when it appears near the end of a sentence. Like other generalizations about emphasis, these have limited application; they can inform a writer's judgment but cannot substitute for it.

Look closely at each pair of sentences that you created in Exercise 6D. When you place first one idea into a verbal phrase and then the other, what happens? Does the emphasis shift? Which sentence sounds better to your ear? What other factors affect the emphasis?

On the whole, do your sentences confirm the generalizations or complicate them?

Reducing Clauses to Create Verbal Phrases

Back in Chapter 5, you reduced adjective clauses to phrases by eliminating the subject and/or the verb. In some sentences, the reduction changed an adjective clause to a verbal phrase — so that, for example, "the language that is spoken in the family" became "the language *spoken in the family.*" Similarly, "gay people that are supporting his campaign" became "gay people *supporting his campaign.*"

Adverb clauses can sometimes be reduced to verbal phrases as well:

When he entered Yale in 1968, Gates was part of the college's first "large" group of blacks.

<u>Entering Yale in 1968</u>, Gates was part of the college's first "large" group of blacks.

After he finished his degree at Yale, Gates studied English and American literature in Cambridge.

<u>After finishing his degree at Yale</u>, Gates studied English and American literature in Cambridge.

In the first pair, the subordinator *when* disappears, while in the second pair, the subordinator *after* is retained. In both cases, the subject is eliminated and the verb changes to an *-ing* verbal.

As you edit your prose, you may sometimes decide that, for the sake of conciseness, clarity, rhythm, or emphasis, you wish to reduce a subordinate clause to a verbal phrase.

EXERCISE 6F

The passages below are adapted from Henry Louis Gates's essay "The Two Nations of Black America" (p. 164) and Amy Tan's "My Grandmother's Choice" (p. 267). After reading each passage, reduce the underlined clause to a verbal phrase. (Remember that, even when restricted to verbal phrases, you have several options: -ing, -ed, and to.) What do you think? Does the revised passage strike you as more or less effective than the original?

Example

Because it was brimming to overflow with maybe 200 students, the year's first meeting of the Black Student Alliance at Yale looked like Harlem to me! I basked in the warmth that was generated by the comfort of the range of brown colors in that room, but I also shuddered when I contemplated the awesome burden of leadership that we felt.

Sample Response

~~Because it was~~ brimming to overflow with maybe 200 students, the year's first meeting of the Black Student Alliance at Yale looked like Harlem to me! I basked in the warmth ~~that was~~ generated by the comfort of the range of brown colors in that room, but I also shuddered ~~when I contemplated~~ when contemplating the awesome burden of leadership that we felt.

The revised passage does strike me as more effective; it's more concise.

1. These students were not so much a new black middle-class bourgeoisie that had been recruited to scale the ladder of class as the scions of an old and colored middle class that had been recruited to integrate a white male elite. We clung to a soft black nationalist politics because we wanted to keep ourselves on the straight and narrow.

2. For me one crucial scene of instruction on the path of nationalist politics came while I was watching a black program that had been produced by students at Howard. In the film, a student, who was happily dating a white co-ed, comes to see the error of his ways after he meets the activist Maulana Ron Karenga.

3. Our community and our families prepared us to be successful as they told us over and over, "Get all the education you can."

4. Because he wished to show his displeasure, he insulted Jyou Ma's cooking. During one of their raucous dinner arguments, the table was shoved and a pot of boiling soup tipped and spilled all over his niece's neck, which caused a burn that almost killed her.

5. One night he raped her, <u>which made her an outcast</u>. <u>Because she realized that she had no other choice</u>, my grandmother became a concubine to a rich man, and took her young daughter to live on an island near Shanghai. She left her son behind <u>because she wanted to save his face</u>.

Dangling Modifiers

There is probably no grammar term that evokes such apprehension, or such ridicule, as "dangling modifier." When you imagine Miss Grundy — that prototype of fussy English teachers, with stiff posture, pursed lips, and an obsession for grammatical purity — what is she doing? She's smacking a ruler on the desk of a red-faced child, and she's exclaiming "Dangling Modifier!" The other children feel sorry for the mortified young writer, but they can't help snickering as they think about how to deploy the word *dangling* during recess.

Because modifiers are separate from the essential structure of the clause, they can be more or less firmly attached to the clause. If a modifier is not attached carefully — if there's some ambiguity about what it modifies — it is said to dangle. Since verbal phrases are especially prone to dangling, it's worth taking time during proofreading to double-check verbal phrases, making sure they're firmly tethered.

The sentence below illustrates a dangling modifier:

After reading Gates's essay, our understanding of ethnic identity changed.

Who read the essay? Our understanding? That can't be what the writer meant to say. To edit the sentence, insert a noun (or pronoun) that identifies the readers immediately after the verbal phrase, or change the verbal phrase to a different sort of structure — for example, an adverb clause. Because an adverb clause has its own subject-verb pair, there can be no confusion about who's doing what.

After reading Gates's essay, <u>we</u> had a different understanding of ethnic identity.

Edited by inserting the appropriate noun (here, a pronoun) right after the verbal phrase.

<u>After we had read Gates's essay</u>, our understanding of ethnic identity changed.

Edited by changing the verbal phrase to a clause.

Writers, editors, grammarians, and other lovers of language sometimes disagree about whether a dangling modifier really causes ambiguity, whether it really requires editing. A hard-liner might object to the sentence below:

> When learning a new language, it may be necessary to risk social embarrassment in order to interact with native speakers.

Who is learning a new language? It? That doesn't make much sense. And yet . . . any reader would understand this sentence easily enough, and there might be good reason to avoid using words such as *you* or *language learners* in the independent clause. Choices about editing dangling modifiers, like so many other choices writers and editors make, require not just attention to structure but good judgment.

EXERCISE 6G

In each of the sentences below (loosely based on the story "Genetic Engineering"), the verbal phrase is a dangling modifier. Revise the sentence, first by inserting an appropriate noun or pronoun right after the verbal phrase, then by changing the verbal phrase to a clause.

Example
To test my complex theories of suspended animation, a colony of slugs was placed in the basement freezer.

First Revision
To test my complex theories of suspended animation, I placed a colony of slugs in the basement freezer.

Second Revision
Because I wanted to test my complex theories of suspended animation, a colony of slugs was placed in the basement freezer.

1. Discovering the frozen slugs, it seemed best not to ask too many questions.
2. Soon after repairing my record player, the rubber band snapped and the damned thing broke all over again.
3. Choosing between their mother's interest in tanning and their father's interest in science, it was no contest.
4. After visiting my father's office, there was comfort in knowing he had some colleagues who shared his interests.
5. Once completed, the young scientist wished he could redesign his experiment.

6. Having sold their homes on the beach, the engineer's comments about the value of sand were interesting to the fishermen.

7. After selling their homes to retirees from out of state, the property value went up.

Punctuation also affects a reader's understanding of verbal phrases. Any verbal phrase set off by a comma, whether it appears at the beginning or the end of a clause, will attach itself to the clause's subject:

Using a magnifying glass, I studied an old photograph of my father.

I studied an old photograph of my father, using a magnifying glass.

I studied an old photograph of my father using a magnifying glass.

Who was using the magnifying glass? Readers will understand the first two sentences to mean the same thing — that the narrator used a magnifying glass to study a photograph. In the last sentence, the absence of the comma makes a big difference. Now, the narrator studies an image in which his father has a magnifying glass in hand.

Rather than close this chapter with warnings about errors or advice about punctuation, I'd like to return to the main point. Verbal phrases are a versatile syntactic structure, often under-used in the work of undergraduate writers but common in published prose. I urge you to experiment with them in your writing.

EXERCISE 6H

Use verbal phrases to develop sentences whose structure imitates the models by Jane Smiley (p. 237) and Louise Erdrich (p. 139).

Example

Twain came back to the novel and worked on it twice again, once to re-write the chapters containing the feud between the Grangerfords and the Sheperdsons, and later to introduce the Duke and the Dauphin.

Sample Response

My grandmother traveled to Colorado and worked there twice,
independent clause

    once to teach the children of a wealthy ranch family
to *verbal phrase*

and later to write her memoirs.

to *verbal phrase*

Uncle Tom's Cabin was published in 1852, when Twain was seventeen, still living in Hannibal and contributing to his brother's newspapers, still sympathizing with the South.

1. Write a sentence in which you recall your young self affectionately.

_____

independent clause

    when I was _____

    adverb clause (providing your age)

    _____

    -ing *verbal phrase*

    _____

    -ing *verbal phrase*

2. Write a sentence in which you recall your young self more critically.

_____

independent clause

    when I was _____

    adverb clause (providing your age)

    _____

    -ing *verbal phrase*

    _____

    -ing *verbal phrase*

The next morning, waking to a silence where I usually heard my father's noises, hearing a vacancy before I even knew it for sure, I understood that the worst was yet to come.

3. Write a sentence that creates a sober, ominous tone.

    The next morning,

_____

-ing *verbal phrase*

_____

-ing *verbal phrase*

I understood that _____

4. Write a sentence that creates a joyous tone.

The next morning,

_____

-ing *verbal phrase*

_____

-ing *verbal phrase*

I understood that _____

Noun Phrases Working as Modifiers

Appositives and Absolutes

WHAT'S NOT TO LOVE about apposition? Appositives are easy to write, extremely versatile, and risk-free — you rarely see a dangling, misplaced, or otherwise misguided appositive. To the wise writer, appositives are staples, the salt and pepper of modification.

This chapter discusses three kinds of modifiers that belong in every writer's repertoire: noun phrases in apposition, other structures in apposition, and absolute phrases.

Noun Phrases in Apposition

An **appositive** is a noun phrase that appears in a sentence next to another noun phrase with the same referent. In everyday speech, appositives sometimes appear in introductions, as in "This is my brother-in-law, *Jerry Allen*" or "I'd like you to meet Jerry Allen, *my brother-in-law from Texas.*" The two noun phrases *Jerry Allen* and *my brother-in-law from Texas* have the same referent — that is, they refer to the same person — but there is informational value in naming the person both ways. Similarly, an appositive might be placed next to other proper nouns (Thomas Edison, *my children's elementary school*) or, perhaps, used to explain a term (a spiral, *the long glide that Nancy Kerrigan does so beautifully*).

Like verbal phrases, appositives can be thought of as supplements — extra information, added to the clause — or as reductions of separate sentences. Compare the sentences below:

I'd like you to meet Jerry Allen.

I'd like you to meet Jerry Allen. He is my brother-in-law from Texas.

I'd like you to meet Jerry Allen, who is my brother-in-law from Texas.

I'd like you to meet **Jerry Allen**, my brother-in-law from Texas.

In the final sentence, the appositive *my brother-in-law from Texas* serves as a modifier, restating the initial noun, *Jerry Allen*. The use of an appositive makes the final sentence more informative than the first, more concise than the second or third.

In published writing, appositives are quite common. They perform several functions, illustrated below with sentences from Jane Smiley's article "Say It Ain't So, Huck" (p. 237), Oliver Sacks's essay "The Case of the Colorblind Painter" (p. 199), and Louise Erdrich's short story "Shamengwa" (p. 139).

Identifying People

Appositives are often paired with proper nouns, providing identifying information so that readers will understand the significance of a name. Normally the name comes first, then the identification — but, as you see in some of the examples below, the order can be reversed.

Edwin Land—not merely the inventor of the instant Land camera and Polaroid but an experimenter and theorizer of genius—provided a photographic demonstration of color perception even more startling.

Helmholtz's great contemporary, Clerk Maxwell, had also been fascinated by the mystery of color vision from his student days.

When Ophelia takes over the education of **Topsy**, a child who has suffered a most brutal previous upbringing, she discovers that she can do nothing with her until she takes her, literally, to her bosom.

A Kentucky slave, Tom, is sold to pay off a debt to a slave trader, who takes him to New Orleans.

EXERCISE 7A

In this paragraph, Smiley describes the characterization in *Uncle Tom's Cabin*. She introduces many characters in a short space, using appositives to identify them.

1. Underline seven appositives that name or identify people.

The characters appear, one after another, vivified by their attitudes, desires, and opinions as much as by their histories and their fates. Surely Augustine St. Clare, Tom's owner in New Orleans, is an exquisite portrayal of a humane but indecisive man, who knows what he is doing but not how to stop it. Surely Cassy, a fellow slave whom Tom meets on the Legree plantation, is one of the great angry women in all of literature—not only bitter, murderous, and nihilistic but also intelligent and enterprising. Surely the midlife spiritual journey of Ophelia St. Clare, Augustine's Yankee cousin, from self-confident ignorance to affectionate understanding is most convincing, as is Topsy's parallel journey from ignorance and self-hatred to humanity. . . . The slave trader, Haley; Tom's wife, Chloe; Augustine's wife, Marie; Legree's overseers, Sambo and Quimbo—good or evil, they all live.

2. Think of a novel, film, or television program in which the characters are particularly well drawn. Write a paragraph similar to Smiley's: describe the characters, providing an initial identification of each in a brief appositive.

Defining Terms

If Sacks thinks readers need background information to identify Edwin Land and Clerk Maxwell, he can be pretty sure we'll need help with *alexia* and *cerebral achromatopsia*. The sentences below illustrate a characteristic function of appositives in academic writing: in a pair of noun phrases, one introduces a technical term and the other defines it.

This alexia, or inability to read, lasted for five days, but then disappeared.

Total colorblindness caused by brain damage, so-called cerebral achromatopsia, though described more than three centuries ago, remains a rare and important condition.

Filling in Examples or Explanations

Appositives can also pin down the meaning of a word or phrase by providing a concise series of examples. The sentences below track the progress of Mr. I.'s coming to terms with his colorblindness, a slow movement from depression to the determination to get on with life. In each sentence, Sacks uses a pair of noun phrases, one naming a phenomenon in general terms and the other listing specifics.

> His first black-and-white paintings, done in February and March, gave a feeling of **violent forces**—rage, fear, despair, excitement— but these were held in control, attesting to the powers of artistry that could disclose, and yet contain, such intensity of feeling.

> These paintings, even though still in black and white, were full of movement, vitality, and sensuousness; and they went with **a change in his personal life**—a lessening of his withdrawal and the beginnings of a renewed social and sexual life, a lessening of his fears and depression, and a turning back to life.

> He seemed to be turning to **all the visual modes that still remained to him**—form, contour, movement, depth—and exploring them with heightened intensity.

Occasionally an appositive listing specifics will begin the sentence. In the sentences below, the list is, conceptually, the subject of the sentence. But long noun phrases make awkward sentence subjects. By presenting the list in an appositive, then using a simple pronoun as the grammatical subject, the writers make the sentences easy to process:

> The ineffectual Mr. Shelby and his submissive, and subversive, wife; the slave trader Haley; Tom's wife, Chloe; Augustine's wife, Marie; Legree's overseers, Sambo and Quimbo—good or evil, **they all** live.

> Compare: *The ineffectual Mr. Shelby and his submissive, and subversive, wife; the slave trader Haley; Tom's wife, Chloe; Augustine's wife, Marie; and Legree's overseers, Sambo and Quimbo, good or evil, all live.*

> Her strong arms, her kisses, the clean soap smell of her face, her voice calming me—**all of this** was gone.

> Compare: *Her strong arms, her kisses, the clean soap smell of her face, and her voice calming me were gone.*

You can see the same principle at work in the second half of "'The Case of the Colorblind Painter,'" where Sacks summarizes the development of color theory over several centuries. Some of the concepts require rather lengthy explanation. In the passage below, Sacks explains why "classical" color theory is inadequate to explain problems like Mr. I.'s. He keeps the independent clauses relatively simple, packing the explanatory detail into appositives:

> All of this, of course, is very difficult to explain in terms of **classical color theory**—Newton's notion of an invariant relationship between wavelength and color, of a cell-to-cell transmission of wavelength information from the retina to the brain, and of a direct conversion of this information into color. **Such a simple process**—a neurological analogy to the decomposition and recomposition of light through a prism—could hardly account for the complexity of color perception in real life.

I would not describe the above passage as easy to read. Still, a reader can follow the thread of the argument by focusing on the main clauses: this (Mr. I.'s colorblindness) is difficult to explain in terms of classical color theory because it assumes too simple a process for color perception. By tucking the explanations of classical color theory into modifiers, Sacks makes the information available without complicating the essential structure of the clauses.

Renaming with a Twist

Perhaps the most important use of appositives in writing is to rename a person or thing, or to restate an idea, in words that get the reader to see it in a new light. When Jane Smiley points out that several famous nineteenth-century novelists shared her admiration of *Uncle Tom's Cabin*, she presents the group of writers three times:

> The novel was immediately read and acclaimed by **any number of excellent judges**: Charles Dickens, George Eliot, Leo Tolstoy, George Sand—the whole roster of nineteenth-century liberals whose work we read today and try to persuade ourselves that *Huck Finn* is equal to.

The novelists are first alluded to in the noun phrase "any number of excellent judges." Then an appositive specifies the novelists by name. Then another appositive refers to that same set of people but describes them in new language, reminding us of their significance as influential liberals and distinguished authors.

In the examples below, the appositives work in a similar way, restating the ideas so that we look at them from a slightly different angle:

As Mr. I. pointed out, we accept black-and-white photographs or films because they are **representations of the world**—images that we can look at, or away from, when we want.

Now he heard music with no visual accompaniment; this, for him, was **music with its essential chromatic counterpart missing,** music now radically impoverished.

No matter how often the critics "place in context" Huck's use of the word "nigger," they can never excuse or fully hide **the deeper racism of the novel**—the way Twain and Huck use Jim because they really don't care enough about his desire for freedom to let that desire change their plans.

EXERCISE 7B

Combine the sentences in each group by transforming the sentences in boldface into appositives. When you've completed the exercise, compare your sentences to the originals.

Example
All of these women have been promised something by their owners, but, owing to slavery, all of these promises have been broken. **They have been promised love, education, the privilege and joy of raising their own children.** *(See Smiley, para. 12.)*

Sample Response
All of these women have been promised something by their owners—love, education, the privilege and joy of raising their own children—but, owing to slavery, all of these promises have been broken.

1. It is with the feud that the novel begins to fail, because from here on the episodes are mere distractions from the true subject of the work. **The true subject is Huck's affection for and responsibility to Jim.** *(See Smiley, para. 5.)*

2. Harriet Beecher Stowe, active in the abolitionist movement and in the effort to aid and educate escaped slaves, had no such personal conflict

when she sat down to write *Uncle Tom's Cabin*. **Stowe was a New Englander. She was the daughter of Puritans and thinkers.** *(See Smiley, para. 15.)*

3. In these two months he produced dozens of paintings, marked by a singular style. **They were marked by a character he had never shown before.** *(See Sacks, "Colorblind Painter," para. 29.)*

4. Color vision, it seemed—like the other processes of early vision—required no prior knowledge. **The other processes include motion, depth, and form perception.** *(See Sacks, "Colorblind Painter," para. 17.)*

5. Geraldine sometimes drove Shamengwa to fiddling contests, where he could perform in more of a concert setting. **She was a dedicated, headstrong woman who six years back had borne a baby, dumped its father, and earned a degree in education.** *(See Erdrich, para. 4.)*

6. He even won awards. **He won prizes of the cheap sort given at local musical contests. They were engraved plaques and small tin cups set on plastic pedestals.** *(See Erdrich, para. 4.)* ¹

7. My true friend was my fiddle, anyway. **It was the only friend I really needed.** *(See Erdrich, para. 28.)*

8. His was a peaceful death. **It was the sort of death we used to pray to Saint Joseph to give us all.** *(See Erdrich, para. 48.)*

EXERCISE 7C

Add an appositive after the noun phrase in boldface.

Example
Corwin learned to play the violin.

Sample Responses
Corwin, a troubled young man who had been searching for beauty and purpose in his life, learned to play the violin.

Corwin, a lifelong troublemaker and thief, learned to play the violin.

As you develop sentences 1–3, create a positive image of your piano lessons.

1. I'll never forget the day I met **my piano teacher**.

2. She gave lessons in **her living room**.

3. She had **a large, grey cat**.

As you develop sentences 4–6, create a negative image of your piano lessons.

4. I'll never forget the day I met **my piano teacher**.

5. She gave lessons in **her living room**.
6. She had **a large, grey cat**.

You have probably noticed that writers punctuate appositives with a variety of marks. Commas are the default punctuation. But, especially if the appositive is long and complex, containing commas of its own, it's helpful to set it off with more emphatic punctuation such as a colon or dash.

In fiction, you'll sometimes even see appositives punctuated with periods. Here's one of my favorite passages from "Shamengwa":

> The music was more than music—at least, more than what we are used to hearing. The sound connected instantly with **something deep and joyous**. Those powerful moments of true knowledge which we paper over with daily life. The music tapped **our terrors**, too. Things we'd lived through and wanted never to repeat. Shredded imaginings, unadmitted longings, fear, and also surprising pleasures. We can't live at that pitch. But every so often, something shatters like ice, and we fall into the river of our own existence. We are aware. This realization was in the music somehow, or in the way Shamengwa played it.

Other Structures in Apposition

Though the term *appositive* is usually reserved for noun phrases, many structures can be placed in apposition — that is, placed alongside a clause or phrase of the same type, with the same referent. Then the second clause or phrase will be read as a modifier, restating or elaborating on the first.

The sentences below illustrate structures that are frequently placed in apposition.

That Clauses

> The novel took me a couple of days (it was longer than I had remembered), and I closed the cover stunned. Yes, stunned. Not, by any means, by the artistry of the book but by the notion **that this is the novel all American literature grows out of**, that this is a great novel, that this is even a serious novel.

> Mr. I. arrived at his studio with relief, expecting **that the horrible mist would be gone**, that everything would be clear again.

That such a center might exist, that any part of the cortex might be specialized for the perception of color, was immediately contested and continued to be contested for almost a century.

It is at higher levels **that integration occurs,** that color fuses with memories, expectations, associations, and desires to make a world with resonance and meaning for each of us.

Verb Phrases

Newton, in his famous prism experiment in 1666, showed that white light **was composite**—could be decomposed into, and recomposed by, all the colors of the spectrum.

Color constancy, for him [Helmholtz], was a special example of the way in which we **achieve perceptual constancy generally,** make a stable perceptual world from a chaotic sensory flux.

As though her heart, too, were buried underneath that small white headstone in the Catholic cemetery, she **turned cold,** turned away from the rest of us.

Now that I am old and know the ways of grief, I understand that she **felt too much,** loved too much.

I might have **stayed that way,** joined my mother in the darkness from which she could not return.

Prepositional Phrases

Thus, unable to rectify even the inner image, the idea, of various foods, he turned increasingly **to black and white foods**—to black olives and white rice, black coffee and yogurt.

"The sun rose **like a bomb,** like some enormous nuclear explosion," he said later.

Though many of the cases described had other problems, too . . . the crucial lesions seemed to be **in the medial cortex,** in areas homologous to V4 in the monkey.

But always, no matter how hesitantly, it ended up advancing **straight toward the southern rock,** straight toward me.

I do my best to make the small decisions well, and I try not to hunger **for the greater things,** for the deeper explanations.

If you examine all of the sentences in this section carefully, you'll see that the structures placed in apposition fit into the same grammatical slot in the sentence. For example, you could choose any one of Smiley's *that* clauses to complete the sentence below:

I was stunned by the notion	that this is the novel all American literature grows out of.
I was stunned by the notion	that this is a great novel.
I was stunned by the notion	that this is even a serious novel.

Typically, structures in apposition are arranged so that the most general statement of the idea comes first, with the modifier adding specific detail. Look at the example below:

Thus, unable to rectify even the inner image, the idea, of various foods, he turned increasingly **to black and white foods**—to black olives and white rice, black coffee and yogurt.

The more general "to black and white foods" naturally precedes the more specific "to black olives and white rice, black coffee and [white] yogurt."

When the phrases are about equally specific, you can play with the order:

The sun rose **like a bomb,** like some enormous nuclear explosion.

or

The sun rose **like some enormous nuclear explosion,** like a bomb.

I'd like to stress two points: Apposition is easy. And it gives writers access to a wide range of choices for developing sentences with information, ideas, and images.

EXERCISE 7D

If you haven't already done so, read Louise Erdrich's short story "Shamengwa" (p. 139). Then develop each of the following sentences by adding at least one phrase in apposition to the phrase in boldface. The new phrase should echo the first one in structure and meaning; it should contain virtually the same content, reworded so that the reader sees it in a new light. Take your time with this exercise, writing sentences consistent with the meaning and the mood of Erdrich's story.

Examples

Shamengwa's music was **extraordinary**.

Shamengwa's music could make listeners aware **of joys and grief that lay buried in their hearts**.

People's emotions often turn on them.

Sample Responses

Shamengwa's music was extraordinary, hauntingly beautiful.

Shamengwa's music could make listeners aware of joys and grief that lay buried in their hearts, of hidden hopes and secret fears, of memories they had tried to lock away.

People's emotions, their fears and resentments, even their love, often turn on them.

1. Shamengwa's arm was injured in **a childhood accident**.

2. Corwin drove a 1991 Impala **with all the signs of old age and hard use**.

3. The narrator is surprised to discover **how deeply he misses Shamengwa's music**.

4. At Geraldine's urging, Shamengwa tells the story of **how his fiddle came to him**.

5. After the death of her youngest child, Shamengwa's mother **fell into a state of numb despair**.

6. Corwin's sentence was **to study with Shamengwa**.

7. Shamengwa was **proud of Corwin**.

8. **When the moon slipped behind the clouds**, Billy applied pitch to Edwin's canoe.

Absolute Phrases

Especially in descriptive passages, writers sometimes use a modifier called an **absolute phrase**. Like an appositive, an absolute is headed by a noun, but instead of echoing another noun phrase, it modifies the sentence as a whole. Let's begin with some examples from "The Case of the Colorblind Painter" and "Shamengwa":

> He found color television especially hard to bear, its images always unpleasant, sometimes unintelligible.

> He could no longer see clouds in the sky, <u>their whiteness being</u> <u>scarcely distinguishable from the azure, which seemed bleached to a</u> <u>pale grey.</u>

> It was the middle of September on the reservation, <u>the mornings chill,</u> <u>the afternoons warm, the leaves still green and thick in their final</u> <u>sweetness.</u>

> Corwin stood gazing at the coffin, <u>the violin dangling from one hand.</u>

The modifiers in these sentences are absolute phrases. If you study their structure, you will notice some common features. First, each absolute phrase is headed by a noun (*images, whiteness, mornings, afternoons, leaves, violin*). Second, as I've noted, each modifies the sentence as a whole rather than attaching itself to a particular word or phrase.

Absolute phrases are very easy to imagine as separate sentences. Oliver Sacks might have written, "He found color television especially hard to bear. Its images were always unpleasant, sometimes unintelligible." The second sentence is transformed into an absolute phrase by the deletion of the verb. Similarly, the absolute phrases in this sentence represent the deletion of *to be* verbs:

> It was the middle of September on the reservation. The mornings <u>were</u> chill. The afternoons <u>were</u> warm. The leaves <u>were</u> still green and thick in their sweetness.

> It was the middle of September on the reservation, the mornings chill, the afternoons warm, the leaves still green and thick in their sweetness.

Sometimes, absolute phrases retain the verb in its *-ing* form:

> He could no longer see clouds in the sky. Their whiteness <u>was</u> scarcely distinguishable from the azure, which seemed bleached to a pale grey.

> He could no longer see clouds in the sky, their whiteness <u>being</u> scarcely distinguishable from the azure, which seemed bleached to a pale grey.

> Corwin stood gazing at the coffin. The violin <u>dangled</u> from one hand.

> Corwin stood gazing at the coffin, the violin <u>dangling</u> from one hand.

The linguist Martha Kolln[1] points out that absolutes can also be seen as alternatives to prepositional phrases headed by *with*:

Corwin stood gazing at the coffin, <u>with</u> the violin dangling from one hand.

Corwin stood gazing at the coffin, the violin dangling from one hand.

You'll often see absolutes in series, probably because the series permits a writer to break an image down into parts, zooming in for a close-up of one part, then another. For example, in several sentences in "Shamengwa," Erdrich uses absolute phrases in physical descriptions of people, calling our attention to arms and legs, right hand and left hand, shoulders and hands:

So when Geraldine came to trim her father's hair one morning and found him on the floor, <u>his good hand bound behind his back</u>, <u>his ankles tied</u>, she was not surprised to see the lock of the cupboard smashed and the violin gone.

She spent most of her time at the church, <u>her ivory-and-silver rosary draped over her right fist</u>, <u>her left hand wearing the beads smoother, smaller, until I thought one day for sure they would disappear between her fingers</u>.

Corwin had been sitting in the back and now he walked up to the front, <u>his shoulders hunched</u>, <u>hands shoved in his pockets</u>.

EXERCISE 7E

The sentences below are reprinted (and in some cases adapted) from several of the model texts at the end of this book. Combine the sentences by transforming each clause in boldface into an absolute phrase, either by eliminating a *to be* verb or by changing the verb to its *-ing* form.

Example
He was asleep. **His violin was next to his bed. The covers were pulled to his chin.**

Sample Response
He was asleep, his violin next to his bed, the covers pulled to his chin.

1. He saw the sunrise over the highway. **The blazing reds were all turned into black.**

2. It was not just that colors were missing, but that what he did see had a distasteful, "dirty" look. **The whites were glaring. The blacks were cavernous. Everything was wrong, unnatural, stained, and impure.**

3. For Helmholtz, color was a direct expression of the wavelengths of light absorbed by each receptor. **The nervous system just translated one into the other.**

4. Edwin Land used two filters to make the images. **One passed longer wavelengths (a red filter). The other passed shorter wavelengths (a green filter).**

5. Fickle gnomes control the weather, and an air conditioner is powered by a team of squirrels. **Their cheeks are packed with ice cubes.**

6. Gretchen's method of tanning involved baby oil and a series of poses that tended to draw crowds. **The mothers shielded their children's eyes with sand-covered fingers.**

In sentences 7 and 8, reduce the prepositional phrases to absolute phrases. (This is ridiculously easy—all you have to do is cross out *with*. But do take time to listen to the difference.)

Example
The main building seemed to lean heavily to one side, like a cripple, **with the roof sagging toward Canada.**

Sample Response
The main building seemed to lean heavily to one side, like a cripple, the roof sagging toward Canada.

7. All around me the options seemed to be narrowing, as if I were hurtling down a huge black funnel, **with the whole world squeezing in tight.**

8. Down in my chest there was still that leaking sensation, **with something very warm and precious spilling out.**

EXERCISE 7F

Develop each sentence by adding at least two absolute phrases. Visualize an image, then render it for your reader, part by part.

Example
She was all decked out for the prom.

Sample Response
She was all decked out for the prom, her body sheathed in a silky, floor-length gown, hair pulled into an elegant chignon, feet adorned in fashionable sandals, a glittery little purse hanging from her shoulder.

1. I was prepared for my new job.

2. The vampire entered the bedroom.

3. The cottage appeared to be uninhabited.
4. The waiter brought us a hamburger. *(Make the hamburger sound tempting.)*
5. The waiter brought us a hamburger. *(Make the hamburger sound unappetizing.)*

CHAPTER 7 NOTE

[1] Martha Kolln, *Understanding English Grammar* (New York: Macmillan Publishing Company), 1990.

8

Special Effects
Expectations and Exceptions

LINGUISTS AND EDUCATIONAL RESEARCHERS have studied how the mind processes written language. They have observed the order in which syntactic structures are acquired (which structures children master first, which ones take longer) and the speed with which children and adults comprehend sentences. The insights of these researchers can explain why some texts strike us as reader-friendly while others require a hard slog.

Readers want sentences to be easy to process; they want subjects and verbs to behave like subjects and verbs, sentences to be clear and complete, paragraphs to flow smoothly. These are reasonable expectations, and we comply with them because we wish to be understood and, perhaps, to give pleasure.

But occasionally, we don't give readers quite what they expect. Occasionally, we can communicate what we mean more powerfully or more beautifully if we take readers by surprise. This chapter describes readers' expectations primarily in order to recommend that you meet them — stopping along the way to point out some examples of special effects achieved by breaking with convention.

Focus on the Subject

If you've read Chapter 2 , you know all about focus. Writers create well-focused sentences by placing actors — often, human actors — in the subject position of sentences. Well-focused sentences are easy for English speakers to process because they follow the familiar SVO (subject-verb-object) pattern, with the actor and action appearing right up front in the subject-verb positions. A well-focused sentence strikes readers as clear and easy to read precisely because it gives them what they expect, what they intuitively accept as the norm.

The sentences below are simple, straightforward examples of the subject-verb-object order:

Elroy fixed breakfast for me.

I took my suitcase out to the car.

Now, consider another option. In a passive voice construction, the actor is removed from the subject position:

ACTIVE VOICE	PASSIVE VOICE
Elroy fixed breakfast for me.	Breakfast was fixed for me by Elroy.
I took my suitcase out to the car.	My suitcase was taken out to the car by me.

Why might a writer use the passive voice? Writers sometimes make this choice for the sake of paragraph continuity; for example, imagine a paragraph about the three meals:

Breakfast was fixed for me by Elroy. Lunch was Mary Lou's responsibility, and dinner was prepared by Jonathan.

And writers sometimes choose the passive voice in order to create that *by* phrase at the end, giving the actor even more stress than he or she would get in the subject position:

My suitcase was taken out to the car by me! (Where in hell was the bellhop?)

A structure called *it*-cleft provides yet another option for manipulating emphasis.

ACTOR-ACTION WORD ORDER	IT-CLEFT
Elroy fixed breakfast for me.	It was Elroy who fixed breakfast for me.
I took my suitcase out to the car.	It was I who took my suitcase out to the car.

The *it*-cleft highlights the noun phrase immediately following the subject (*it*) and the verb (a form of *be*). The sentences above stress that *it was Elroy* and nobody else who fixed my breakfast; *it was I* and nobody else who carried the suitcase.

Placing a different noun phrase after the subject and verb shifts the stress:

ACTOR-ACTION WORD ORDER	IT-CLEFT
Elroy fixed breakfast for me.	It was breakfast that Elroy fixed for me.
I took my suitcase out to the car.	It was my suitcase that I took out to the car.

In this iteration, the first sentence tells us that *it was breakfast* and no other meal that Elroy fixed, the second that *it was my suitcase* and nothing else (or my suitcase and nobody else's) that I took to the car.

A similar effect can be achieved with the *what*-cleft.

ACTOR-ACTION WORD ORDER	WHAT-CLEFT
Elroy fixed breakfast for me.	What Elroy fixed for me was breakfast.
I took my suitcase out to the car.	What I took out to the car was my suitcase.

The *what*-cleft structure stresses a noun phrase — *breakfast, my suitcase* — by pushing it to the end of the sentence.

The clauses I've been playing with are taken from Tim O'Brien's story "On the Rainy River" where, in fact, he placed the actor in the subject position. If you read the surrounding sentences, you'll see that this is a sober, quiet moment in the story:

> I don't remember saying goodbye. The last night we had dinner together, and I went to bed early, and in the morning Elroy fixed breakfast for me . . .

> At some point later in the morning, it's possible that we shook hands—I just don't remember—but I do know that by the time I'd finished packing the old man had disappeared. Around noon, when I took my suitcase out to the car, I noticed that his old black pickup truck was no longer parked in front of the house. . . . I washed up the breakfast dishes, left his two hundred dollars on the kitchen counter, and drove south toward home.

At this point, O'Brien writes the lean, clear prose that most of us strive for on most occasions.

By contrast, let's look at some special occasions. Here is the first sentence of "On the Rainy River":

> This is one story I've never told before.

O'Brien opens his story with a sentence that, like the *it*-cleft and *what*-cleft, violates our expectations for word order. If the sentence began with the actor as subject, it would read "I've never told this story before." To my mind, O'Brien's version is more effective because it stresses the story rather than the storyteller; it promises that this story to which I'm about to commit my time is something special. This effect is heightened in the sentences that follow:

> This is one story I've never told before. Not to anyone. Not to my parents, not to my brother or sister, not even to my wife.

The story is a long-held secret — and he's telling it to me! "This is one story" . . . this is some story. I'm hooked.

Louise Erdrich's story "Shamengwa" also opens with an unconventional sentence. The word order is inverted, the verb appearing before the subject:

> At the edge of our reservation settlement there <u>lived</u> an old <u>man</u> whose arm was twisted up winglike along his side, and who was for that reason named for a butterfly—Shamengwa.

If Erdrich had begun her sentence with the actor as subject, it would read:

> An old <u>man</u> whose arm was twisted up winglike along his side, and who was for that reason named for a butterfly—Shamengwa—<u>lived</u> there at the edge of our reservation settlement.

That will never do. The noun phrase, modified as it is by two adjective clauses, is just too long to occupy the subject position; the reader has to wait too long to reach the verb. How about this one:

> An old <u>man</u> <u>lived</u> there at the edge of our reservation settlement. His arm was twisted up winglike along his side, and he was for that reason named for a butterfly—Shamengwa.

Better, I think, but still not as effective as Erdrich's sentence for pulling the reader into the world of the story.

The point is this. The injunction to name the actor and action early in a sentence, in the subject-verb position, is a reliable guideline, and writers comply with it most of the time. "Except," as Dr. Seuss might say, "when they don't. Because, sometimes, they won't."

EXERCISE 8A

Practice the *it*-cleft and *what*-cleft constructions by revising these sentences. Use the unconventional word order to stress the phrase in boldface.

Example
it-cleft

My mother lost a baby boy to diphtheria when I was but four years old, and **that loss** turned my mother to the Church.

Sample Response
My mother lost a baby boy to diphtheria when I was but four years old, and it was that loss that turned my mother to the Church.

Example
what-cleft

Diphtheria took her youngest child from her.

Sample Response
What took her youngest child from her was diphtheria.

1. *it*-cleft

   About that time, I received a terrible kick from the cow.

2. *it*-cleft

   The cow's kick injured Shamengwa's arm.

3. *what*-cleft

   The cow's kick injured Shamengwa's arm.

4. *it*-cleft

   On the first hot afternoon in early May, I opened my window.

5. *it*-cleft

   I heard **the sound of Corwin's music.**

6. *what*-cleft

   I heard **the sound of Corwin's music.**

7. *it*-cleft

   The narrator finally learned the story of the violin's past.

8. *what*-cleft

   The date on the letter, 1897, stuck in my mind, woke me in the middle of the night.

EXERCISE 8B

Examine these sentences from "On the Rainy River" and "Shamengwa." First you see the sentence with conventional SVO word order; then you see it as it appears in the story. Read each sentence in its context. Then try to account for the writer's choice, whether by speculating about the reason(s) that may have motivated the writer or by describing the effect of the sentence on you as you read. Attend to such matters as emphasis and paragraph continuity.

Example

I've told most of this before, or at least hinted at it, but I have never told the full truth.

Most of this I've told before, or at least hinted at, but what I have never told is the full truth. *(See O'Brien, para. 13.)*

Sample Analysis

The first clause, "most of this I've told before," is very close to "this is one story I've never told before," the opening sentence in "On the Rainy River." Consequently, it echoes the first sentence and weaves the theme of speech vs. silence throughout the story. The second clause uses the what-cleft to stress both "I have never told" and "the full truth." This promises that what's coming is the full truth.

1. The raw fact of terror was beyond all this, or at the very center.

   Beyond all this, or at the very center, was the raw fact of terror. *(See O'Brien, para. 9.)*

2. The Rainy River, wide as a lake in places, was off to my right, and Canada was beyond the Rainy River.

   Off to my right was the Rainy River, wide as a lake in places, and beyond the Rainy River was Canada. *(See O'Brien, para. 16.)*

3. Elroy must've understood some of this.

   Some of this Elroy must've understood. *(See O'Brien, para. 29.)*

4. A black case of womanly shape that fastened on the side with two brass locks was there, lashed to a crosspiece in the bow.

   There, lashed to a crosspiece in the bow, was a black case of womanly shape that fastened on the side with two brass locks. *(See Erdrich, para. 36.)*

5. And that is why I will play no other fiddle.

   And that is why no other fiddle will I play. *(See Erdrich, para. 37.)*

Completeness and Explicitness

Readers find sentences easy to read if they are complete and explicit, so that the syntactic structure of every phrase is immediately identifiable. For example, of the two sentences below, the second is easier to process:

> The stories you read in childhood shape your personality.
>
> The stories <u>that</u> you read in childhood shape your personality.

In this sentence, the relative pronoun *that* is optional; both sentences are perfectly correct, and you'll see sentences just like them everywhere in published prose. But readers grasp the second more easily, presumably because the presence of *that* signals the adjective clause, indicating how to piece the sentence together.

The same phenomenon can be observed when *that* introduces other structures, in this case a noun clause:

> I noticed his old black pickup truck was no longer parked in front of the house.
>
> I noticed <u>that</u> his old black pickup truck was no longer parked in front of the house.

In this pair, it's easier to see why the absence of *that* slows processing. As you read the first sentence, you would certainly understand *I noticed* as the subject and verb, and you might well interpret the next noun phrase, *his old black pickup truck,* as the object. But you'd be wrong: the object is the whole clause. (What did I notice? That the pickup truck was gone.) In the second sentence, the presence of *that* signals the beginning of a clause in the object position, so there's no risk of a misreading.

As I pointed out in Chapter 3, the presence of function words can be similarly helpful in lists. In her essay on the American response to the 9/11 terror attacks, Arundhati Roy quotes President Bush:

> "They hate our freedoms—our freedom of religion, our freedom of speech, our freedom to vote and assemble and disagree with each other."

> "They hate our freedoms—our freedom of religion, freedom of speech, freedom to vote and assemble and disagree with each other."

Later in the essay, Roy similarly repeats a function word in a list:

> In fact, the problem for an invading army is that Afghanistan has no conventional coordinates or signposts to plot on a military map—no big cities, no highways, no industrial complexes, no water treatment plants.

> In fact, the problem for an invading army is that Afghanistan has no conventional coordinates or signposts to plot on a military map—no big cities, highways, industrial complexes, water treatment plants.

In either case, the second version is clear enough, but Bush's speechwriter chose to include the determiner *our* before every noun phrase, and Roy chose to include *no* four times. One effect of this repetition is to emphasize the meaning: these freedoms are *ours,* Afghanistan has *no* signs of advanced industrialism. Another effect is to promote easy processing. In short, to accommodate readers, writers usually make grammatical structures complete and explicit, using function words to signal syntactic relationships.

Because complete grammatical units are the norm, sentences that omit an expected word or phrase can be quite striking. Here, in three grammatically complete sentences, is the opening to "On the Rainy River":

> This is one story I've never told before. I haven't told it to anyone. I haven't told it to my parents, to my brother or sister, or even to my wife.

And here, again, is the opening as it appears in print:

> This is one story I've never told before. Not to anyone. Not to my parents, not to my brother or sister, not even to my wife.

O'Brien repeats the function word *not* — but he omits the grammatical core of the second and third sentences, writing just prepositional phrases punctuated with periods. He violates the expectation of explicitness and completeness, leaving it to the reader to find a grammatical home for the prepositional phrases by linking them to the first sentence.

O'Brien's second and third sentences are **fragments**, units punctuated as sentences but missing an independent clause. Fragments call attention to themselves; readers notice them, and reactions can range from puzzlement to admiration. To my ear, O'Brien's fragments make his prose sound like a speaking voice, especially in passages like these:

> In June of 1967, a month after graduating from Macalester College, I was drafted to fight a war I hated. I was twenty-one years old. Young, yes, and politically naïve, but even so the American war in Vietnam seemed to me wrong.

> In any case those were my convictions, and back in college I had taken a modest stand against the war. Nothing radical, no hothead stuff, just ringing a few doorbells for Gene McCarthy, composing a few tedious, uninspired editorials for the campus newspaper.

O'Brien also favors fragments in passages describing emotional turmoil, where the scraps of language recreate the turbulent current of the narrator's thoughts and feelings:

> I remember a sound in my head. It wasn't thinking, just a silent howl. A million things all at once — I was too good for this war. Too smart, too compassionate, too everything. It couldn't happen. . . . A mistake, maybe — a foul-up in the paperwork.

Fragments appear in all genres of writing. They are infrequent in academic writing because its purposes are best served by explicitness and because, for better or worse, academic writers maintain a formal tone. Fragments are more frequent in fiction, where we value the artfulness of special effects.

EXERCISE 8C

In the paragraph below, Erdrich describes the character Corwin Peace. Read the paragraph carefully, then work with it.

Corwin was one of those I see again and again. A bad thing waiting for a worse thing to happen. A mistake, but one that we kept trying to salvage, because he was so young. Some thought he had no redeeming value whatsoever. A sociopath. A clever manipulator, who drugged himself dangerous each weekend. Others pitied him and blamed his behavior on his mother's drinking. F.A.E. F.A.S. A.D.D. He wore those initials after his name the way educated people append their degrees. Still others thought they saw something in him that could be saved—perhaps the most dangerous idea of all. . . . He was, unfortunately, good-looking, with the features of an Edward Curtis subject, though the crack and vodka were beginning to make him puffy.

1. Underline the fragments.
2. Rewrite the paragraph so that it contains only complete grammatical sentences, retaining the meaning as much as possible. What do you think? Are there places where your revisions improve the paragraph?

EXERCISE 8D

This passage is adapted from Tim O'Brien's "On the Rainy River" (p. 171). It continues the description of the narrator's reaction to receiving a draft notice.

I was a *liberal,* for Christ sake: If they needed fresh bodies, why not draft some back-to-the-stone-age hawk? Why not draft some dumb jingo in his hard hat and Bomb Hanoi button, or one of LBJ's pretty daughters, or Westmoreland's whole handsome family—nephews and nieces and baby grandson. There should be a law, I thought. If you support a war, if you think it's worth the price, that's fine, but you have to put your own precious fluids on the line. You have to head for the front and hook up with an infantry unit and help spill the blood. And you have to bring along your wife, or your kids, or your lover. There should be a law, I thought.

1. Rewrite the passage so that it has at least three fragments, using the material provided but cutting some units loose from their grammatical mooring in the sentences.
2. What do you think? Are there places where your revisions improve the passage? Compare your choices to O'Brien's. *(See para. 4.)*

Sentence Variety

Prose flows. It has a pace, a rhythm — and readers find it most pleasing when the rhythm is varied, with the pace speeding up or slowing down at appropriate points, the reader's voice sometimes rising, sometimes falling. Virginia Woolf said that when she wrote, she heard the rhythm first, and she filled in words to keep up with it.

The passage below appears about halfway through "On the Rainy River." These are not the kind of paragraphs that will echo in your mind for the rest of the afternoon; they don't come from a turning point in the story, they don't offer high drama. But they flow easily, as you'll hear if you read them aloud:

We spent six days together at the Tip Top Lodge. Just the two of us. Tourist season was over, and there were no boats on the river, and the wilderness seemed to withdraw into a great permanent stillness. Over those six days Elroy Berdahl and I took most of our meals together. In the mornings we sometimes went out on long hikes into the woods, and at night we played Scrabble or listened to records or sat reading in front of his big stone fireplace. At times I felt the awkwardness of an intruder, but Elroy accepted me into his quiet routine without fuss or ceremony. He took my presence for granted, the same way he might've sheltered a stray cat—no wasted sighs or pity—and there was never any talk about it. Just the opposite. What I remember more than anything is the man's willful, almost ferocious silence. In all that time together, all those hours, he never asked the obvious questions: Why was I there? Why alone? Why so preoccupied? If Elroy was curious about any of this, he was careful never to put it into words.

My hunch, though, is that he already knew. At least the basics. After all, it was 1968, and guys were burning draft cards, and Canada was just a boat ride away. Elroy Berdahl was no hick. His bedroom, I remember, was cluttered with books and newspapers. He killed me at the Scrabble board, barely concentrating, and on those occasions when speech was necessary he had a way of compressing large thoughts into small, cryptic packets of language. One evening, just at sunset, he pointed up at an owl circling over the violet-lighted forest to the west.

"Hey, O'Brien," he said. "There's Jesus."

Analyzing the paragraphs for sentence variety, you immediately notice the wide range of sentence lengths. The shortest sentences — "Why alone?" "There's Jesus" — contain just two words; the longest (beginning "In the mornings we sometimes went out") contains 33. There is no unbroken sequence of long sentences (more than 25 words), and the only extended sequence of short sentences (fewer than 15 words) is the one that ends the first paragraph.

We'll return to sentence length in a moment. But first, I'd like to point out two other kinds of variation. One way of classifying sentences is to note their functions. Sentences fall into four categories: declaratives (statements), interrogatives (questions), imperatives (commands), and exclamations. The previous passage, like most prose, relies primarily on declarative sentences. But the string of declaratives is interrupted by questions near the end of the first paragraph and by the quoted exclamation in the last.

Another way to classify sentences is to consider the complexity of their structure, observing the mix of independent clauses, dependent clauses, and modifiers. Here's how the first paragraph shakes out:

We spent six days together at the Tip Top Lodge.	*one independent clause*
Just the two of us.	*fragment*
Tourist season was over, and there were no boats on the river, and the wilderness seemed to withdraw into a great permanent stillness.	*three independent clauses joined by and*
Over those six days Elroy Berdahl and I took most of our meals together.	*one independent clause*
In the mornings we sometimes went out on long hikes into the woods, and at night we played Scrabble or listened to records or sat reading in front of his big stone fireplace.	*two independent clauses joined by and; the second clause contains a coordinate series*
At times I felt the awkwardness of an intruder, but Elroy accepted me into his quiet routine without fuss or ceremony.	*two independent clauses joined by but*
He took my presence for granted, the same way he might've sheltered a stray cat—no wasted sighs or pity—and there was never any talk about it.	*two independent clauses joined by and; the first clause contains an appositive and another noun phrase set off by dashes*

Just the opposite.	*fragment*
What I remember more than anything is the man's willful, almost ferocious silence.	*one independent clause;* what-*cleft*
In all that time together, all those hours, he never asked the obvious questions:	*one independent clause; introductory prepositional phrase contains an appositive*
Why was I there?	*one independent clause*
Why alone?	*fragment*
Why so preoccupied?	*fragment*
If Elroy was curious about any of this, he was careful never to put it into words.	*one dependent clause, one independent clause*

The second paragraph is equally varied in terms of the sentences' complexity.

It may well be that O'Brien, like Woolf, writes with his ear, producing sentences that vary in length, function, and complexity in response to an intuitive sense of what sounds right. Actually, I suspect that most of us write that way. We hear the music of language around us every day from birth — perhaps before birth — so that, as we write, we reach for words that will capture the right sound as well as the right meaning.

EXERCISE 8E

Analyze sentence variety in this passage from "Shamengwa."

Shamengwa was a man of refinement, who prepared himself carefully to meet life every day. In the Ojibwa language that is spoken on our reservation, *owehzhee* is the way men get themselves up—pluck stray hairs, brush each tooth, make a precise part in their hair, and, these days, press a sharp crease down the front of their blue jeans—in order to show that, although the government has tried in every way possible to destroy their manhood, they are undefeatable. *Owehzhee.* We still look good and we know it. The old man was never seen in disarray, and yet there was more to it.

He played the fiddle. How he played the fiddle! Although his arm was so twisted and disfigured that his shirts had to be carefully altered and pinned to accommodate the gnarled shape, he had agility in that arm, even strength. Ever since he was very young, Shamengwa had, with the aid of a white silk scarf, tied his elbow into a position that allowed the elegant hand and fingers at the end of the damaged arm full play across the fiddle's strings. With his other hand, he drew the bow.

1. How many words are in the shortest sentence?

2. How many words are in the longest sentence?

3. How many sentences are short, with fewer than 15 words?

4. How many are long, with more than 25 words?

5. Are there sequences of three or more very short sentences in a row?

6. Are there sequences of long sentences?

7. Where does Erdrich use something other than declarative sentences—questions, commands, exclamations, or fragments? (Think about the effect of these sentences, considering why she may have chosen to set them apart.)

EXERCISE 8F

If you'd like to examine sentence variety in an essay rather than a short story, work with this paragraph from Arundhati Roy's article "The Algebra of Infinite Justice" (p. 188).

For strategic, military and economic reasons, it is vital for the U.S. government to persuade its public that their commitment to freedom and democracy and the American Way of Life is under attack. In the current atmosphere of grief, outrage, and anger, it's an easy notion to peddle. However, if that were true, it's reasonable to wonder why the symbols of America's economic and military dominance—the World Trade Centre and the Pentagon—were chosen as the targets of the attacks. Why not the Statue of Liberty? Could it be that the stygian anger that led to the attacks has its taproot not in American freedom and democracy, but in the U.S. government's record of commitment and support to exactly the opposite things—to military and economic terrorism, insurgency, military dictatorship, religious bigotry, and unimaginable genocide (outside America)? It must be hard for ordinary Americans, so recently bereaved, to look up at the world with their eyes full of tears and encounter what might appear to them to be indifference. It isn't indifference. It's just augury. An absence of surprise. The tired wisdom of knowing that what goes around eventually comes around.

1. How many words are in the shortest sentence?
2. How many words are in the longest sentence?
3. How many sentences are short, with fewer than 15 words?
4. How many are long, with more than 25 words?
5. Are there sequences of three or more very short sentences in a row?
6. Are there sequences of long sentences?
7. Where does Roy use something other than declarative sentences—questions, commands, exclamations, or fragments? (Think about the effect of these sentences, considering why she may have chosen to set them apart.)

Sentence length is always a topic of interest to writers, editors, and teachers. Short sentences have much to recommend them: they are easy for readers to process, and they are easy for writers to produce. For very young or unskilled writers, short sentences seem a safe choice because they don't present many opportunities for error. And some professional writers, especially those who create technical documents, prefer short sentences, seeking an average sentence length of 15 to 20 words.

Long sentences have their virtues as well. If you have read Chapters 4 through 7, you have seen that the use of modifiers makes it possible for a writer to be specific and precise — and of course, the more modification, the longer the sentence. And there is a relationship between sentence length and intellectual sophistication. Children write short sentences; as they mature, the average sentence length in their writing moves steadily upward. In some publications, especially academic journals and high-prestige magazines like *Granta* and *The New Yorker*, average sentence length climbs toward 25 words.

But in the end, we come back to the importance of variety. Even in a genre where generally short-ish sentences and a low words-per-sentence average are preferred, it's risky to write one short sentence after another after another: the prose is likely to sound choppy and childlike. Even in a genre where generally long-ish sentences and a high words-per-sentence average are preferred, it's risky to write an unbroken sequence of long sentences or to let a sentence extend beyond, say, 60 words: the prose is likely to strike readers as dense and difficult.

Let's have a look at some passages in which Louise Erdrich and Tim O'Brien have taken the risk.

In the following passage, Erdrich renders a pivotal moment in Shamengwa's story, relying heavily on very short sentences:

The dream was simple. A voice. *Go to the lake and sit by the southern rock. Wait there. I will come to you.*
I decided to follow these instructions. I took my bedroll, a scrap of jerky, and a loaf of bannock, and sat myself down on the crackling lichen of the southern rock. That plate of stone jutted out into the water, which dropped off from its edges into a green-black depth. From that rock, I could see all that happened on the water. I put tobacco down for the spirits. All day I sat there waiting. Flies bit me. The wind boomed in my ears. Nothing happened. I curled up when the light left and I slept. Stayed on the next morning. The next day, too. It was the first time that I had ever slept out on the shores, and I began to understand why people said of the lake that there was no end to it, even though it was bounded by rocks.

Sentence length in this passage ranges from 2 words in the second sentence to 39 words in the last sentence. Still, the short sentences stand out because there are so many of them and because they are so very short. The passage has two series of short sentences, one describing the dream and the other describing the young Shamengwa's experience sitting beside the lake. Erdrich tells us how to read the first set of short sentences: they are a dream. And so we know how to read the second set as well. As I read about Shamengwa sitting on the southern rock, I imagine his frame of mind — dreamlike, surreal. Shamengwa is prepared — and by the rhythm of the prose, the reader is prepared — to accept a boat without an oarsman, floating across the lake with the gift of a violin.

Very short or very long sentences also indicate an altered consciousness in several passages of "On the Rainy River." The final crisis, the moment when the narrator's struggle with his conscience finally tears him apart, takes place as he sits in a boat on the river, the Canadian shore just twenty yards away:

My whole life seemed to spill out into the river, swirling away from me, everything I had ever been or ever wanted to be. I couldn't get my breath; I couldn't stay afloat; I couldn't tell which way to swim. A hallucination, I suppose, but as real as anything I would ever feel. . . . A squad of cheerleaders did cartwheels along the banks of the Rainy River; they had megaphones and pompoms and smooth brown thighs. The crowd swayed left and right. A marching band played fight songs. All my aunts and uncles were there, and Abraham Lincoln, and Saint George, and a nine-year-old girl named Linda who had died of a brain tumor back in fifth grade, and several members of the United States

Senate, and a blind poet scribbling notes, and LBJ, and Huck Finn, and Abbie Hoffman, and all the dead soldiers back from the grave, and the many thousands who were later to die—villagers with terrible burns, little kids without arms or legs—yes, and the Joint Chiefs of Staff were there, and a couple of popes, and a first lieutenant named Jimmy Cross, and the last surviving veteran of the American Civil War, and Jane Fonda dressed up as Barbarella, and an old man sprawling beside a pigpen, and my grandfather, and Gary Cooper, and a kind-faced woman carrying an umbrella and a copy of Plato's *Republic*, and a million ferocious citizens waving flags of all shapes and colors—people in hard hats, people in headbands—they were all whooping and chanting and urging me toward one shore or the other.

O'Brien follows this remarkable kaleidoscope of images with a return to the aluminum boat, rocking on the river. Elroy Berdahl "remained quiet. He kept fishing. . . . He made it real." The final paragraphs describing Berdahl's patient watchfulness and then the narrator's preparations to return home bring the reader back to earth with a conventional blend of sentences, varied in length but no longer extreme.

Very short sentences in sequence, or very long sentences, create special effects. Readers are surprised to see them. Brought up short, they read with special attention — and the writer has an opportunity to heighten the impact of words describing something frightening, something tumultuous, something magical.

EXERCISE 8G

In a paragraph of 100 to 200 words, describe a recent dream. Write two versions of your paragraph, keeping the content essentially the same, but experimenting with sentence variety:

1. Minimize sentence variety. Write every sentence in one or two clauses, and don't let the sentence length drop below 10 words or rise above 15. Try to make the prose sound dull, plodding, or singsong.

2. Maximize sentence variety. Experiment with different sentence types (questions, commands, exclamations) and with extreme sentence lengths—very short sentences and/or an ultra-long sentence like O'Brien's. Be as artful as you can, using the unconventional sentences to heighten the paragraph's effect.

Model Texts
for Writers

Louise Erdrich

Shamengwa

Louise Erdrich was born in 1954 into a family of storytellers. With the encouragement of her parents, who were teachers in Wahpeton, North Dakota, she began writing as a child, and she developed the storyteller's habit of observing the people around her closely, listening for the rhythms of everyday speech. In 1972, she enrolled in Dartmouth College as part of the college's first class to include women. During her undergraduate years, she published several poems, and her first book was a poetry collection. But she soon returned to storytelling, and today she is best known for her short stories and novels.

While at Dartmouth, Erdrich studied English and creative writing. She also took classes in the Native American Studies program directed by Michael Dorris, a young anthropologist who would later become her husband and coauthor. Her studies prompted her to explore the Ojibwa heritage of her mother's family. After graduating from Dartmouth, Erdrich enrolled in a program in creative writing at Johns Hopkins, earning her M.A. in 1979. She now lives in Minneapolis, Minnesota, where she owns Birchbark Books. In collaboration with her sister Heid Erdrich, she organizes the annual Turtle Mountain Writers' Workshop.

Many of Erdrich's stories take place among the Ojibwa people of North Dakota and Minnesota. "Shamengwa" is typical of her fiction, telling the stories of several characters—an aging musician, a young ruffian who steals his violin, two brothers who played the same violin long ago—presenting them as individuals but embedding them in a network of relationships and a series of events by which they are bound together. The theme of relationships being ruptured and repaired is echoed by the story's structure: it is told from multiple points of view, but it begins and ends in the voice of a tribal judge whose purpose is to preserve the community. Storytelling itself has the function of preserving community: the narrator's responsibility, he says, is "to keep watch over this little patch of earth, to judge its miseries and tell its stories."

Louise Erdrich is widely admired for her skill as a stylist. Critics often describe her writing as "lyrical": even when she is writing prose, the language is poetic, with a gentle rhythm, striking images, and frequent use of metaphor. Erdrich's novels include *Love Medicine* (1984), *The Beet Queen* (1986), *Tracks* (1988), *The Bingo Palace* (1994), *The Antelope Wife* (1998), and *The Painted Drum* (2005). She has written a memoir of motherhood, *The Blue Jay's Dance: A Birth Year* (2003), and several children's books.

"Shamengwa" was published in *The New Yorker* in December 2002 and reprinted in *The Best American Short Stories of 2003*, edited by Walter Mosley.

I

At the edge of our reservation settlement there lived an old man whose arm was twisted up winglike along his side, and who was for that reason named for a butterfly — Shamengwa. Other than his arm, he was an extremely well-made person. Anyone could see that he had been handsome, and he still cut a graceful figure, slim and of medium height. His head was covered with a startling thick mane of white hair, which he was proud of. Every few weeks, he had it carefully trimmed and styled by his daughter, Geraldine, who travelled in from the bush just to do it.

Shamengwa was a man of refinement, who prepared himself carefully to meet life every day. In the Ojibwa language that is spoken on our reservation, *owehzhee* is the way men get themselves up — pluck stray hairs, brush each tooth, make a precise part in their hair, and, these days, press a sharp crease down the front of their blue-jeans — in order to show that, although the government has tried in every way possible to destroy their manhood, they are undefeatable. *Owehzhee*. We still look good and we know it. The old man was never seen in disarray, and yet there was more to it.

He played the fiddle. How he played the fiddle! Although his arm was so twisted and disfigured that his shirts had to be carefully altered and pinned to accommodate the gnarled shape, he had agility in that arm, even strength. Ever since he was very young, Shamengwa had, with the aid of a white silk scarf, tied his elbow into a position that allowed the elegant hand and fingers at the end of the damaged arm full play across the fiddle's strings. With his other hand, he drew the bow. When I try to explain the sound he made, I come to some trouble with words. Inside became outside when Shamengwa played music. Yet inside to outside does not half sum it up. The music was more than music — at least, more than what we are used to hearing. The sound connected instantly with something deep and joyous. Those powerful moments of true knowledge which we paper over with daily life. The music tapped our terrors, too. Things we'd lived through and wanted never to repeat. Shredded imaginings, unadmitted longings, fear, and also surprising pleasures. We can't live at that pitch. But, every so often, something shatters like ice, and we fall into the river of our own existence. We are aware. This realization was in the music, somehow, or in the way Shamengwa played it.

Thus Shamengwa wasn't wanted at every party. The wild joy his jigs and reels brought forth might just as easily send people crashing onto the rocks of their roughest memories and they'd end up stunned and addled or crying in their beer. So it is. People's emotions often turn on them. Geraldine, a dedicated, headstrong woman who six years back had borne a baby, dumped its father, and earned a degree in education, sometimes drove Shamengwa to fiddling contests, where he could perform in more of a concert setting. He even won awards, prizes of the cheap sort given at local musical contests — engraved plaques and small tin cups set on plastic pedestals. These he placed on a triangle scrap of shelf high in one corner of his house. The awards were never dusted, and sometimes, when his grandchild asked him to take them down for her to play with, they came apart. Shamengwa didn't care. He was, however, fanatical about his violin.

He treated this instrument with the reverence we accord our drums, 5 which are considered living beings and require from us food, water, shelter, and love. He fussed over it, stroked it clean with a soft cotton handkerchief, laid it carefully away in the cupboard every night in a leather case that he kept as well polished as his shoes. The case was lined with velvet that had been faded by time from a heavy blood red to a pallid and streaked violet. I don't know violins, but his was thought to be exceptionally beautiful; it was generally understood to be old and quite valuable, too. So when Geraldine came to trim her father's hair one morning and found him on the floor, his good hand bound behind his back, his ankles tied, she was not surprised to see the lock of the cupboard smashed and the violin gone.

I am a tribal judge, and things come to me through the grapevine of the court system or the tribal police. Gossip, rumors, scuttlebutt, B.S., or just flawed information. I always tune in, and I even take notes on what I hear around. It's sometimes wrong, or exaggerated, but just as often it contains a germ of useful truth. In this case, for instance, the name Corwin Peace was on people's lips, although there was no direct evidence that he had committed the crime.

Corwin was one of those I see again and again. A bad thing waiting for a worse thing to happen. A mistake, but one that we kept trying to salvage, because he was so young. Some thought he had no redeeming value whatsoever. A sociopath. A clever manipulator, who drugged himself dangerous each weekend. Others pitied him and blamed his behavior on his mother's drinking. F.A.E. F.A.S. A.D.D. He wore those initials after his name the way educated people append their degrees. Still others thought they saw something in him that could be saved — perhaps the most dangerous idea of all. He was a petty dealer with a string of girlfriends. He was, unfortunately, good-looking, with the features of an Edward Curtis subject, though the crack and vodka were beginning to make him puffy.

Drugs now travel the old fur-trade routes, and where once Corwin would have sat high on a bale of buffalo robes and sung travelling songs to the screeching of an oxcart, now he drove a 1991 Impala with hubcaps missing and its back end dragging. He drove it hard and he drove it all cranked up, but he was rarely caught, because he travelled such erratic hours. He drove without a license — it had long ago been taken from him. D.U.I. And he was always looking for money — scamming, betting, shooting pool, even now and then working a job that, horrifyingly, put him on the other side of a counter frying Chinese chicken strips. He was one of those whom I kept track of because I imagined I'd be seeing the full down-arcing shape of his life's trajectory. I wanted to make certain that if I had to put him away I could do it and sleep well that same night. So far, he had confirmed this.

As the days passed, Corwin lay low and picked up his job at the deep fryer. He made one of those rallying attempts that gave heart to so many of his would-be saviors. He straightened out, stayed sober, and used his best manners, and when questioned was convincingly hopeful about his prospects and affable about his failures. "I'm a jackass," he admitted, "but I never sank so low as to rip off the old man's fiddle." Yet he had, of course. And, while we waited for him to make his move, there was the old man, who quickly began to fail. I had not realized how much I loved to hear him play — sometimes out on his scrubby back lawn after dusk, sometimes at those little concerts, and other times just for groups of people who would gather round. After weeks had passed, a dull spot opened and I ached with surprising poignance for Shamengwa's loss, which I honestly shared, so that I had to seek him out and sit with him as if it would help to mourn the absence of his music together. I wanted to know, too, whether, if the violin did not turn up, we could get together and buy him a new, perhaps even better instrument. So I sat in Shamengwa's little front room one afternoon and tried to find an opening.

"Of course," I said, "we think we know who took your fiddle. We've got our eye on him."

Shamengwa swept his hair back with the one graceful hand and said, as he had many times, "I was struck from behind."

Where he'd hit the ground, his cheekbone had split and the white of his eye was an angry red. He moved with a stiff, pained slowness, the rigidity of a very old person. He lowered himself piece by piece into a padded brown rocking chair and gazed at me, or past me, really. I soon understood that although he spoke quietly and answered questions, he was not fully engaged in the conversation. In fact, he was only half present, and somewhat dishevelled, irritable as well, neither of which I'd ever seen in him before. His shirt was buttoned wrong, the plaid askew, and he hadn't shaved that morning. His breath was sour, and he didn't seem at all glad that I had come.

We sat together in a challenging silence until Geraldine brought two mugs of hot, strong, sugared tea and got another for herself. Shamengwa's hand shook as he lifted the cup, but he drank. His face cleared a bit as the tea went down, and I decided that there would be no better time to put forth my idea.

"Uncle," I said, "we would like to buy a new fiddle for you."

Shamengwa said nothing, but put down the cup and folded his hands in his lap. He looked past me and frowned in a thoughtful way.

"Wouldn't he like a new violin?" I appealed to Geraldine. She shook her head as if she were both annoyed with me and exasperated with her father. We sat in silence. I didn't know where to go from there.

Shamengwa had leaned back in his chair and closed his eyes. I thought he might be trying to get rid of me. But I was stubborn and did not want to go. I wanted to hear Shamengwa's music again.

"Oh, tell him about it, Daddy," Geraldine said at last.

Shamengwa leaned forward and bent his head over his hands as though he were praying.

20   I relaxed now and understood that I was going to hear something. It was that breathless gathering moment I've known just before composure cracks, the witness breaks, the truth comes out. I am familiar with it, and although this was not exactly a confession, it was, as it turned out, something not generally known on the reservation.

II

My mother lost a baby boy to diphtheria when I was but four years old, Shamengwa said, and it was that loss that turned my mother to the Church. Before that, I remember my father playing chansons, reels, and jigs on his fiddle, but after the baby's death he put the fiddle down and took the Holy Communion. My mother out of grief became strict with my father, my older sister, and me. Where before we'd had a lively house that people liked to visit, now there was quiet. No wine and no music. We kept our voices down because our noise hurt, my mother said, and there was no laughing or teasing by my father, who had once been a dancing and hilarious man.

I don't believe my mother meant things to change so, but the sorrow she bore was beyond her strength. As though her heart, too, were buried underneath that small white headstone in the Catholic cemetery, she turned cold, turned away from the rest of us. Now that I am old and know the ways of grief, I understand she felt too much, loved too hard, and was afraid to lose us as she had lost my brother. But to a little boy these things are hidden. It only seemed to me that, along with that baby, I had lost her love. Her strong arms, her kisses, the clean soap smell of her face, her voice calming me — all of this was gone. She was like a statue in a church. Every so often we would find her in the kitchen, standing still, staring through the wall. At first we touched her clothes, petted her hands. My father kissed her, spoke gently into her ear, combed her hair into a shawl around her shoulders. Later, after we had given up, we just walked around her as you would a stump. My sister took up the cooking, and gradually we accepted that the lively, loving mother we had known wasn't going to return. We didn't try to coax her out. She spent most of her time at the church, her ivory-and-silver rosary draped over her right fist, her left hand wearing the beads smoother, smaller, until I thought one day for sure they would disappear between her fingers.

We lived right here then, but in those days trees and bush still surrounded us. There were no houses to the west. We pastured our horses where the Dairy Queen now stands. One day, while my family was in town and I was home with a cold, I became restless. I began to poke around, and soon enough I came across the fiddle that my mother had forced my father to stop playing. There it was. I was alone with it. I was only five or six years old, but I could balance a fiddle and I remembered how my father had used the bow. I got sound out of it all right, though nothing pleasing. The noise made my bones shiver. I put the fiddle back carefully, well before my parents came home, and climbed underneath my blankets when they walked into the yard. I pretended to sleep, not because I wanted to keep up the appearance of being sick but because I could not bear to return to the way things had been. Something had changed. Something had disrupted the nature of all that I knew. This deep thing had to do with the fiddle.

After that, I contrived, as often as I could, to stay alone in the house. As soon as everyone was gone I took the fiddle from its hiding place, and I tuned it to my own liking. I learned how to play it one string at a time, and I started to fit these sounds together. The sequence of notes made my brain itch. It became a torment for me to have to put away the fiddle when my family came home. Sometimes, if the wind was right, I sneaked the fiddle from the house and played out in the woods. I was always careful that the wind should carry my music away to the west, where there was no one to hear it. But one day the wind may have shifted. Or perhaps my mother's ears were more sensitive than my sister's and my father's. Because when I came back into the house I found her staring out the window, to the west. She was excited, breathing fast. Did you hear it? She cried out. Did you hear it? Terrified to be discovered, I said no. She was very agitated, and my father had a hard time calming her. After he finally got her to sleep, he sat at the table with his head in his hands. I tiptoed around the house, did the chores. I felt terrible not telling him that my music was what she'd heard. But now, as I look back, I consider my silence the first decision I made as a true musician. An artist. My playing was more important to me than my father's pain. It was that clear. I said nothing, but after that I was all the more sly and twice as secretive.

25   It was a question of survival, after all. If I had not found the music, I would have died of the silence. There are ways of being abandoned even when your parents are right there.

We had two cows, and I did the milking in the morning and evening. Lucky, because if my parents forgot to cook at least I had the milk. I can't say I really ever suffered from a stomach kind of hunger, but another kind of human hunger bit me. I was lonely. It was about that time that I received a terrible kick from the cow, an accident, as she was usually mild. A wasp sting, perhaps, caused her to lash out in surprise. She caught my arm and, although I had no way of knowing it, shattered the bone. Painful? Oh, for certain it was, but my parents did not think to take me to a doctor. They did not notice, I suppose. I did tell my father about it, but he only nodded, pretending that he had heard, and went back to whatever he was doing.

The pain in my arm kept me awake, and at night, when I couldn't distract myself, I moaned in my blankets by the stove. But worse was the uselessness of the arm in playing the fiddle. I tried to prop it up, but it fell like a rag doll's arm. I finally hit upon a solution. I started tying up my broken arm, just as I do now. I had, of course, no idea that it would heal that way and that as a result I would be considered a permanent cripple. I only knew that with the arm tied up I could play, and that playing saved my life. So I was, like most artists, deformed by my art. I was shaped.

School is where I got the name I carry now. Shamengwa, the black-and-orange butterfly. It was a joke on my "wing arm." Although a nun told me that a picture of a butterfly in a painting of Our Lady was meant to represent the Holy Spirit, I didn't like the name at first. My bashfulness about the shape of my arm caused me to avoid people even once I was older, and I made no friends. Human friends. My true friend was my fiddle, anyway, the only friend I really needed. And then I lost that friend.

My parents had gone to church, but there was on that winter's day some problem with the stove. Smoke had filled the nave at the start of Mass and everyone was sent straight home. When my mother and father arrived, I was deep into my playing. They listened, standing at the door rooted by the surprise of what they heard, for how long I do not know. I had not heard the door open and, with my eyes shut, had not seen the light thereby admitted. Finally, I noticed the cold breeze that swirled around me, turned, and we stared at one another with a shocked gravity that my father broke at last by asking, "How long?"

I did not answer, although I wanted to. *Seven years. Seven years!* 30
He led my mother in. They shut the door behind them. Then he said, in a voice of troubled softness, "Keep on."

So I played, and when I stopped he said nothing.

Discovered, I thought the worst was over. But the next morning, waking to a silence where I usually heard my father's noises, hearing a vacancy before I even knew it for sure, I understood that the worst was yet to come. My playing had woken something in him. That was the reason he left. But I don't know why he had to take the violin. When I saw that it was missing, all breath left me, all thought, all feeling. For a while after that I was the same as my mother. In our loss, we were cut off from the true, bright, normal routines of living. I might have stayed that way, joined my mother in the darkness from which she could not return. I might have lived on in that diminished form, if I had not had a dream.

The dream was simple. A voice. *Go to the lake and sit by the southern rock. Wait there. I will come to you.*

I decided to follow these instructions. I took my bedroll, a scrap 35
of jerky, and a loaf of bannock, and sat myself down on the crackling lichen of the southern rock. That plate of stone jutted out into the water, which dropped off from its edges into a green-black depth. From that rock, I could see all that happened on the water. I put tobacco down for the spirits. All day, I sat there waiting. Flies bit me. The wind boomed in my ears. Nothing happened. I curled up when the light left and I slept. Stayed on the next morning. The next day, too. It was the first time that I had ever slept out on the shores, and I began to understand why people said of the lake that there was no end to it, even though it was bounded by rocks. There were rivers flowing in and flowing out, secret currents, six kinds of weather working on its surface and a hidden terrain beneath. Each wave washed in from somewhere unseen and washed out again to somewhere unknown. I saw birds, strange-feathered and unfamiliar, passing through on their way to somewhere

else. Listening to the water, I was for the first time comforted by sounds other than my fiddle-playing. I let go. I thought I might just stay there forever, staring at the blue thread of the horizon. Nothing mattered. When a small bit of the horizon's thread detached, darkened, proceeded forward slowly, I observed it with only mild interest. The speck seemed to both advance and retreat. It wavered back and forth. I lost sight of it for long stretches, then it popped closer, over a wave.

It was a canoe. But either the paddler was asleep in the bottom or the canoe was drifting. As it came nearer, I decided for sure that it must be adrift, it rode so lightly in the waves, nosing this way, then the other. But always, no matter how hesitantly, it ended up advancing straight toward the southern rock, straight toward me. I watched until I could clearly see there was nobody in it. Then the words of my dream returned. *I will come to you.* I dove in eagerly, swam for the canoe — I had learned, as boys do, to compensate for my arm, and although my stroke was peculiar, I was strong. I thought perhaps the canoe had been badly tied and slipped its mooring, but no rope trailed. Perhaps high waves had coaxed it off a beach where its owner had dragged it up, thinking it safe. I pushed the canoe in to shore, then pulled it up behind me, wedged it in a cleft between two rocks. Only then did I look inside. There, lashed to a crosspiece in the bow, was a black case of womanly shape that fastened on the side with two brass locks.

That is how my fiddle came to me, Shamengwa said, raising his head to look steadily at me. He smiled, shook his fine head, and spoke softly. And that is why no other fiddle will I play.

III

Corwin shut the door to his room. It wasn't really his room, but some people were letting him stay in their basement in return for several favors. Standing on a board propped on sawhorses, he pushed his outspread fingers against the panel of the false ceiling. He placed the panel to one side and groped up behind it among wires and underneath a pad of yellow fiberglass insulation, until he located the handle of the case. He bore it down to the piece of foam rubber that served as his mattress and through which, every night, he felt the hard cold of the concrete floor seep into his legs. He had taken the old man's fiddle because he needed money, but he hadn't thought much about where he would sell it or who would buy it. Then he had an inspiration. One of the women in the house went to Spirit Lake every weekend to stay with her boyfriend's family. He'd put the fiddle in the trunk and hitch along. They'd let him out at Miracle Village Mall, and he'd take the violin there and sell it to a music lover.

Corwin got out of the car and carried the violin into the mall. There are two kinds of people, he thought, the givers and the takers. I'm a taker. Render unto Corwin what is due him. His favorite movie of recent times was about a cop with such a twisted way of looking at the world that you couldn't tell if he was evil or good — you only knew that he could seize your mind with language. Corwin had a thing for language. He inhaled it from movies, rap and rock music, television. It rubbed around inside him, word against word. He thought he was writing poems sometimes in his thoughts, but the poems would not come out. The words stuck in odd configurations and made patterns that raced across the screen of his shut eyes and off the edge, down his temples and into the darkness of his neck. So when he walked through the air-lock doors into the warm cathedral-like space of the central food court, his brain was a mumble.

Taking a seat, peering at the distracted-looking shoppers, he quickly understood that none of them was likely to buy the fiddle. He walked into a music store and tried to show the instrument to the manager, who said only, "Nah, we don't take used." Corwin walked out again. He tried a few people. They shied away or turned him down flat.

"Gotta regroup," Corwin told himself, and went back to sit on the length of bench he had decided to call his own. That was where he got the idea that became a gold mine. He remembered a scene from a TV show, a clip of a musician in a city street. He was playing a saxophone or something of that sort, and at his feet there was an open instrument case. A woman stopped and smiled and threw a dollar in the case. Corwin took the violin out and laid the open case invitingly at his feet. He took the fiddle in one hand and drew the bow across the strings with the other. It made a terrible, strange sound. The screech echoed in the food court and several people raised their lips from the waxed-paper food wrappers to look at Corwin. He looked back at them, poised and frozen. It was a moment of drama — he had them. An audience. He had to act instantly or lose them. Instinctively, he gave a flowery, low bow, as though he were accepting an ovation. There were a few murmurs of amusement. Someone even applauded. These sounds acted on Corwin

40

Peace at once, more powerfully than any drug he had tried. A surge of unfamiliar zeal filled him, and he took up the instrument again, threw back his hair, and began to play a swift, silent passage of music.

His mimicry was impeccable. Where had he learned it? He didn't know. He didn't touch the bow to the strings, but he played music all the same. Music ricocheted around between his ears. He could hardly keep up with what he heard. His body spilled over with drama. When the music in his head stopped, he dipped low and did the splits, which he'd learned from Prince videos. He held the violin and the bow overhead. Applause broke over him. A skein of dazzling sound.

They picked up Corwin Peace pretending to play the fiddle in a Fargo mall, and brought him to me. I have a great deal of latitude in sentencing. In spite of myself, I was intrigued by Corwin's unusual treatment of the instrument, and I decided to set a precedent. First, I cleared my decision with Shamengwa. Then I sentenced Corwin to apprentice himself with the old master. Six days a week, two hours each morning. Three hours of practice after work. He would either learn to play the violin or he would do time. In truth, I didn't know who was being punished, the boy or the old man. But at least now, from Shamengwa's house, we began to hear the violin again.

It was the middle of September on the reservation, the mornings chill, the afternoons warm, the leaves still green and thick in their final sweetness. All the hay was mowed. The wild rice was beaten flat. The radiators in the tribal offices went on at night, but by noon we had to open the windows to cool off. The woodsmoke of parching fires and the spent breeze of diesel entered then, and sometimes the squall of Corwin's music from down the hill. The first weeks were not promising. Then the days turned uniformly cold, we kept the windows shut, and until spring the only news of Corwin's progress came through his probation officer. I didn't expect much. It was not until the first hot afternoon in early May that I opened my window and actually heard Corwin playing.

45   "Not half bad," I said that night when I visited Shamengwa. "I listened to your student."

"He's clumsy as hell, but he's got the fire," Shamengwa said, touching his chest. I could tell that he was proud of Corwin, and I allowed myself to consider the possibility that something as idealistic as putting an old man and a hard-core juvenile delinquent together had worked, or hadn't, anyway, ended up a disaster. The lessons and the relationship outlasted, in fact, the sentence. Fall came, and we closed the windows again. In spring, we opened them, and once or twice heard Corwin playing. Then Shamengwa died. His was a peaceful death, the sort of death we used to pray to St. Joseph to give us all. He was asleep, his violin next to the bed, covers pulled to his chin. Found in the morning by Geraldine.

There was a large funeral with the usual viewing, at which people filed up to his body and tucked flowers and pipe tobacco and small tokens into Shamengwa's coffin to accompany him into the earth. Geraldine placed a monarch butterfly upon his shoulder. She said that she had found it that morning on the grille of her car. Halfway through the service, she stood up and took the violin from the coffin, where it had been tucked up close to her father.

"A few months ago, Dad told me that when he died I was to give this violin to Corwin Peace," she told everyone. "And so I'm offering it to him now. And I've already asked him to play us one of Dad's favorites today."

Corwin had been sitting in the back and now he walked up to the front, his shoulders hunched, hands shoved in his pockets. The sorrow in his face surprised me. It made me uneasy to see such a direct show of emotion in one who had been so volatile. But Corwin's feelings seemed directed once he took up the fiddle and began to play. He played a chanson everyone knew, a song typical of our people because it began tender and slow, then broke into a wild strangeness that pricked our pulses and strained our breath. Corwin played with passion, if not precision, and there was enough of the old man's energy in his music that by the time he'd finished everybody was in tears.

Then came the shock. Amid the dabbing of eyes and discreet nose-blowing, Corwin stood gazing into the coffin at his teacher, the violin dangling from one hand. Beside the coffin there was an ornate Communion rail. Corwin raised the violin high and smashed it on the rail, once, twice, three times, to do the job right. I was in the front pew, and I jumped from my seat as though I'd been prepared for something like this. I grasped Corwin's arm as he laid the violin carefully back beside Shamengwa, but then I let him go, for I recognized that his gesture was spent. My focus moved from Corwin to the violin itself, because I saw,

50

sticking from its smashed wood, a roll of paper. I drew the paper out. It was old and covered with a stiff, antique flow of writing. The priest, somewhat shaken, began the service again. I put the roll of paper into my jacket pocket and returned to my seat. I didn't exactly forget to read it. There was just so much happening after the funeral, what with the windy burial and then the six-kinds-of-fry-bread supper in the Knights of Columbus Hall, that I didn't get the chance to sit still and concentrate. It was evening and I was at home, comfortable in my chair with a bright lamp turned on behind me, so the radiance fell over my shoulder, before I finally read what had been hidden in the violin for so many years.

IV

I, Baptiste Parentheau, also known as Billy Peace, leave to my brother Edwin this message, being a history of the violin which on this day of Our Lord August 20, 1897, I send out onto the waters to find him.

A recapitulation to begin with: Having read of LaFountaine's mission to the Iroquois, during which that priest avoided having his liver plucked out before his eyes by nimbly playing the flute, our own Father Jasprine thought it wise to learn to play a musical instrument before he ventured forth into the wastelands past the Lake of the Woods. Therefore, he set off with music as his protection. He studied and brought along his violin, a noble instrument, which he played less than adequately. If the truth were told, he'd have done better not to impose his slight talents on the Ojibwa. Yet, as he died young and left the violin to his altar boy, my father, I should say nothing against good Jasprine. I should, instead, be grateful for the joys his violin afforded my family. I should be happy in the hours that my father spent tuning and then playing the thing, and in the devotion that my brother and I eagerly gave to it. Yet, as things ended so hard between my brother and myself because of the instrument, I find myself imagining that we never knew the violin, that I'd never played its music or understood its voice. For when my father died he left the fiddle to both my brother Edwin and myself, with the stipulation that were we unable to decide who should have it, then we were to race for it as true sons of the great waters, by paddling our canoes.

55   When my brother and I heard this declaration read, we said nothing. There was nothing to say, for as much as it was true that we loved

each other, we both wanted that violin. Each of us had given it years of practice, each of us had whispered into its hollow our sorrows and taken hold of its joys. That violin had soothed our wild hours, courted our wives. But now we were done with the passing of it back and forth. And if it had to belong to one of us two brothers I determined that it would be me.

Two nights before we took our canoes out, I conceived of a sure plan. When the moon slipped behind clouds and the world was dark, I went out to the shore with a pannikin of heated pitch. I had decided to interfere with Edwin's balance. Our canoes were so carefully constructed that each side matched ounce for ounce. By thickening the seams on one side with a heavy application of pitch, I'd throw off Edwin's paddle stroke enough, I was sure, to give me a telling advantage.

Ours is a wide lake and full of islands. It is haunted by birds who utter sarcastic or sad cries. One loses sight of others easily, and sound travels skewed, bouncing off the rock cliffs. There are flying skeletons, floating bogs, caves containing the spirits of little children, and black moods of weather. We love it well, and we know its secrets — in some part, at least. Not all. And not the secret that I put in motion.

We were to set off on the far northern end of the lake and arrive at the south, where our uncles had lit fires and brought the violin, wrapped in red cloth, in its fancy case. We started out together, joking. Edwin, you remember how we paddled through the first two narrows, laughing as we exaggerated our efforts, and how I said, as what I'd done with the soft pitch weighed on me, "Maybe we should share the damn thing after all."

You laughed and said that our uncles would be disappointed, waiting there, and that when you won the contest things would be as they were before, except all would know that Edwin was the faster paddler. I promised you the same. Then you swerved behind a skim of rock and took your secret shortcut. As I paddled, I had to stop occasionally and bail. At first I thought that I had sprung a slow leak, but in time I understood. While I was painting on extra pitch, you were piercing the bottom of my canoe. I was not, in fact, in any danger, and when the wind shifted all of a sudden and it began to storm — no thunder or lightning, just a buffet of cold rain — I laughed and thanked you. For the water I took on actually helped to steady me. I rode lower, and stayed on course. But you foundered. It was worse to be set off balance. You must have overturned.

60 The bonfires die to coals on the south shore. I curl in blankets but I do not sleep. I am keeping watch. At first when you are waiting for someone, every shadow is an arrival. Then the shadows become the very substance of dread. We hunt for you, call your name until our voices are worn to whispers. No answer. In one old man's dream everything goes around the other way, the not-sun-way, counterclockwise, which means that the dream is of the spirit world. And then he sees you there in his dream, going the wrong way, too.

The uncles have returned to their houses, pastures, children, wives. I am alone on the shore. As the night goes black, I sing for you. As the sun comes up, I call across the water. White gulls answer. As the time goes on, I begin to accept what I have done. I begin to know the truth of things.

They have left the violin here with me. Each night I play for you, brother, and when I can play no more I'll lash our fiddle into the canoe and send it out to you, to find you wherever you are. I won't have to pierce the bottom so it will travel the bed of the lake. Your holes will do the trick, brother, as my trick did for you.

V

Of course, the canoe did not sink to the bottom of the lake. Nor did it stray. The canoe and its violin eventually found a different Peace, through the person of Shamengwa. The fiddle had searched long, I had no doubt of that. For what stuck in my mind, what woke me in the middle of the night, was the date on the letter: 1897. The violin had spoken to Shamengwa and called him out onto the lake more than twenty years later.

"How about that?" I said to Geraldine. "Can you explain such a thing?"

65 She looked at me steadily.

"We know nothing" is what she said.

I was to marry her. We took in Corwin. The violin lies buried in the arms of the man it saved, while the boy it also saved plays for money now and prospers here on the surface of the earth. I do my work. I do my best to make the small decisions well, and I try not to hunger for the greater things, for the deeper explanations. For I am sentenced to keep watch over this little patch of earth, to judge its miseries and tell its stories. That's who I am. *Mii'sago iw.*

Henry Louis Gates Jr.

Sin Boldly

Henry Louis Gates Jr. is a professor at Harvard University, where he chaired the Department of African and African American Studies from 1991 to 2006. He is currently director of the W. E. B. Du Bois Institute for African and African American Research.

In his 1994 memoir, *Colored People*, Gates describes his early life in Piedmont, West Virginia, the small mill town where he grew up. His father was a millworker, his mother a housecleaner; both were avid readers, with high expectations for their sons' academic success. Gates began elementary school in 1956, the year after the school was integrated in response to the Supreme Court's order in *Brown v. Board of Education*. Following in the footsteps of his brother Rocky, six years his senior, Gates was an excellent student, and he went on to Potomac State College of West Virginia.

In 1969, at the end of his freshman year, Gates transferred to Yale. He quickly distinguished himself: in his senior year, he was one of twelve students selected as "scholars of the house," which meant that he was freed from his classes and permitted to work independently on a single project. After graduating from Yale *summa cum laude* in history, he earned a Mellon Fellowship to support study at Cambridge. There, he earned his M.A. and Ph.D. in English literature and began his career as a literary critic specializing in early African American writing.

Gates has written in many genres. As a young man, he was a journalist, writing for the *Yale Daily News* and working briefly as a correspondent for *Time*. He has written a column for the *New York Times* and many articles for *The New Yorker*. As a scholar, Gates has written books of literary theory and criticism, biography, and cultural criticism. He has edited encyclopedias of African American history and culture, and he wrote a PBS mini-series, *The Wonders of the African World* (2000), as well two documentaries, *America Beyond the Color Line* (2004) and *African American Lives* (2008).

Gates's writing often blends his scholarly interest in African American life and literature with reflections on his personal experiences—his childhood in Piedmont, his involvement in the politicized world of academia during the last decades of the twentieth century, his travels to Africa, his interactions with America's leading artists, entertainers, and intellectuals. You'll hear a sampling of his narrative voice in "Sin Boldly," a chapter from *Colored People* recounting his first year after high school.

In 1968, three of the Fearsome Foursome graduated from high school. Soul Moe was called upon to serve his country in Vietnam, and Swano and I would head down to Potomac State. (Roland had been held back a couple of years.) I gave the valedictory address at graduation, defying tradition by writing my own speech — surreptitiously, because this was not allowed. All through the last six weeks of marking period I had practiced delivering the traditional prepared speech with Miss Twigg, our senior English teacher, then had gone home to rehearse my real speech with Mama. Mama had a refined sense of vocal presentation and a wonderful sense of irony and timing. My speech was about Vietnam, abortion, and civil rights, about the sense of community our class shared, since so many of us had been together for twelve years, about the individual's rights and responsibilities in his or her community, and about the necessity to defy norms out of love. I searched the audience for Miss Twigg's face, just to see her expression when I read the speech! She turned as red as a beet, but she liked the speech, and as good as told me so with a big wink at the end of the ceremony.

My one year at Potomac State College of West Virginia University, in Keyser, all of five miles away, was memorable for two reasons: because of my English classes with Duke Anthony Whitmore and my first real love affair, with Maura Gibson.

I came to Potomac State to begin that long, arduous trek toward medical school. I enrolled in August 1968, a week before Labor Day, and I was scared to death. While I had been a good student at Piedmont High, I had no idea how well I would fare in the big-time competition of a college class that included several of the best students from Keyser High, as well as bright kids from throughout the state. I had never questioned my decision to attend Potomac State; it was inevitable: you went there after Piedmont High, as sure as the night follows the day. My uncles Raymond and David had attended it in the fifties, my brother in the early sixties, and my cousin Greg had begun the year before. I would attend too, then go off to "the university" — in Morgantown — to become a doctor.

Greg had told me about life on campus, about the freedom of choice, about card parties in the Union, and, of course, about the women. But be had also told me one thing early in his freshman year that had stayed with me throughout my senior year in Piedmont. "There's an English teacher down there," he had said, "who's going to blow your mind."

"What's his name?" I responded.   5

"Duke Anthony Whitmore," he replied.

"*Duke?*" I said. "What kind of name is Duke? Is he an Englishman?"

"No, dummy," Greg replied. "He's a white guy from Baltimore."

So as I nervously slouched my way through registration a year later, I found myself standing before the ferocious Mr. Gallagher, who enjoyed the reputation of being tough. He gave me the name of my adviser.

I looked at the name; it was not Whitmore. "Can I be assigned to   10
Mr. Whitmore?" I ventured. "Because I've heard quite a lot about him from my cousin."

"You'll have to ask him," Mr. Gallagher said. "He's over there."

I made my way to Mr. Whitmore's table, introduced myself tentatively, stated my case, telling him my cousin Greg had said that he was a great teacher, a wonderful inspiration, etc., etc. What Greg had really said was: "This guy Whitmore is *crazy*, just like you!" It was love at first sight, at least for me. And that, in retrospect, was the beginning of the end of my twelve-year-old dream of becoming a doctor.

Learning English and American literature from the Duke was a game to which I looked forward every day. I had always loved English and had been blessed with some dedicated and able teachers. But reading books was something I had always thought of as a pastime, certainly not as a vocation. The Duke made the study of literature an alluring prospect.

Duke Whitmore did not suffer fools gladly. He did not suffer fools at all. Our classes — I enrolled in everything he taught, despite his protests, which I have to say weren't very strenuous — soon came to be dominated by three or four voices. We would argue and debate just about everything from Emerson and Thoreau to the war in Vietnam and racial discrimination. He would recite a passage from a poem or play, then demand that we tell him, rapid-fire, its source.

15 "*King Lear*," I responded one day.

"What act, what scene, Mr. Gates?" he demanded.

"Act Three, Scene Four," I shouted out blindly, not having the faintest clue as to whether the passage that he had recited was from *Hamlet* or the Book of Job.

"Exactly," he responded with a certain twinkle in his eye. "Sin boldly," he would tell me later, citing Martin Luther. My reckless citation was wrong, of course, but he wished to reward me for my audacity.

It was a glorious experience. Words and thoughts, ideas and visions, came alive for me in his classroom. It was he who showed me, by his example, that ideas had a life of their own and that there were other professions as stimulating and as rewarding as being a doctor.

20 After an academically successful year, Professor Whitmore encouraged me to transfer to the Ivy League. I wrote to Harvard, Yale, and Princeton. Since I had cousins who had gone to Harvard and Princeton, I decided to try for Yale. I sent off the application and took a summer job in the personnel office of the paper mill. I'd been hired for the express purpose of encouraging a few black people to transfer into the craft unions; I recruited them and administered the necessary tests. In three months, each union had been integrated, with barely an audible murmur from its members. Things were changing in Piedmont — a little.

Though we didn't become an item until our freshman year at Potomac State, Maura Gibson and I had known each other from a distance in high school. I used to run into her at the bowling alley and at Jimmy's Pizza next door. She was sharp on her feet and loved to argue. Once, she took me to task for talking about race so much. You can't talk about the weather without bringing up race, she charged. I was embarrassed about that at first, then pleased.

Once we were at college, Maura and I started having long talks on the phone, first about nothing at all and then about everything. The next thing I remember happening between us was parking in her green Dodge up in the colored cemetery on Radical Hill, near where just about all the Keyser colored, and much of the white trash, lived. "Radical" is a synonym in the valley for tacky or ramshackle. I'm not sure which came first, the name or what it came to mean. That's where we were when Horse Lowe (the coach of the college's football team and the owner of the property that abuts the colored cemetery) put his big red face into Maura's window, beat on the windshield with his fist, then told me to get the hell off his property.

Horse Lowe would wait until a couple had begun to pet heavily, then he'd sneak up on the car. He liked to catch you exposed. Even so, we used to park up there all the time. I figured that he'd get tired of throwing us out before I got tired of parking.

On weekends during the summer of 1969, I'd drive over to Rehoboth Beach, in Delaware, to see Maura, who was working as a waitress at a place called the Crab Pot. I'd leave work on Friday at about four o'clock, then drive all the way to Delaware, through Washington and the Beltway, past Baltimore and Annapolis, over the Chesapeake Bridge, past Ocean City, arriving at Rehoboth before midnight, with as much energy as if I had just awakened. We'd get a motel room after her shift ended, and she'd bring a bushel of crabs, steamed in the hot spice called Old Bay. We'd get lots of ice-cold Budweiser and we'd have a feast, listening to Junior Walker play his saxophone, play "What Does It Take" over and over and over again. "What does it take to win your love for me? . . ."

Since Maura was white, I felt that I was making some sort of vague political statement, especially in the wake of Sammy Davis, Jr., and *Guess Who's Coming to Dinner*. Others concurred. We were hassled at the beach. Somehow, for reasons having to do with nudity and sensuality, blacks were not allowed to walk along most beachfronts or attend resorts. I personally integrated many places at Rehoboth Beach that summer.

I was used to being stared at and somewhat used to being the only black person on the beach, or in a restaurant, or at a motel. But I hadn't quite realized how upset people could be until the day that some white guy sicced his Saint Bernard on me as Maura and I walked by. Certainly Maura and I had been no strangers to controversy, but we usually took pains not to invite it. Back home, we had sneaked around at first, hiding in cemeteries and in a crowd of friends, almost never being seen together in public alone. Until we were found out — by her father, of all people. A man called "'Bama," of all things.

It was the evening we had agreed to meet at the big oak tree on Spring Street in Keyser, near one of her friends' houses. I picked her up in my '57 Chevrolet, and we went up to harass the Horse. Afterward, I dropped her off, then drove the five miles back to Piedmont. By the time I got home, Maura had called a dozen times. It turned out that her father had followed her down the street and hidden behind a tree while she waited, had watched her climb into my car. He knew the whole thing.

And he, no progressive on race matters, was sickened and outraged.

Soon, it seemed, all of the Valley knew the whole thing, and everybody had an opinion about it. We were apparently the first interracial couple in Mineral County, and there was hell to pay. People began making oblique threats, in the sort of whispers peculiar to small towns. When friends started warning my parents about them, they bought me a '69 Mustang so I could travel to and from school — and the colored graveyard — safely. (The Chevy had taken to conking out unpredictably.) Some kids at Potomac State started calling us names, anonymously, out of dormitory windows. And in the middle of all this chaos, 'Bama Gibson, Maura's father, decided he was going to run for mayor.

30   Lawd, Lawd, Lawd.

In his own redneck way, 'Bama Gibson was a perfectly nice man, but he was not exactly mayoral material. He had been a postman and became some sort of supervisor at the post office. He was very personable, everybody liked him, and he knew everybody's business, the way a postman in any small town does. With the whole town talking about how terrible it was that his daughter was dating a colored boy, and the men giving him their sympathy and declaring what they'd do to that nigger if that nigger ever touched their daughter, old 'Bama up and announced his candidacy.

Dr. Church, former president of the college, was the obvious front-runner. People were saying he'd already started to measure the mayor's office for new curtains. Certainly no one would have given 'Bama any hope of beating Dr. Church, even before my nappy head came on the horizon. *With you on these crackers' minds,* Daddy told me, *he's got two chances: slim and none. Boy, how do you* get *into all this trouble?*

Meantime, at the height of the campaign, Roland, Jerry, Swano, and I decided to integrate the Swordfish, a weekend hangout where all the college kids went to listen to a live band — usually E. G. Taylor and the Sounds of Soul, a white band with a black, Eugene Taylor, as lead singer. Eugene could *sing*. He wasn't so great with learning the words, but that Negro could warble. He'd make up words as he went along, using sounds similar to those he could not remember but making no sense.

Still, we wanted the right to hear Eugene mess up James Brown's words, same as anybody else, so we started to plot our move. Late one Friday night, when the Swordfish was rocking and packed, we headed up New Creek in our Soul Mobile, which we had washed for the occasion, even replacing the old masking tape over the holes in the roof. The Fearsome Foursome made their date with destiny. We were silent as we drove into the parking lot. There was nothing left to say. We were scared to death but just had to get on with it.

We parked the car and strolled up the stairs to the Swordfish. Since there was no cover charge, we walked straight into the middle of the dance floor. That's when the slo-mo started, an effect exacerbated by the strobe lights. Everybody froze: the kids from Piedmont and Keyser who had grown up with us; the students from Potomac State; the rednecks and crackers from up the hollers, the ones who came to town once a week all dressed up in their Sears, Roebuck perma-pressed drawers, their Thom McAn semi-leather shoes, their ultimately *white* sox, and their hair slicked back and wet-looking. The kids of rednecks, who liked to drink gallons of 3.2 beer, threaten everybody within earshot, and puke all over themselves — they froze too, their worst nightmare staring them in the face.

After what seemed like hours but was probably less than a minute, a homely white boy with extra-greasy blond hair recovered and began to shout "Niggers" as his face assumed the ugly mask of hillbilly racism. I stared at this white boy's face, which turned redder and redder as *he* turned into the Devil, calling on his boys to kick our asses: calling us niggers and niggers and niggers to help them summon up their courage. White boys started moving around us, forming a circle around ours. Our good friends from Keyser and Potomac State were still frozen, embarrassed that we were *in* there, that we had violated their space, dared to cross the line. No help from them. (I lost lots of friends that night.) Then, breaking through the circle of rednecks, came the owner, who started screaming: Get out of here! Get out of here! and picked up Fisher and slammed his head against the wall. It wasn't easy to see because of all the smoke and because of the strobe effect of the flashing blue lights, but I remember being surprised at how Roland's Afro had

35

kept its shape when his head sprang back off the wall, the way a basket-ball keeps its shape no matter how much or how hard you dribble it.

Moe and I hauled Fisher off the ground, with Swano's broad shoulders driving through the 'necks the way Bubba Smith used to do for the Baltimore Colts. I wondered if Roland's head would stop bleeding. Fuck you, motherfucker, I heard myself say. We're gonna shut your racist ass down. We're gonna shut your ass down, repeated Moe and Swano in chorus. Take a good look around you, you crackers, cuz this is your last time here.

We dragged Fisher to the car, ducking the bottles and cans as we sped away. Roland's head had stopped its bleeding by the time we passed Potomac Valley Hospital, which we called the meat factory because one of the doctors was reputed to be such a butcher, so we drove on past it and headed for my house. What'll y'all do now? Daddy asked as Mama bandaged Roland Fisher's head.

And yes, the place was shut down. We called the State Human Rights Commission on Monday, and the commissioner, Carl Glass, came up to Piedmont a few days later. He interviewed the four of us separately, and then he went out to the Swordfish and interviewed the proprietor, who by this time had told everybody white and colored in Keyser that he was going to get that troublemaker Gates. He swore to the commissioner that he would close down before he let niggers in. The commissioner took him at his word and sent an official edict telling him to integrate or shut down. As the man promised, he shut it down. And that is why the Swordfish nightclub is now Samson's Family Restaurant, run by a very nice Filipino family.

40   Well, all of this broke out in the middle of 'Bama Gibson's campaign to be the first postman elected as Mayor of Keyser, West Virginia, The Friendliest City in the U.S.A., as the road sign boasted — to which we chorused "bullshit" whenever we passed it.

The whole town talked about this campaign, from sunup to sundown. And there were some curious developments. Our family doctor, Dr. Staggers (our high school principal, Mr. Staggers's son), went out of his way to tell me that lots of his friends, well-educated and liberal, had decided to suspend disbelief and vote for 'Bama, just to prove (as he put it) that Keyser is not Birmingham. Then the colored people, who never voted, decided to register and turn out for good ole 'Bama. The college kids at Potomac State, the ones not busy calling Maura "nigger-lover" from their dormitory windows, turned out in droves. And all the romantics who lived in Keyser, those who truly respected the idea of love and passion, voted for 'Bama. All both of them. Bizarrely enough, the election was turning into a plebiscite on interracial relationships.

I stayed out of Keyser on the day of the election, terrified that I'd already caused Maura's father to lose. If it's close, there's no sense aggravating the ones sitting on the fence, rubbing their nose in it, Daddy had said. And so I waited for Maura's phone call, which came around eleven-thirty and informed me that we had nothing more to worry about, her father had trampled Dr. Church. No longer would the police follow us, daring us to go even one mile over the speed limit. That's what she told me, and I could scarcely believe it. I started parking my car on red lines and in front of fire hydrants, just to test her assertion. She was right.

It was also because of 'Bama's new office that I learned that the West Virginia State Police had opened a file on me in Mineral County, which identified me for possible custodial detention if and when race riots started. Maura gave me the news late one night, whispering it over the phone. Old 'Bama, whom victory had made magnanimous, had wanted me to know and to be warned.

I remember feeling sick and scared . . . and then, when that passed, a little flattered. I was eighteen, had scarcely been outside Mineral County, and someone in authority decided I was dangerous? I mean, *I* liked to think so. But that an official establishment should collude with my fantasies of importance was quite another matter.

I took it as a sign that it was time for me to leave the Valley and go Elsewhere. I did leave it, that very fall, packing my bags for New Haven. But leaving it *behind* was never a possibility. It did not take me long to realize that.

The "Personal Statement" for my Yale application began: "My grandfather was colored, my father was Negro, and I am black." And it concluded: "As always, whitey now sits in judgment of me, preparing to cast my fate. It is your decision either to let me blow with the wind as a non-entity or to encourage the development of self. Allow me to prove myself."

I wince at the rhetoric today, but they let me in.

Henry Louis Gates Jr.

The Two Nations of Black America

In "The Two Nations of Black America," Henry Louis Gates Jr. argues that Black America has achieved "the best of times and the worst of times," with unprecedented opportunity but a persistent problem of widespread poverty. Published in the *Brookings Review* in 1998, the article summarizes key points from *The Future of the Race*, coauthored by Gates and Cornel West.

For a biographical sketch of Gates, see page 155.

Six black men, each intellectually superior in his own way, graduated from Yale College in the class of 1966. Each had managed, through some luck and a lot of pluck, to penetrate the ironclad barriers that had kept the blacks matriculating at Yale to a fixed number for several decades. When I entered Yale two years later, 95 black men and women entered with me.

We were, to a person, caught up in the magic of the moment. Our good fortune was to have been selected to be part of the first "large" group of blacks included in Yale's commitment to educate "1,000 male leaders" each year. But we wondered: what would becoming a true black leader entail — for ourselves and for our people outside those hallowed Ivy walls? What sort of sacrifices and obligations did this special ticket to success bring along with it? We worried about this — out loud, often, and noisily.

Mostly we did our worrying in our long languid dinners in the colleges or in bull sessions in our suites, but our ritualized worrying space was our weekly meetings of the Black Student Alliance at

Yale, headed by our black and shining prince, Glenn de Chabert. Our first item of business was always "recruitment," how to get more black students to join us at New Haven. "This place is lily white," de Chabert would complain. "We are flies in the buttermilk." Brimming to overflow with maybe 200 students, the year's first meeting of the BSAY looked like Harlem to me! I basked in the warmth generated by the comfort of the range of brown colors in that room, but I also shuddered (as unnoticeably as I could) as I contemplated the awesome burden of leadership that we felt or were made to feel, fulfilling our obligations to "help the community." After all, "the revolution" was unfolding around the country and we, along with students like us at Harvard, Columbia, Princeton, Amherst, and Wesleyan, were to be its vanguard. This burden was no mere abstraction. The trial of New Haven's Black Panthers, and of one of their leaders, Bobby Seale, was under way just a block or two away at New Haven's federal courthouse.

It astonishes me today how sharp my black colleagues were, how thoughtful beyond their years, how mature. For some reason, I long assumed that most of these guys were up from the ghetto, first generation college. After all, our uniforms of the day, dashikis and blue jeans, obliterated our variety of social distinctions. Names like Baskerville and Irving, Reed and Robinson, Schmoke and de Chabert, Barrington Parker the Third, meant nothing particular to me. Only later would I discover that my contemporaries were no strangers to the idea of college. Had it not been for affirmative action, we would have met at Howard or Morehouse. They were not so much a new black middle-class bourgeoisie recruited to scale the ladder of class as the scions of an old and colored middle class, recruited to integrate a white male elite. We clung to a soft black nationalist politics to keep ourselves to the straight and narrow.

For me one crucial scene of instruction on the path of a more or less nationalist politics came while I was watching a black program that had been produced by students at Howard. In the film, a student, happily dating a white co-ed, comes to see the error of his ways after a campus visit by Maulana Ron Karenga. What a figure Karenga was — brown bald head, African robes, dark sun glasses. This was one bad dude, bad enough to make this guy in the film turn his back on love and come on home! I'm not sure it had ever occurred to me before this that there was "a way to be 'black,'" that one could be in the program or outside of it.

Of course I knew what an Uncle Tom was, but even Uncle Tom was still part of the extended family. No one ever talked about banishing him from the tribe. Before this. But this was a new day. A new generation, a vanguard within the vanguard of civil rights leadership, was demanding Black Power, the right to take over, and declaring venerable elders like Martin Luther King, Jr., to be too old, too tired, too Milquetoast to be effective keepers of Black Power's incandescent flare. Dr. King was especially symptomatic, moving away as he had done from an exclusively race-based politics to a more broadly conceived analysis that would bring "poor people" together. Where did a movement based on poverty leave all of us who were discovering an Afro-coifed dashiki-clad "blackness" long forcibly hidden from our view? Even the Black Panthers, Marxists that they claimed to be, manipulated the trappings of nationalist garb and rhetoric to maximize their appeal in a program that would eventually lead out of the black community and straight into a coalition with the brown and red and white truly poor.

J. Edgar Hoover and his FBI, apparently, were not aware of, or especially concerned about, what Freud called "the narcissism of tiny differences" within the black movement. For Hoover, the Panthers were black, they were radical, they were Communist-inspired. And they could be dealt with.

Systematic repression has a curious way of hampering the evolution of a movement. And not only were the Black Panthers repressed, Dr. King was assassinated — in retrospect the most dramatic act of violent repression in the wing of the movement that was beginning to embrace a class-based organizing principle that sought to reorder American society. Dr. King was killed. People like Huey Newton were imprisoned. And people as unlike as Elijah Mohammed and Vernon Jordan, Jesse Jackson, and my new compatriots at Yale were being invited to integrate a newly expanded American upper middle class. The vanguard of black cultural nationalist political consciousness, in other words, became the vanguard in the race's broad movement across the great divide that had for so long prevented genuine economic mobility up the great American ladder of class.

Somehow, in the late sixties, in the aftermath of the King assassination, what was held to be "authentically" black began to change. Ghetto culture was valorized; the "bourgeois" lifestyle that the old guard leaders of the civil rights establishment embodied was held to be too great a price to pay for our freedom, or at least to admit to. We wanted to be "real," to "be down with the people," to be successful, yes, but to appear to be "black" at the same time. And to be black was to be committed to a revolution of values, of mores and manners, of economic relationships. We were "a people." The best way to dramatize this kinship was to dress, walk, talk like a "brother."

Above all, being black meant that we were at one with "the revolu-   10
tion" standing tall and firm in defense of "the people," and that revolutionary vanguard, the persecuted and harassed Black Panther Party for Self-Defense. We went on strike on April 15, 1970, two weeks before Nixon and Henry Kissinger invaded Cambodia. We struck because Bobby Seale, we felt deeply, was not being tried fairly just down the street, bound and gagged as he was at the worst moment of the trial. The strike rally was glorious. It seemed as if 100,000 people crowded onto the New Haven Green on May Day of 1970. Kingman Brewster, Yale's dynamic president, offered them food and shelter in the residential colleges. Each stained glass window of the sacred cathedral of learning that we called "Sterling" stood intact at week's end. De Chabert had never spoken more impressively, never been more daring or inspiring.

However, graduation inevitably came, calling us to the newly expanded opportunities in graduate and professional schools and then on to similarly expanded opportunities in the broader professional and academic world. I went off to Cambridge, England, and when I returned a few years later to teach at Yale, so very much had changed. Any pretense that black admissions would be anything but staunchly and firmly middle class had ended during my absence. The new black middle class was perpetuating itself. Affirmative action, under assault by the Supreme Court's 1978 Bakke decision and wounded, still was functioning to increase the size of the middle class exponentially by a factor of four. Meanwhile, the gradual disappearance of industrial jobs in the cities was cutting off that upwardly mobile class escalator that so many in the middle class had been able to scale.

Thenceforth, in one of the most curious social transformations in the class structure in recent American history, two tributaries began to flow, running steadily into two distinct rivers of aspiration and achievement. By 1990, the black middle class, imperiled though it might feel itself to be, had never been larger, more prosperous, or more relatively secure. Simultaneously, the pathological behavior that results from extended impoverishment engulfed a large part of a black underclass that seemed unable to benefit from a certain opening up of American society that the civil rights movement had long envisioned and had finally made possible, if only for some. And for the first time ever, that inability to benefit seemed permanent.

Gangsterism became the handmaiden of hopelessness. Even middle-class children, well-educated, often, and well-heeled, found value in publicly celebrating a "gangsta" lifestyle. Cultural forms such as Rap and Hip Hop, "the CNN of the black community," valorized violence, homophobia, misogyny, anti-Semitism, and a curious form of masochistic self-destruction. And then life began to imitate art — the gangsterism of the art of Hip Hop liberalized itself in the reciprocal murders of Tupac and Biggie Smalls — and the bizarre nightmare inversion of popular black values manifested itself in a most public way.

Which brings us to the present — for the African-American community, the best of times and the worst of times. We have the largest black middle class in our history and the largest black underclass. In 1990, 2,280,000 black men were in prison, or probation, or parole, while 23,000 earned a college degree. That's a ratio of 99 to 1, compared with a ratio of 6 to 1 for white men.

15   What do we do about this? What do we not do?

First of all, we have to stop feeling guilty about our success. Too many of us have what psychologists call "the guilt of the survivor," deep anxieties about leaving the rest of our fellow blacks in the inner city of despair. We need to feel the commitment to service, not to guilt. Our community and our families prepared us to be successful. "Get all the education you can" they told us over and over — and we did.

Second, we don't have to fail in order to be black. As odd and as crazy as this sounds. Far too many young black kids say that succeeding is "white." Had any of us said this sort of thing when we were growing up, our families and friends would have checked us into a mental institution. We need more success individually and collectively.

Third, we don't have to pretend any longer that 35 million people can ever possibly be members of the same economic class. The entire population of Canada is 27 million. Canadians are not all members of one economic class. Nor do they speak with one single voice, united behind one single leader. As each of us knows, we have never been members of one social or economic class and never will be. The best we can strive for is that the class differentials within the black community — the bell curve of class — cease their lopsided ratios because of the pernicious nature of racial inequality.

So how do we do this? How do we "fight the power" in a post–civil rights world in which Bull Connors and George Wallace are no longer the easy targets? A world in which the rhetoric of the civil rights era sounds hollow and empty? A world in which race differences and class differentials have been ground together in a crucible of misery and squalor, in such a way that few of us can tell where one stops and the other begins? I certainly have no magic cures.

But we do know that the causes of poverty within the black community are both structural and behavioral. Scholars as diverse as philosopher Cornel West and sociologist William Julius Wilson have pointed this out, and we are foolish to deny it. A household composed of a 16-year-old mother, a 32-year-old grandmother, and a 48-year-old great grandmother cannot possibly be a site for hope and optimism. Our task, it seems to me, is to lobby for those social programs that have been demonstrated to make a difference for those motivated to seize these expanded opportunities.   20

More important, we have to demand a structural change in this country, the equivalent of a Marshall Plan for the cities. We have to take people off welfare, train them for occupations relevant to a 21st-century, high-tech economy, and put them to work. Joblessness, as Wilson maintains, is our biggest crisis.

And while I favor such incentives as tax breaks to generate new investment in inner cities, youth apprenticeships with corporations, expanded tax credits for earned income, and tenant ownership of inner-city property, we have to face the reality that most of our inner cities are simply not going to become overnight oases of prosperity. We should think about moving black inner-city workers to the jobs rather than hold our breath and wait for new factories to resettle in the inner city.

It is only by confronting the twin realities of white racism, on the one hand, and our failures to take the initiative and break the cycle of poverty, on the other, that we, the remnants of W. E. B. Du Bois's Talented Tenth, will be able to assume a renewed leadership role for, and with, the black community. To continue to repeat the same old stale formulas; to blame "the man" for oppressing us all, in exactly the same ways; to scapegoat Koreans, Jews, or even Haitians for the failure of black Americans to seize local entrepreneurial opportunities is to fail to accept our role as leaders of our own community. Not to demand that each member of the black community accept individual responsibility for her or his behavior — whether that behavior assumes the form of black-on-black homicide, gang members violating the sanctity of the church, unprotected sexual activity, gangster rap lyrics, whatever — is for us to function merely as ethnic cheerleaders selling woof tickets from campus or suburbs, rather than saying the difficult things that may be unpopular with our fellows. Being a leader does not necessarily mean being loved; loving one's community means daring to risk estrangement and alienation from it in the short run in order to break the cycle of poverty and despair in which we find ourselves, over the long run. For what is at stake is nothing less than the survival of our country, and the African-American people themselves.

Those of us on campus can also reach out to those of us left behind on the streets. The historically black colleges and universities and Afro-American Studies departments in this country can institutionalize sophomore and junior year internships for community development through organizations such as the Children's Defense Fund. Together we can combat teenage pregnancies, black-on-black crime, and the spread of AIDS from drug abuse and unprotected sexual relations, and counter the spread of despair and hopelessness in our communities. Dr. King did not die so that half of us would make it, half of us perish, forever tarnishing two centuries of agitation for our equal rights. We, the members of the Talented Tenth, must accept our historical responsibility and live Dr. King's credo that none of us is free until all of us are free. And that all of us are brothers and sisters, as Dr. King said so long ago — white and black, Protestant and Catholic, Gentile and Jew and Muslim, rich and poor — even if we are not brothers-in-law.

Tim O'Brien

On the Rainy River

Tim O'Brien was born in 1946 in Austin, Minnesota, to an insurance salesman and an elementary school teacher. Both of his parents were veterans: his father had been in the Navy in Iwo Jima and Okinawa during World War II, and his mother had served with the WAVES (Women Accepted for Volunteer Emergency Service). As a child, O'Brien spent time reading in the county library, learning to perform magic tricks, and playing baseball (his first piece of fiction was called "Timmy of the Little League").

O'Brien attended Macalester College in Saint Paul, Minnesota, majoring in political science. When he graduated in 1968, he hoped to join the State Department as a diplomat—but instead, just weeks after graduation, he was drafted into the Army. O'Brien nearly fled to Canada: during his training in Fort Lewis, Washington, he planned to desert, but he went only as far as Seattle before turning back. In 1969, at the age of 22, he went to Quang Ngai, Vietnam, first as a rifleman and later as a radio telephone operator and clerk. He completed a 13-month tour of duty, earning a Purple Heart and a Bronze Star.

After his return to the United States in 1970, O'Brien enrolled in Harvard's doctoral program in government and spent his summers working as an intern for the *Washington Post*. He became a full-time national affairs reporter, covering Senate hearings and political events. Several years later, O'Brien left both his graduate work and his job at the *Post* to pursue a career as a writer. In a memoir, seven novels, and many short stories, O'Brien has explored the question of moral responsibility: Who is responsible for the 58,000 American soldiers and more than a million Vietnamese people killed in battle between 1965 and 1975?

"On the Rainy River" describes a young man who has to choose between going to Vietnam and fleeing to Canada to evade the draft. He blames the war on everyone—the president, the joint chiefs of staff, the knee-jerk patriots in his hometown—but ultimately takes his place among them, choosing to go to war. His decision precipitates the events of the book, *The Things They Carried*, just as O'Brien's own conflicted decision to go to war set the course of his life, first as a soldier and then as a writer.

The Things They Carried (1990) was a finalist for both the Pulitzer Prize and the National Book Critics Circle Award. O'Brien's other significant books include *If I Die in a Combat Zone, Box Me Up and Ship Me Home* (1973), *Going after Cacciato* (1978), *The Nuclear Age* (1985), and *In the Lake of the Woods* (1994). Tim O'Brien lives in Texas with his wife and son. He teaches creative writing at Texas State University.

This is one story I've never told before. Not to anyone. Not to my parents, not to my brother or sister, not even to my wife. To go into it, I've always thought, would only cause embarrassment for all of us, a sudden need to be elsewhere, which is the natural response to a confession. Even now, I'll admit, the story makes me squirm. For more than twenty years I've had to live with it, feeling the shame, trying to push it away, and so by this act of remembrance, by putting the facts down on paper, I'm hoping to relieve at least some of the pressure on my dreams. Still, it's a hard story to tell. All of us, I suppose, like to believe that in a moral emergency we will behave like the heroes of our youth, bravely and forthrightly, without thought of personal loss or discredit. Certainly that was my conviction back in the summer of 1968. Tim O'Brien: a secret hero. The Lone Ranger. If the stakes ever became high enough — if the evil were evil enough, if the good were good enough — I would simply tap a secret reservoir of courage that had been accumulating inside me over the years. Courage, I seemed to think, comes to us in finite quantities, like an inheritance, and by being frugal and stashing it away and letting it earn interest, we steadily increase our moral capital in preparation for that day when the account must be drawn down. It was a comforting theory. It dispensed with all those bothersome little acts of daily courage; it offered hope and grace to the repetitive coward; it justified the past while amortizing the future.

In June of 1968, a month after graduating from Macalester College, I was drafted to fight a war I hated. I was twenty-one years old. Young, yes, and politically naive, but even so the American war in Vietnam seemed to me wrong. Certain blood was being shed for uncertain reasons. I saw no unity of purpose, no consensus on matters of philosophy or history or law. The very facts were shrouded in uncertainty: Was it a civil war? A war of national liberation or simple aggression? Who started it, and when, and why? What really happened to the USS *Maddox* on that dark night in the Gulf of Tonkin? Was Ho Chi Minh a Communist stooge, or a nationalist savior, or both, or neither? What about the Geneva Accords? What about SEATO and the Cold War? What about dominoes? America was divided on these and a thousand other issues, and the debate had spilled out across the floor of the United States Senate and into the streets, and smart men in pinstripes could not agree on even the most fundamental matters of public policy. The only certainty that summer was moral confusion. It was my view then, and still is, that you don't make war without knowing why. Knowledge, of course, is always imperfect, but it seemed to me that when a nation goes to war it must have reasonable confidence in the justice and imperative of its cause. You can't fix your mistakes. Once people are dead, you can't make them undead.

In any case those were my convictions, and back in college I had taken a modest stand against the war. Nothing radical, no hothead stuff, just ringing a few doorbells for Gene McCarthy, composing a few tedious, uninspired editorials for the campus newspaper. Oddly, though, it was almost entirely an intellectual activity. I brought some energy to it, of course, but it was the energy that accompanies almost any abstract endeavor; I felt no personal danger, I felt no sense of an impending crisis in my life. Stupidly, with a kind of smug removal that I can't begin to fathom, I assumed that the problems of killing and dying did not fall within my special province.

The draft notice arrived on June 17, 1968. It was a humid afternoon, I remember, cloudy and very quiet, and I'd just come in from a round of golf. My mother and father were having lunch out in the kitchen. I remember opening up the letter, scanning the first few lines, feeling the blood go thick behind my eyes. I remember a sound in my head. It wasn't thinking, just a silent howl. A million things all at once — I was too *good* for this war. Too smart, too compassionate, too everything. It couldn't happen. I was above it. I had the world dicked — Phi Beta Kappa and summa cum laude and president of the student body and a full-ride scholarship for grad studies at Harvard. A mistake, maybe — a foul-up in the paperwork. I was no soldier. I hated Boy Scouts. I hated camping out. I hated dirt and tents and mosquitoes. The sight of blood made me queasy, and I couldn't tolerate authority, and I didn't know a rifle from a slingshot. I was a *liberal*, for Christ sake: If they needed fresh bodies, why not draft some back-to-the-stone-age hawk? Or some dumb jingo in his hard hat and Bomb Hanoi button, or one of LBJ's pretty daughters, or Westmoreland's whole handsome family — nephews and nieces and baby grandson. There should be a law, I thought. If you support a war, if you think it's worth the price, that's fine, but you have to put your own precious fluids on the line. You have to head for the front and hook up with an infantry unit and help spill the blood. And you have to bring along your wife, or your kids, or your lover. A *law*, I thought.

5   I remember the rage in my stomach. Later it burned down to a smoldering self-pity, then to numbness. At dinner that night my father asked what my plans were.

"Nothing," I said. "Wait."

I spent the summer of 1968 working in an Armour meat-packing plant in my hometown of Worthington, Minnesota. The plant specialized in pork products, and for eight hours a day I stood on a quarter-mile assembly line — more properly, a disassembly line — removing blood clots from the necks of dead pigs. My job title, I believe, was Declotter. After slaughter, the hogs were decapitated, split down the length of the belly, pried open, eviscerated, and strung up by the hind hocks on a high conveyer belt. Then gravity took over. By the time a carcass reached my spot on the line, the fluids had mostly drained out, everything except for thick clots of blood in the neck and upper chest cavity. To remove the stuff, I used a kind of water gun. The machine was heavy, maybe eighty pounds, and was suspended from the ceiling by a heavy rubber cord. There was some bounce to it, an elastic up-and-down give, and the trick was to maneuver the gun with your whole body, not lifting with the arms, just letting the rubber cord do the work for you. At one end was a trigger; at the muzzle end was a small nozzle and a steel roller brush. As a carcass passed by, you'd lean forward and swing the gun up against the clots and squeeze the trigger, all in one motion, and the brush would whirl and water would come shooting out and you'd hear a quick splattering sound as the clots dissolved into a fine red mist.

It was not pleasant work. Goggles were a necessity, and a rubber apron, but even so it was like standing for eight hours a day under a lukewarm blood-shower. At night I'd go home smelling of pig. It wouldn't go away. Even after a hot bath, scrubbing hard, the stink was always there — like old bacon, or sausage, a dense greasy pig-stink that soaked deep into my skin and hair. Among other things, I remember, it was tough getting dates that summer. I felt isolated; I spent a lot of time alone. And there was also that draft notice tucked away in my wallet.

In the evenings I'd sometimes borrow my father's car and drive aimlessly around town, feeling sorry for myself, thinking about the war and the pig factory and how my life seemed to be collapsing toward slaughter. I felt paralyzed. All around me the options seemed to be narrowing, as if I were hurtling down a huge black funnel, the whole world squeezing in tight. There was no happy way out. The government had ended most graduate school deferments; the waiting lists for the National Guard and Reserves were impossibly long; my health was solid; I didn't qualify for CO status — no religious grounds, no history as a pacifist. Moreover, I could not claim to be opposed to war as a matter of general principle. There were occasions, I believed, when a nation was justified in using military force to achieve its ends, to stop a Hitler or some comparable evil, and I told myself that in such circumstances I would've willingly marched off to the battle. The problem, though, was that a draft board did not let you choose your war.

Beyond all this, or at the very center, was the raw fact of terror. I did not want to die. Not ever. But certainly not then, not there, not in a wrong war. Driving up Main Street, past the courthouse and the Ben Franklin store, I sometimes felt the fear spreading inside me like weeds. I imagined myself dead. I imagined myself doing things I could not do — charging an enemy position, taking aim at another human being.

At some point in mid-July I began thinking seriously about Canada. The border lay a few hundred miles north, an eight-hour drive. Both my conscience and my instincts were telling me to make a break for it, just take off and run like hell and never stop. In the beginning the idea seemed purely abstract, the word Canada printing itself out in my head; but after a time I could see particular shapes and images, the sorry details of my own future — a hotel room in Winnipeg, a battered old suitcase, my father's eyes as I tried to explain myself over the telephone.

I could almost hear his voice, and my mother's. Run, I'd think. Then I'd think, Impossible. Then a second later I'd think, *Run*.

It was a kind of schizophrenia. A moral split. I couldn't make up my mind. I feared the war, yes, but I also feared exile. I was afraid of walking away from my own life, my friends and my family, my whole history, everything that mattered to me. I feared losing the respect of my parents. I feared the law. I feared ridicule and censure. My hometown was a conservative little spot on the prairie, a place where tradition counted, and it was easy to imagine people sitting around a table down at the old Gobbler Café on Main Street, coffee cups poised, the conversation slowly zeroing in on the young O'Brien kid, how the damned sissy had taken off for Canada. At night, when I couldn't sleep, I'd sometimes carry on fierce arguments with those people. I'd be screaming at them, telling them how much I detested their blind, thoughtless, automatic acquiescence to it all, their simple minded patriotism, their prideful ignorance, their love-it-or-leave-it platitudes, how they were sending me off to fight a war they didn't understand and didn't want to understand. I held them responsible. By God, yes, I *did*. All of them — I held them personally and individually responsible — the polyestered Kiwanis boys, the merchants and farmers, the pious churchgoers, the chatty housewives, the PTA and the Lions club and the Veterans of Foreign Wars and the fine upstanding gentry out at the country club. They didn't know Bao Dai from the man in the moon. They didn't know history. They didn't know the first thing about Diem's tyranny, or the nature of Vietnamese nationalism, or the long colonialism of the French — this was all too damned complicated, it required some reading — but no matter, it was a war to stop the Communists, plain and simple, which was how they liked things, and you were a treasonous pussy if you had second thoughts about killing or dying for plain and simple reasons.

I was bitter, sure. But it was so much more than that. The emotions went from outrage to terror to bewilderment to guilt to sorrow and then back again to outrage. I felt a sickness inside me. Real disease.

Most of this I've told before, or at least hinted at, but what I have never told is the full truth. How I cracked. How at work one morning, standing on the pig line, I felt something break open in my chest. I don't know what it was. I'll never know. But it was real, I know that much, it was a physical rupture — a cracking-leaking-popping feeling. I remember dropping my water gun. Quickly, almost without thought, I took off my apron and walked out of the plant and drove home. It was midmorning, I remember, and the house was empty. Down in my chest there was still that leaking sensation, something very warm and precious spilling out, and I was covered with blood and hog-stink, and for a long while I just concentrated on holding myself together. I remember taking a hot shower. I remember packing a suitcase and carrying it out to the kitchen, standing very still for a few minutes, looking carefully at the familiar objects all around me. The old chrome toaster, the telephone, the pink and white Formica on the kitchen counters. The room was full of bright sunshine. Everything sparkled. My house, I thought. My life. I'm not sure how long I stood there, but later I scribbled out a short note to my parents.

What it said, exactly, I don't recall now. Something vague. Taking off, will call, love Tim.

I drove north.

15

It's a blur now, as it was then, and all I remember is a sense of high velocity and the feel of the steering wheel in my hands. I was riding on adrenaline. A giddy feeling, in a way, except there was the dreamy edge of impossibility to it — like running a dead-end maze — no way out — it couldn't come to a happy conclusion and yet I was doing it anyway because it was all I could think of to do. It was pure flight, fast and mindless. I had no plan. Just hit the border at high speed and crash through and keep on running. Near dusk I passed through Bemidji, then turned northeast toward International Falls. I spent the night in the car behind a closed-down gas station a half mile from the border. In the morning, after gassing up, I headed straight west along the Rainy River, which separates Minnesota from Canada, and which for me separated one life from another. The land was mostly wilderness. Here and there I passed a motel or bait shop, but otherwise the country unfolded in great sweeps of pine and birch and sumac. Though it was still August, the air already had the smell of October, football season, piles of yellow-red leaves, everything crisp and clean. I remember a huge blue sky. Off to my right was the Rainy River, wide as a lake in places, and beyond the Rainy River was Canada.

For a while I just drove, not aiming at anything, then in the late morning I began looking for a place to lie low for a day or two. I was exhausted, and scared sick, and around noon I pulled into an old fishing resort called the Tip Top Lodge. Actually it was not a lodge at all, just eight or nine tiny yellow cabins clustered on a peninsula that jutted northward into the Rainy River. The place was in sorry shape. There was a dangerous wooden dock, an old minnow tank, a flimsy tar paper boathouse along the shore. The main building, which stood in a cluster of pines on high ground, seemed to lean heavily to one side, like a cripple, the roof sagging toward Canada. Briefly, I thought about turning around, just giving up, but then I got out of the car and walked up to the front porch.

The man who opened the door that day is the hero of my life. How do I say this without sounding sappy? Blurt it out — the man saved me. He offered exactly what I needed, without questions, without any words at all. He took me in. He was there at the critical time — a silent, watchful presence. Six days later, when it ended, I was unable to find a proper way to thank him, and I never have, and so, if nothing else, this story represents a small gesture of gratitude twenty years overdue.

Even after two decades I can close my eyes and return to that porch at the Tip Top Lodge. I can see the old guy staring at me. Elroy Berdahl: eighty-one years old, skinny and shrunken and mostly bald. He wore a flannel shirt and brown work pants. In one hand, I remember, he carried a green apple, a small paring knife in the other. His eyes had the bluish gray color of a razor blade, the same polished shine, and as he peered up at me I felt a strange sharpness, almost painful, a cutting sensation, as if his gaze were somehow slicing me open. In part, no doubt, it was my own sense of guilt, but even so I'm absolutely certain that the old man took one look and went right to the heart of things — a kid in trouble. When I asked for a room, Elroy made a little clicking sound with his tongue. He nodded, led me out to one of the cabins, and dropped a key in my hand. I remember smiling at him. I also remember wishing I hadn't. The old man shook his head as if to tell me it wasn't worth the bother.

20   "Dinner at five-thirty," he said. "You eat fish?"

"Anything," I said.

Elroy grunted and said, "I'll bet."

We spent six days together at the Tip Top Lodge. Just the two of us. Tourist season was over, and there were no boats on the river, and the wilderness seemed to withdraw into a great permanent stillness. Over those six days Elroy Berdahl and I took most of our meals together. In the mornings we sometimes went out on long hikes into the woods, and at night we played Scrabble or listened to records or sat reading in front of his big stone fireplace. At times I felt the awkwardness of an intruder, but Elroy accepted me into his quiet routine without fuss or ceremony. He took my presence for granted, the same way he might've sheltered a stray cat — no wasted sighs or pity — and there was never any talk about it. Just the opposite. What I remember more than anything is the man's willful, almost ferocious silence. In all that time together, all those hours, he never asked the obvious questions: Why was I there? Why alone? Why so preoccupied? If Elroy was curious about any of this, he was careful never to put it into words.

My hunch, though, is that he already knew. At least the basics. After all, it was 1968, and guys were burning draft cards, and Canada was just a boat ride away. Elroy Berdahl was no hick. His bedroom, I remember, was cluttered with books and newspapers. He killed me at the Scrabble board, barely concentrating, and on those occasions when speech was necessary he had a way of compressing large thoughts into small, cryptic packets of language. One evening, just at sunset, he pointed up at an owl circling over the violet-lighted forest to the west. "Hey, O'Brien," he said. "There's Jesus."

The man was sharp — he didn't miss much. Those razor eyes. Now and then he'd catch me staring out at the river, at the far shore, and I could almost hear the tumblers clicking in his head. Maybe I'm wrong, but I doubt it.

One thing for certain, he knew I was in desperate trouble. And he knew I couldn't talk about it. The wrong word — or even the right word — and I would've disappeared. I was wired and jittery. My skin felt too tight. After supper one evening I vomited and went back to my cabin and lay down for a few moments and then vomited again; another time, in the middle of the afternoon, I began sweating and couldn't shut it off. I went through whole days feeling dizzy with sorrow. I couldn't sleep; I couldn't lie still. At night I'd toss around in bed, half awake, half dreaming, imagining how I'd sneak down to the beach and quietly push one of the old man's boats out into the river and start paddling my way toward Canada. There were times when I thought I'd gone off the psychic edge. I couldn't tell up from down, I was just falling, and late in the night I'd lie there watching weird pictures spin through my head. Getting chased by the Border Patrol — helicopters and searchlights and barking dogs — I'd be crashing through the woods, I'd be down on my hands and knees — people shouting out my name — the law closing in on all sides — my hometown draft board and the FBI and the Royal Canadian Mounted Police. It all seemed crazy and impossible. Twenty-one years old, an ordinary kid with all the ordinary dreams and ambitions, and all I wanted was to live the life I was born to — a mainstream life — I loved baseball and hamburgers and cherry Cokes — and now I was off on the margins of exile, leaving my country forever, and it seemed so impossible and terrible and sad.

I'm not sure how I made it through those six days. Most of it I can't remember. On two or three afternoons, to pass some time, I helped Elroy get the place ready for winter, sweeping down the cabins and hauling in the boats, little chores that kept my body moving. The days were cool and bright. The nights were very dark. One morning the old man showed me how to split and stack firewood, and for several hours we just worked in silence out behind his house. At one point, I remember, Elroy put down his maul and looked at me for a long time, his lips drawn as if framing a difficult question, but then he shook his head and went back to work. The man's self-control was amazing. He never pried. He never put me in a position that required lies or denials. To an extent, I suppose, his reticence was typical of that part of Minnesota, where privacy still held value, and even if I'd been walking around with some horrible deformity — four arms and three heads — I'm sure the old man would've talked about everything except those extra arms and heads. Simple politeness was part of it. But even more than that, I think, the man understood that words were insufficient. The problem had gone beyond discussion. During that long summer I'd been over and over the various arguments, all the pros and cons, and it was no longer a question that could be decided by an act of pure reason. Intellect had come up against emotion. My conscience told me to run, but some irrational and powerful force was resisting, like a weight pushing me toward the war. What it came down to, stupidly, was a sense of shame. Hot, stupid shame. I did not want people to think badly of me. Not my parents, not my brother and sister, not even the folks down at the Gobbler Café. I was ashamed to be there at the Tip Top Lodge. I was ashamed of my conscience, ashamed to be doing the right thing.

Some of this Elroy must've understood. Not the details, of course, but the plain fact of crisis.

Although the old man never confronted me about it, there was one 30 occasion when he came close to forcing the whole thing out into the open. It was early evening, and we'd just finished supper, and over coffee and dessert I asked him about my bill, how much I owed so far. For a long while the old man squinted down at the tablecloth.

"Well, the basic rate," he said, "is fifty bucks a night. Not counting meals. This makes four nights, right?"

I nodded. I had three hundred and twelve dollars in my wallet.

Elroy kept his eyes on the tablecloth. "Now that's an on-season price. To be fair, I suppose we should knock it down a peg or two." He leaned back in his chair. "What's a reasonable number, you figure?"

"I don't know," I said. "Forty?"

"Forty's good. Forty a night. Then we tack on food — say another 35 hundred? Two hundred sixty total?"

"I guess."

He raised his eyebrows. "Too much?"

"No, that's fair. It's fine. Tomorrow, though . . . I think I'd better take off tomorrow."

Elroy shrugged and began clearing the table. For a time he fussed with the dishes, whistling to himself as if the subject had been settled. After a second he slapped his hands together.

"You know what we forgot?" he said. "We forgot wages. Those odd 40 jobs you done. What we have to do, we have to figure out what your time's worth. Your last job — how much did you pull in an hour?"

"Not enough," I said.

"A bad one?"

"Yes. Pretty bad."

Slowly then, without intending any long sermon, I told him about my days at the pig plant. It began as a straight recitation of the facts, but before I could stop myself I was talking about the blood clots and the water gun and how the smell had soaked into my skin and how I couldn't wash it away. I went on for a long time. I told him about wild hogs squealing in my dreams, the sounds of butchery, slaughterhouse sounds, and how I'd sometimes wake up with that greasy pig-stink in my throat.

When I was finished, Elroy nodded at me. 45

"Well, to be honest," he said, "when you first showed up here, I wondered about all that. The aroma, I mean. Smelled like you was awful damned fond of pork chops." The old man almost smiled. He made a snuffling sound, then sat down with a pencil and a piece of paper. "So what'd this crud job pay? Ten bucks an hour? Fifteen?"

"Less."

Elroy shook his head. "Let's make it fifteen. You put in twenty-five hours here, easy. That's three hundred seventy-five bucks total wages. We subtract the two hundred sixty for food and lodging, I still owe you a hundred and fifteen."

He took four fifties out of his shirt pocket and laid them on the table.

50 "Call it even," he said.

"No."

"Pick it up. Get yourself a haircut."

The money lay on the table for the rest of the evening. It was still there when I went back to my cabin. In the morning, though, I found an envelope tacked to my door. Inside were the four fifties and a two-word note that said EMERGENCY FUND.

The man knew.

55 Looking back after twenty years, I sometimes wonder if the events of that summer didn't happen in some other dimension, a place where your life exists before you've lived it, and where it goes afterward. None of it ever seemed real. During my time at the Tip Top Lodge I had the feeling that I'd slipped out of my own skin, hovering a few feet away while some poor yo-yo with my name and face tried to make his way toward a future he didn't understand and didn't want. Even now I can see myself as I was then. It's like watching an old home movie: I'm young and tan and fit. I've got hair — lots of it. I don't smoke or drink. I'm wearing faded blue jeans and a white polo shirt. I can see myself sitting on Elroy Berdahl's dock near dusk one evening, the sky a bright shimmering pink, and I'm finishing up a letter to my parents that tells what I'm about to do and why I'm doing it and how sorry I am that I'd never found the courage to talk to them about it. I ask them not to be angry. I try to explain some of my feelings, but there aren't enough words, and so I just say that it's a thing that has to be done. At the end of the letter I talk about the vacations we used to take up in this north country, at a

place called Whitefish Lake, and how the scenery here reminds me of those good times. I tell them I'm fine. I tell them I'll write again from Winnipeg or Montreal or wherever I end up.

On my last full day, the sixth day, the old man took me out fishing on the Rainy River. The afternoon was sunny and cold. A stiff breeze came in from the north, and I remember how the little fourteen-foot boat made sharp rocking motions as we pushed off from the dock. The current was fast. All around us, I remember, there was a vastness to the world, an unpeopled rawness, just the trees and the sky and the water reaching out toward nowhere. The air had the brittle scent of October.

For ten or fifteen minutes Elroy held a course upstream, the river choppy and silver-gray, then he turned straight north and put the engine on full throttle. I felt the bow lift beneath me. I remember the wind in my ears, the sound of the old outboard Evinrude. For a time I didn't pay attention to anything, just feeling the cold spray against my face, but then it occurred to me that at some point we must've passed into Canadian waters, across that dotted line between two different worlds, and I remember a sudden tightness in my chest as I looked up and watched the far shore come at me. This wasn't a daydream. It was tangible and real. As we came in toward land, Elroy cut the engine, letting the boat fishtail lightly about twenty yards off shore. The old man didn't look at me or speak. Bending down, he opened up his tackle box and busied himself with a bobber and a piece of wire leader, humming to himself, his eyes down.

It struck me then that he must've planned it. I'll never be certain, of course, but I think he meant to bring me up against the realities, to guide me across the river and to take me to the edge and to stand a kind of vigil as I chose a life for myself.

I remember staring at the old man, then at my hands, then at Canada. The shoreline was dense with brush and timber. I could see tiny red berries on the bushes. I could see a squirrel up in one of the birch trees, a big crow looking at me from a boulder along the river. That close — twenty yards — and I could see the delicate latticework of the leaves, the texture of the soil, the browned needles beneath the pines, the configurations of geology and human history. Twenty yards. I could've done it. I could've jumped and started swimming for my life. Inside me, in my chest, I felt a terrible squeezing pressure. Even now, as

I write this, I can still feel that tightness. And I want you to feel it — the wind coming off the river, the waves, the silence, the wooded frontier. You're at the bow of a boat on the Rainy River. You're twenty-one years old, you're scared, and there's a hard squeezing pressure in your chest.

60 What would you do?

Would you jump? Would you feel pity for yourself? Would you think about your family and your childhood and your dreams and all you're leaving behind? Would it hurt? Would it feel like dying? Would you cry, as I did?

I tried to swallow it back. I tried to smile, except I was crying.

Now, perhaps, you can understand why I've never told this story before. It's not just the embarrassment of tears. That's part of it, no doubt, but what embarrasses me much more, and always will, is the paralysis that took my heart. A moral freeze: I couldn't decide, I couldn't act, I couldn't comport myself with even a pretense of modest human dignity.

All I could do was cry. Quietly, not bawling, just the chest-chokes.

65 At the rear of the boat Elroy Berdahl pretended not to notice. He held a fishing rod in his hands, his head bowed to hide his eyes. He kept humming a soft, monotonous little tune. Everywhere, it seemed, in the trees and water and sky, a great worldwide sadness came pressing down on me, a crushing sorrow, sorrow like I had never known it before. And what was so sad, I realized, was that Canada had become a pitiful fantasy. Silly and hopeless. It was no longer a possibility. Right then, with the shore so close, I understood that I would not do what I should do. I would not swim away from my hometown and my country and my life. I would not be brave. That old image of myself as a hero, as a man of conscience and courage, all that was just a threadbare pipe dream. Bobbing there on the Rainy River, looking back at the Minnesota shore, I felt a sudden swell of helplessness come over me, a drowning sensation, as if I had toppled overboard and was being swept away by the silver waves. Chunks of my own history flashed by. I saw a seven-year-old boy in a white cowboy hat and a Lone Ranger mask and a pair of holstered six-shooters; I saw a twelve-year-old Little League shortstop pivoting to turn a double play; I saw a sixteen-year-old kid decked out for his first prom, looking spiffy in a white tux and a black bow tie, his hair cut short and flat, his shoes freshly polished. My whole life seemed to spill out into the river, swirling away from me, everything I had ever been

or ever wanted to be. I couldn't get my breath; I couldn't stay afloat; I couldn't tell which way to swim. A hallucination, I suppose, but it was as real as anything I would ever feel. I saw my parents calling to me from the far shoreline. I saw my brother and sister, all the townsfolk, the mayor and the entire Chamber of Commerce and all my old teachers and girlfriends and high school buddies. Like some weird sporting event: everybody screaming from the sidelines, rooting me on — a loud stadium roar. Hotdogs and popcorn — stadium smells, stadium heat. A squad of cheerleaders did cartwheels along the banks of the Rainy River; they had megaphones and pompoms and smooth brown thighs. The crowd swayed left and right. A marching band played fight songs. All my aunts and uncles were there, and Abraham Lincoln, and Saint George, and a nine-year-old girl named Linda who had died of a brain tumor back in fifth grade, and several members of the United States Senate, and a blind poet scribbling notes, and LBJ, and Huck Finn, and Abbie Hoffman, and all the dead soldiers back from the grave, and the many thousands who were later to die — villagers with terrible burns, little kids without arms or legs — yes, and the Joint Chiefs of Staff were there, and a couple of popes, and a first lieutenant named Jimmy Cross, and the last surviving veteran of the American Civil War, and Jane Fonda dressed up as Barbarella, and an old man sprawled beside a pigpen, and my grandfather, and Gary Cooper, and a kind-faced woman carrying an umbrella and a copy of Plato's *Republic*, and a million ferocious citizens waving flags of all shapes and colors — people in hard hats, people in headbands — they were all whooping and chanting and urging me toward one shore or the other. I saw faces from my distant past and distant future. My wife was there. My unborn daughter waved at me, and my two sons hopped up and down, and a drill sergeant named Blyton sneered and shot up a finger and shook his head. There was a choir in bright purple robes. There was a cabbie from the Bronx. There was a slim young man I would one day kill with a hand grenade along a red clay trail outside the village of My Khe.

The little aluminum boat rocked softly beneath me. There was the wind and the sky.

I tried to will myself overboard.

I gripped the edge of the boat and leaned forward and thought, *Now*.

I did try. It just wasn't possible.

70   All those eyes on me — the town, the whole universe — and I couldn't risk the embarrassment. It was as if there were an audience to my life, that swirl of faces along the river, and in my head I could hear people screaming at me. Traitor! they yelled. Turncoat! Pussy! I felt myself blush. I couldn't tolerate it. I couldn't endure the mockery, or the disgrace, or the patriotic ridicule. Even in my imagination, the shore just twenty yards away, I couldn't make myself be brave. It had nothing to do with morality. Embarrassment, that's all it was.

And right then I submitted.

I would go to the war — I would kill and maybe die — because I was embarrassed not to.

That was the sad thing. And so I sat in the bow of the boat and cried.

It was loud now. Loud, hard crying.

75   Elroy Berdahl remained quiet. He kept fishing. He worked his line with the tips of his fingers, patiently, squinting out at his red and white bobber on the Rainy River. His eyes were flat and impassive. He didn't speak. He was simply there, like the river and the late-summer sun. And yet by his presence, his mute watchfulness, he made it real. He was the true audience. He was a witness, like God, or like the gods, who look on in absolute silence as we live our lives, as we make our choices or fail to make them.

"Ain't biting," he said.

Then after a time the old man pulled in his line and turned the boat back toward Minnesota.

I don't remember saying goodbye. That last night we had dinner together, and I went to bed early, and in the morning Elroy fixed breakfast for me. When I told him I'd be leaving, the old man nodded as if he already knew. He looked down at the table and smiled.

At some point later in the morning it's possible that we shook hands — I just don't remember — but I do know that by the time I'd finished packing the old man had disappeared. Around noon, when I took my suitcase out to the car, I noticed that his old black pickup truck was no longer parked in front of the house. I went inside and waited for a while, but I felt a bone certainty that he wouldn't be back. In a way, I thought, it was appropriate. I washed up the breakfast dishes, left his two hundred dollars on the kitchen counter, got into the car, and drove south toward home.

The day was cloudy. I passed through towns with familiar names, 80 through the pine forests and down to the prairie, and then to Vietnam, where I was a soldier, and then home again. I survived, but it's not a happy ending. I was a coward. I went to the war.

Arundhati Roy

The Algebra of Infinite Justice

Arundhati Roy came to the attention of the reading public in 1996 when her novel, *The God of Small Things*, was published to great critical acclaim. The novel, praised for its lush, lyrical prose, won the 1997 Booker Prize for fiction. Translated into forty languages, the book has been an international bestseller, with more than six million copies sold.

The God of Small Things is set in Kerala, the state in South India where Roy spent her childhood. The novel is dedicated to Roy's mother, Mary Roy — a woman who defied convention by marrying outside her community (she was a Syrian Christian, her husband a Hindu), then divorcing. Mary Roy was well known for having challenged inheritance laws that discriminated against women, and she supported herself by founding and running an independent school. Arundhati Roy attended the school until she was sixteen, when she left Kerala for Delhi. Roy grew up with "no caste, no religion, no supervision"; she credits her upbringing with her ability to step outside her own culture and address global political and economic issues.

Roy's professional experiences are diverse: she was trained as an architect, worked briefly at India's National Institute for Urban Affairs, wrote two movie scripts, and acted in the film *Massey Saab* before writing *The God of Small Things*. She has not written a second novel; instead, she has directed her energies to political writing and activism. Her nonfiction books include *The Greater Common Good* (1999), *The Cost of Living* (1999), *Power Politics* (2001), *The Algebra of Infinite Justice* (2002), *War Talk* (2003), *Public Power in the Age of Empire* (2004), and *An Ordinary Person's Guide to Empire* (2004).

"The Algebra of Infinite Justice" was originally published in *The Guardian* on September 29, 2001, two weeks after the attack on the World Trade Center. Roy calls for an analysis of the September 11 attacks that takes not just an American point of view but a global perspective. She establishes a strong position from the start, warning that the immediate American response—rage, expressed in an eagerness to go to war—is short-sighted. The essay's tone sharpens as Roy recalls the economic and military dominance that characterized America's role in international affairs in the late twentieth century. Roy has been criticized for the fervor of her expression. However, she defends the right, even the obligation, of the writer to take a strong position in the face of injustice:

> When people try to dismiss those who ask the big public questions as being emotional, it is a strategy to avoid debate. Why should we be scared of being angry? Why should we be scared of our feelings, if they're based on facts? The whole framework of reason versus passion is ridiculous, because often passion is based on reason . . . I'm a writer. I have a point of view. I have feelings about the things I write about—and I'm going to express them.

Arundhati Roy was awarded the Lannan Foundation's Prize for Cultural Freedom in 2002 and the Sydney Peace Prize in 2004. In 2005, she gave the opening speech at the World Tribunal on Iraq. She lives in New Delhi.

In the aftermath of the unconscionable September 11 suicide attacks on the Pentagon and the World Trade Centre, an American newscaster said: "Good and evil rarely manifest themselves as clearly as they did last Tuesday. People who we don't know massacred people who we do. And they did so with contemptuous glee." Then he broke down and wept.

Here's the rub: America is at war against people it doesn't know, because they don't appear much on TV. Before it has properly identified or even begun to comprehend the nature of its enemy, the U.S. government has, in a rush of publicity and embarrassing rhetoric, cobbled together an "international coalition against terror," mobilised its army, its air force, its navy and its media, and committed them to battle.

The trouble is that once America goes off to war, it can't very well return without having fought one. If it doesn't find its enemy, for the sake of the enraged folks back home, it will have to manufacture one.

Once war begins, it will develop a momentum, a logic, and a justification of its own, and we'll lose sight of why it's being fought in the first place.

What we're witnessing here is the spectacle of the world's most powerful country reaching reflexively, angrily, for an old instinct to fight a new kind of war. Suddenly, when it comes to defending itself, America's streamlined warships, cruise missiles, and F-16 jets look like obsolete, lumbering things. As deterrence, its arsenal of nuclear bombs is no longer worth its weight in scrap. Box-cutters, penknives, and cold anger are the weapons with which the wars of the new century will be waged. Anger is the lock pick. It slips through customs unnoticed. Doesn't show up in baggage checks.

5   Who is America fighting? On September 20, the FBI said that it had doubts about the identities of some of the hijackers. On the same day President George Bush said, "We know exactly who these people are and which governments are supporting them." It sounds as though the president knows something that the FBI and the American public don't.

In his September 20 address to the U.S. Congress, President Bush called the enemies of America "enemies of freedom." "Americans are asking, 'Why do they hate us?'" he said. "They hate our freedoms — our freedom of religion, our freedom of speech, our freedom to vote and assemble and disagree with each other." People are being asked to make two leaps of faith here. First, to assume that The Enemy is who the U.S. government says it is, even though it has no substantial evidence to support that claim. And second, to assume that The Enemy's motives are what the U.S. government says they are, and there's nothing to support that either.

For strategic, military, and economic reasons, it is vital for the U.S. government to persuade its public that their commitment to freedom and democracy and the American Way of Life is under attack. In the current atmosphere of grief, outrage, and anger, it's an easy notion to peddle. However, if that were true, it's reasonable to wonder why the symbols of America's economic and military dominance — the World Trade Centre and the Pentagon — were chosen as the targets of the attacks. Why not the Statue of Liberty? Could it be that the stygian anger that led to the attacks has its taproot not in American freedom and democracy, but in the U.S. government's record of commitment and support to exactly the opposite things — to military and economic terrorism, insurgency, military dictatorship, religious bigotry, and unimaginable genocide (outside America)? It must be hard for ordinary Americans, so recently bereaved, to look up at the world with their eyes full of tears and encounter what might appear to them to be indifference. It isn't indifference. It's just augury. An absence of surprise. The tired wisdom of knowing that what goes around eventually comes around. American people ought to know that it is not them but their government's policies that are so hated. They can't possibly doubt that they themselves, their extraordinary musicians, their writers, their actors, their spectacular sportsmen, and their cinema are universally welcomed. All of us have been moved by the courage and grace shown by firefighters, rescue workers, and ordinary office staff in the days since the attacks.

America's grief at what happened has been immense and immensely public. It would be grotesque to expect it to calibrate or modulate its anguish. However, it will be a pity if, instead of using this as an opportunity to try to understand why September 11 happened, Americans use it as an opportunity to usurp the whole world's sorrow to mourn and avenge only their own. Because then it falls to the rest of us to ask the hard questions and say the harsh things. And for our pains, for our bad timing, we will be disliked, ignored, and perhaps eventually silenced.

The world will probably never know what motivated those particular hijackers who flew planes into those particular American buildings. They were not glory boys. They left no suicide notes, no political messages; no organisation has claimed credit for the attacks. All we know is that their belief in what they were doing outstripped the natural human instinct for survival, or any desire to be remembered. It's almost as though they could not scale down the enormity of their rage to anything smaller than their deeds. And what they did has blown a hole in the world as we knew it. In the absence of information, politicians, political commentators, and writers (like myself) will invest the act with their own politics, with their own interpretations. This speculation, this analysis of the political climate in which the attacks took place, can only be a good thing.

But war is looming large. Whatever remains to be said must be said   10
quickly. Before America places itself at the helm of the "international

coalition against terror," before it invites (and coerces) countries to actively participate in its almost godlike mission — called Operation Infinite Justice until it was pointed out that this could be seen as an insult to Muslims, who believe that only Allah can mete out infinite justice, and was renamed Operation Enduring Freedom — it would help if some small clarifications are made. For example, Infinite Justice/ Enduring Freedom for whom? Is this America's war against terror in America or against terror in general? What exactly is being avenged here? Is it the tragic loss of almost 7,000 lives, the gutting of five million square feet of office space in Manhattan, the destruction of a section of the Pentagon, the loss of several hundreds of thousands of jobs, the bankruptcy of some airline companies, and the dip in the New York Stock Exchange? Or is it more than that? In 1996, Madeleine Albright, then the U.S. secretary of state, was asked on national television what she felt about the fact that 500,000 Iraqi children had died as a result of U.S. economic sanctions. She replied that it was "a very hard choice," but that, all things considered, "we think the price is worth it." Albright never lost her job for saying this. She continued to travel the world representing the views and aspirations of the U.S. government. More pertinently, the sanctions against Iraq remain in place. Children continue to die.

So here we have it. The equivocating distinction between civilisation and savagery, between the "massacre of innocent people" or, if you like, "a clash of civilisations" and "collateral damage." The sophistry and fastidious algebra of infinite justice. How many dead Iraqis will it take to make the world a better place? How many dead Afghans for every dead American? How many dead women and children for every dead man? How many dead mojahedin for each dead investment banker? As we watch mesmerised, Operation Enduring Freedom unfolds on TV monitors across the world. A coalition of the world's superpowers is closing in on Afghanistan, one of the poorest, most ravaged, war-torn countries in the world, whose ruling Taliban government is sheltering Osama bin Laden, the man being held responsible for the September 11 attacks.

The only thing in Afghanistan that could possibly count as collateral value is its citizenry. (Among them, half a million maimed orphans. There are accounts of hobbling stampedes that occur when artificial limbs are airdropped into remote, inaccessible villages.) Afghanistan's economy is in a shambles. In fact, the problem for an invading army is that Afghanistan has no conventional coordinates or signposts to plot on a military map — no big cities, no highways, no industrial complexes, no water treatment plants. Farms have been turned into mass graves. The countryside is littered with land mines — ten million is the most recent estimate. The American army would first have to clear the mines and build roads in order to take its soldiers in.

Fearing an attack from America, one million citizens have fled from their homes and arrived at the border between Pakistan and Afghanistan. The UN estimates that there are eight million Afghan citizens who need emergency aid. As supplies run out — food and aid agencies have been asked to leave — the BBC reports that one of the worst humanitarian disasters of recent times has begun to unfold. Witness the infinite justice of the new century. Civilians starving to death while they're waiting to be killed.

In America there has been rough talk of "bombing Afghanistan back to the stone age." Someone please break the news that Afghanistan is already there. And if it's any consolation, America played no small part in helping it on its way. The American people may be a little fuzzy about where exactly Afghanistan is (we hear reports that there's a run on maps of the country), but the U.S. government and Afghanistan are old friends.

In 1979, after the Soviet invasion of Afghanistan, the CIA and Pakistan's ISI (Inter Services Intelligence) launched the largest covert operation in the history of the CIA. Their purpose was to harness the energy of Afghan resistance to the Soviets and expand it into a holy war, an Islamic jihad, which would turn Muslim countries within the Soviet Union against the communist regime and eventually destabilise it. When it began, it was meant to be the Soviet Union's Vietnam. It turned out to be much more than that. Over the years, through the ISI, the CIA funded and recruited almost 100,000 radical mojahedin from forty Islamic countries as soldiers for America's proxy war. The rank and file of the mojahedin were unaware that their jihad was actually being fought on behalf of Uncle Sam. (The irony is that America was equally unaware that it was financing a future war against itself.)

In 1989, after being bloodied by ten years of relentless conflict, the Russians withdrew, leaving behind a civilisation reduced to rubble.

Civil war in Afghanistan raged on. The jihad spread to Chechnya, Kosovo, and eventually to Kashmir. The CIA continued to pour in money and military equipment, but the overheads had become immense, and more money was needed. The mojahedin ordered farmers to plant opium as a "revolutionary tax". The ISI set up hundreds of heroin laboratories across Afghanistan. Within two years of the CIA's arrival, the Pakistan-Afghanistan borderland had become the biggest producer of heroin in the world, and the single biggest source of the heroin on American streets. The annual profits, said to be between $100 billion and $200 billion, were ploughed back into training and arming militants.

In 1995, the Taliban — then a marginal sect of dangerous, hardline fundamentalists — fought its way to power in Afghanistan. It was funded by the ISI, that old cohort of the CIA, and supported by many political parties in Pakistan. The Taliban unleashed a regime of terror. Its first victims were its own people, particularly women. It closed down girls' schools, dismissed women from government jobs, and enforced sharia laws under which women deemed to be "immoral" are stoned to death, and widows guilty of being adulterous are buried alive. Given the Taliban government's human rights track record, it seems unlikely that it will in any way be intimidated or swerved from its purpose by the prospect of war, or the threat to the lives of its civilians.

After all that has happened, can there be anything more ironic than Russia and America joining hands to re-destroy Afghanistan? The question is, can you destroy destruction? Dropping more bombs on Afghanistan will only shuffle the rubble, scramble some old graves, and disturb the dead.

20 The desolate landscape of Afghanistan was the burial ground of Soviet communism and the springboard of a unipolar world dominated by America. It made the space for neocapitalism and corporate globalisation, again dominated by America. And now Afghanistan is poised to become the graveyard for the unlikely soldiers who fought and won this war for America.

And what of America's trusted ally? Pakistan too has suffered enormously. The U.S. government has not been shy of supporting military dictators who have blocked the idea of democracy from taking root in the country. Before the CIA arrived, there was a small rural market for opium in Pakistan. Between 1979 and 1985, the number of heroin addicts grew from zero to one-and-a-half million. Even before September 11, there were three million Afghan refugees living in tented camps along the border. Pakistan's economy is crumbling. Sectarian violence, globalisation's structural adjustment programmes, and drug lords are tearing the country to pieces. Set up to fight the Soviets, the terrorist training centres and madrasahs, sown like dragon's teeth across the country, produced fundamentalists with tremendous popular appeal within Pakistan itself. The Taliban, which the Pakistan government has supported, funded, and propped up for years, has material and strategic alliances with Pakistan's own political parties.

Now the U.S. government is asking (asking?) Pakistan to garotte the pet it has hand-reared in its backyard for so many years. President Musharraf, having pledged his support to the U.S., could well find he has something resembling civil war on his hands.

India, thanks in part to its geography, and in part to the vision of its former leaders, has so far been fortunate enough to be left out of this Great Game. Had it been drawn in, it's more than likely that our democracy, such as it is, would not have survived. Today, as some of us watch in horror, the Indian government is furiously gyrating its hips, begging the U.S. to set up its base in India rather than Pakistan. Having had this ringside view of Pakistan's sordid fate, it isn't just odd, it's unthinkable, that India should want to do this. Any third world country with a fragile economy and a complex social base should know by now that to invite a superpower such as America in (whether it says it's staying or just passing through) would be like inviting a brick to drop through your windscreen.

Operation Enduring Freedom is ostensibly being fought to uphold the American Way of Life. It'll probably end up undermining it completely. It will spawn more anger and more terror across the world. For ordinary people in America, it will mean lives lived in a climate of sickening uncertainty: Will my child be safe in school? Will there be nerve gas in the subway? A bomb in the cinema hall? Will my love come home tonight? There have been warnings about the possibility of biological warfare — smallpox, bubonic plague, anthrax — the deadly payload of innocuous crop-duster aircraft. Being picked off a few at a time may end up being worse than being annihilated all at once by a nuclear bomb.

The U.S. government, and no doubt governments all over the world, will use the climate of war as an excuse to curtail civil liberties, deny free speech, lay off workers, harass ethnic and religious minorities, cut back on public spending, and divert huge amounts of money to the defence industry. To what purpose? President Bush can no more "rid the world of evil-doers" than he can stock it with saints. It's absurd for the U.S. government to even toy with the notion that it can stamp out terrorism with more violence and oppression. Terrorism is the symptom, not the disease. Terrorism has no country. It's transnational, as global an enterprise as Coke or Pepsi or Nike. At the first sign of trouble, terrorists can pull up stakes and move their "factories" from country to country in search of a better deal. Just like the multinationals.

Terrorism as a phenomenon may never go away. But if it is to be contained, the first step is for America to at least acknowledge that it shares the planet with other nations, with other human beings who, even if they are not on TV, have loves and griefs and stories and songs and sorrows and, for heaven's sake, rights. Instead, when Donald Rumsfeld, the U.S. defence secretary, was asked what he would call a victory in America's new war, he said that if he could convince the world that Americans must be allowed to continue with their way of life, he would consider it a victory.

The September 11 attacks were a monstrous calling card from a world gone horribly wrong. The message may have been written by Bin Laden (who knows?) and delivered by his couriers, but it could well have been signed by the ghosts of the victims of America's old wars. The millions killed in Korea, Vietnam, and Cambodia; the 17,500 killed when Israel — backed by the U.S. — invaded Lebanon in 1982; the 200,000 Iraqis killed in Operation Desert Storm; the thousands of Palestinians who have died fighting Israel's occupation of the West Bank. And the millions who died, in Yugoslavia, Somalia, Haiti, Chile, Nicaragua, El Salvador, the Dominican Republic, Panama, at the hands of all the terrorists, dictators, and genocidists whom the American government supported, trained, bankrolled, and supplied with arms. And this is far from being a comprehensive list.

For a country involved in so much warfare and conflict, the American people have been extremely fortunate. The strikes on September 11 were only the second on American soil in over a century. The first was Pearl Harbour. The reprisal for this took a long route, but ended with Hiroshima and Nagasaki. This time the world waits with bated breath for the horrors to come.

Someone recently said that if Osama bin Laden didn't exist, America would have had to invent him. But, in a way, America did invent him. He was among the jihadis who moved to Afghanistan in 1979 when the CIA commenced its operations there. Bin Laden has the distinction of being created by the CIA and wanted by the FBI. In the course of a fortnight he has been promoted from suspect to prime suspect and then, despite the lack of any real evidence, straight up the charts to being "wanted dead or alive."

From all accounts, it will be impossible to produce evidence (of the sort that would stand scrutiny in a court of law) to link Bin Laden to the September 11 attacks. So far, it appears that the most incriminating piece of evidence against him is the fact that he has not condemned them.

From what is known about the location of Bin Laden and the living conditions in which he operates, it's entirely possible that he did not personally plan and carry out the attacks — that he is the inspirational figure, "the CEO of the holding company." The Taliban's response to U.S. demands for the extradition of Bin Laden has been uncharacteristically reasonable: produce the evidence, then we'll hand him over. President Bush's response is that the demand is "non-negotiable."

(While talks are on for the extradition of CEOs — can India put in a side request for the extradition of Warren Anderson of the U.S.? He was the chairman of Union Carbide, responsible for the Bhopal gas leak that killed 16,000 people in 1984. We have collated the necessary evidence. It's all in the files. Could we have him, please?)

But who is Osama bin Laden really? Let me rephrase that. What is Osama bin Laden? He's America's family secret. He is the American president's dark doppelganger. The savage twin of all that purports to be beautiful and civilised. He has been sculpted from the spare rib of a world laid to waste by America's foreign policy: its gunboat diplomacy, its nuclear arsenal, its vulgarly stated policy of "full-spectrum dominance," its chilling disregard for non-American lives, its barbarous military interventions, its support for despotic and dictatorial regimes, its merciless economic agenda that has munched through the economies of poor countries like a cloud of locusts. Its marauding multinationals who are taking over the air we breathe, the ground we stand on, the water we drink, the thoughts we think. Now that the family secret has been spilled, the twins are blurring into one another and gradually becoming interchangeable. Their guns, bombs, money, and drugs have been going around in the loop for a while. (The Stinger missiles that will greet U.S. helicopters were supplied by the CIA. The heroin used by America's drug addicts comes from Afghanistan. The Bush administration recently gave Afghanistan a $43 million subsidy for a "war on drugs" . . .)

Now Bush and Bin Laden have even begun to borrow each other's rhetoric. Each refers to the other as "the head of the snake." Both invoke God and use the loose millenarian currency of good and evil as their terms of reference. Both are engaged in unequivocal political crimes. Both are dangerously armed — one with the nuclear arsenal of the obscenely powerful, the other with the incandescent, destructive power of the utterly hopeless. The fireball and the ice pick. The bludgeon and the axe. The important thing to keep in mind is that neither is an acceptable alternative to the other.

35   President Bush's ultimatum to the people of the world — "If you're not with us, you're against us" — is a piece of presumptuous arrogance. It's not a choice that people want to, need to, or should have to make.

Oliver Sacks

From The Case of the Colorblind Painter

When Oliver Sacks was born in 1933, he was already on the path toward a life in science. His father was a physician in general practice, his mother a surgeon, and they lived in London near a large extended family that included mathematicians, chemists, and other physical scientists.

Sacks's childhood was interrupted by World War II when, like many London children, he was sent away from the city. At the age of six, he went with his brother Michael to the village of Braefield, where they were safe from bombs but endured loneliness, scarcity (their diet was mostly turnips and beetroot), and the cruelty of a sadistic headmaster. Returning to London in 1943, Oliver sought kindness and order. He found it in the company of his Uncle Dave, a chemist who encouraged the boy's fascination with metals and helped him build his own laboratory.

As he grew older, Sacks's interest shifted from chemistry to medicine; he studied at Oxford University, graduating in 1958 with a medical degree from Queen's College. Three years later, he relocated to the United States, serving as an intern at Mount Zion Hospital in San Francisco and as a resident in neurology at UCLA. In 1965, he settled in New York.

As a neurologist, Sacks has written dozens of articles for medical journals. But his most influential writing appears in narrative case studies of patients with neurological disorders, written for a general audience. In the late 1960s, he worked at Beth Abraham Hospital with a group of patients who had been rendered speechless and immobile by a type of encephalitis. When he treated the patients with an experimental drug, L-dopa, they were revived. Sacks collected stories of the patients' recovery in *Awakenings*, published in 1973 and adapted into a 1990 film starring Robert De Niro and Robin Williams.

Sacks has written about neurological conditions such as Tourette's syndrome and autism for *The New Yorker* and the *New York Review of Books*. His ten books include *The Man Who Mistook His Wife for a Hat* (1985), *An Anthropologist on Mars* (1995), *The Island of the Colorblind* (1996), and *Musicophilia: Tales of Music and the Brain* (2007).

As the editor of *The Best American Science Writing of 2003*, Sacks wrote an introductory essay explaining what he values in writing:

> The best science writing, it seems to me, has a swiftness and naturalness, a transparency and clarity, not clogged with pretentiousness or literary artifice. The science writer gives himself or herself to the subject completely, does not intrude on it in an annoying or impertinent way, and yet gives a personal warmth and perspective to every word. . . . It is, at best, a wonderful fusion, as factual as a news report, as imaginative as a novel.

"The Case of the Colorblind Painter" appears in *An Anthropologist on Mars*.

Early in March 1986 I received the following letter:

> I am a rather successful artist just past 65 years of age. On January 2nd of this year I was driving my car and was hit by a small truck on the passenger side of my vehicle. When visiting the emergency room of a local hospital, I was told I had a concussion. While taking an eye examination, it was discovered that I was unable to distinguish letters or colors. The letters appeared to be Greek letters. My vision was such that everything appeared to me as viewing a black and white television screen. Within days, I could distinguish letters and my vision became that of an eagle — I can see a worm wriggling a block away. The sharpness of focus is incredible. BUT — I AM ABSOLUTELY COLOR BLIND. I have visited ophthalmologists who know nothing about this color-blind business. I have visited neurologists, to no avail. Under hypnosis I still can't distinguish colors. I have been involved in all kinds of tests. You name it. My brown dog is dark grey. Tomato juice is black. Color TV is a hodge-podge. . . .

Had I ever encountered such a problem before, the writer continued; could I explain what was happening to him — and could I help?

This seemed an extraordinary letter. Colorblindness, as ordinarily understood, is something one is born with — a difficulty distinguishing red and green, or other colors, or (extremely rarely) an inability to see any colors at all, due to defects in the color-responding cells, the cones, of the retina. But clearly this was not the case with my correspondent, Jonathan I. He had seen normally all his life, had been born with a full complement of cones in his retinas. He had *become* colorblind, after sixty-five years of seeing colors normally — *totally* colorblind, as if "viewing a black and white television screen." The suddenness of the event was incompatible with any of the slow deteriorations that can befall the retinal cone cells and suggested instead a mishap at a much higher level, in those parts of the brain specialized for the perception of color.

Total colorblindness caused by brain damage, so-called cerebral achromatopsia, though described more than three centuries ago, remains a rare and important condition. It has intrigued neurologists because, like all neural dissolutions and destructions, it can reveal to us the mechanisms of neural construction — specifically, here, how the brain "sees" (or makes) color. Doubly intriguing is its occurrence in an artist, a painter for whom color has been of primary importance, and who can directly paint as well as describe what has befallen him, and thus convey the full strangeness, distress, and reality of the condition.

Color is not a trivial subject but one that has compelled, for hundreds of years, a passionate curiosity in the greatest artists, philosophers, and natural scientists. The young Spinoza wrote his first treatise on the rainbow; the young Newton's most joyous discovery was the composition of white light; Goethe's great color work, like Newton's, started with a prism; Schopenhauer, Young, Helmholtz, and Maxwell, in the last century, were all tantalized by the problem of color; and Wittgenstein's last work was his *Remarks on Colour*. And yet most of us, most of the time, overlook its great mystery. Through such a case as Mr. I.'s we can trace not only the underlying cerebral mechanisms or physiology but the phenomenology of color and the depth of its resonance and meaning for the individual.

On getting Mr. I.'s letter, I contacted my good friend and colleague Robert Wasserman, an ophthalmologist, feeling that together we needed to explore Mr. I.'s complex situation and, if we could, help   5 him. We first saw him in April 1986. He was a tall, gaunt man, with a sharp, intelligent face. Although obviously depressed by his condition, he soon warmed to us and began talking with animation and humor. He constantly smoked as he talked; his fingers, restless, were stained with nicotine. He described a very active and productive life as an artist, from his early days with Georgia O'Keeffe in New Mexico, to painting backdrops in Hollywood during the 1940s, to working as an Abstract Expressionist in New York during the 1950s and later as an art director and a commercial artist.

We learned that his accident had been accompanied by a transient amnesia. He had been able, evidently, to give a clear account of himself and his accident to the police at the time it happened, late on the afternoon of January 2, but then, because of a steadily mounting headache, he went home. He complained to his wife of having a headache and feeling confused, but made no mention of the accident. He then fell into a long, almost stuporous sleep. It was only the next morning, when his wife saw the side of the car stove in, that she asked him what had happened. When she got no clear answer ("I don't know. Maybe somebody backed into it") she knew that something serious must have happened.

Mr. I. then drove off to his studio and found on his desk a carbon copy of the police accident report. He had had an accident, but somehow, bizarrely, had lost his memory of it. Perhaps the report would jolt his memory. But lifting it up, he could make nothing of it. He saw print of different sizes and types, all clearly in focus, but it looked like "Greek" or "Hebrew" to him.[1] A magnifying glass did not help; it simply became *large* "Greek" or "Hebrew." (This alexia, or inability to read, lasted for five days, but then disappeared.)

Feeling now that he must have suffered a stroke or some sort of brain damage from the accident, Jonathan I. phoned his doctor, who arranged for him to be tested at a local hospital. Although, as his original letter indicates, difficulties in distinguishing colors were detected at this time, in addition to his inability to read, he had no subjective sense of the alteration of colors until the next day.

---

[1] I asked Mr. I. later if he knew Greek or Hebrew; he said no, there was just the sense of an unintelligible foreign language; perhaps, he added, "cuneiform" would be more accurate. He saw forms, he knew they had to have meaning, but could not imagine what this meaning might be.

That day he decided to go to work again. It seemed to him as if he were driving in a fog, even though he knew it to be a bright and sunny morning. Everything seemed misty, bleached, greyish, indistinct. He was flagged down by the police close to his studio: he had gone through two red lights, they said. Did he realize this? No, he said, he was not aware of having passed through any red lights. They asked him to get out of the car. Finding him sober, but apparently bewildered and ill, they gave him a ticket and suggested he seek medical advice.

Mr. I. arrived at his studio with relief, expecting that the horrible   10
mist would be gone, that everything would be clear again. But as soon as he entered, he found his entire studio, which was hung with brilliantly colored paintings, now utterly grey and void of color. His canvases, the abstract color paintings he was known for, were now greyish or black and white. His paintings — once rich with associations, feelings, meanings — now looked unfamiliar and meaningless to him. At this point the magnitude of his loss overwhelmed him. He had spent his life as a painter; now even his art was without meaning, and he could no longer imagine how to go on.

The weeks that followed were very difficult. "You might think," Mr. I. said, "loss of color vision, what's the big deal? Some of my friends said this, my wife sometimes thought this, but to me, at least, it was awful, disgusting." He *knew* the colors of everything, with an extraordinary exactness (he could give not only the names but the numbers of colors as these were listed in a Pantone chart of hues he had used for many years). He could identify the green of van Gogh's billiard table in this way unhesitatingly. He *knew* all the colors in his favorite paintings, but could no longer see them, either when he looked or in his mind's eye. Perhaps he knew them, now, only by verbal memory.

It was not just that colors were missing, but that what he did see had a distasteful, "dirty" look, the whites glaring, yet discolored and off-white, the blacks cavernous — everything wrong, unnatural, stained, and impure.[2]

Mr. I. could hardly bear the changed appearances of people ("like animated grey statues") any more than he could bear his own appearance in the mirror: he shunned social intercourse and found sexual

---

[2] Similarly, a patient of Dr. Antonio Damasio, with achromatopsia from a tumor, thought everything and everyone looked "dirty," even finding new-fallen snow unpleasant and dirty.

intercourse impossible. He saw people's flesh, his wife's flesh, his own flesh, as an abhorrent grey; "flesh-colored" now appeared "rat-colored" to him. This was so even when he closed his eyes, for his vivid visual imagery was preserved but was now without color as well.

The "wrongness" of everything was disturbing, even disgusting, and applied to every circumstance of daily life. He found foods disgusting due to their greyish, dead appearance and had to close his eyes to eat. But this did not help very much, for the mental image of a tomato was as black as its appearance. Thus, unable to rectify even the inner image, the idea, of various foods, he turned increasingly to black and white foods — to black olives and white rice, black coffee and yogurt. These at least appeared relatively normal, whereas most foods, normally colored, now appeared horribly abnormal. His own brown dog looked so strange to him now that he even considered getting a Dalmatian.

15   He encountered difficulties and distresses of every sort, from the confusion of red and green traffic lights (which he could now distinguish only by position) to an inability to choose his clothes. (His wife had to pick them out, and this dependency he found hard to bear; later, he had everything classified in his drawers and closet — grey socks here, yellow there, ties labeled, jackets and suits categorized, to prevent otherwise glaring incongruities and confusions.) Fixed and ritualistic practices and positions had to be adopted at the table; otherwise he might mistake the mustard for the mayonnaise, or, if he could bring himself to use the blackish stuff, ketchup for jam.[3]

---

[3] In 1688, in *Some Uncommon Observations about Vitiated Sight*, Robert Boyle described a young woman in her early twenties whose eyesight had been normal until she was eighteen, when she developed a fever, was "tormented with blisters," and, with this, "deprived of her sight." When she was presented with something red, "she look'd attentively upon it, but told me, that to her, it did not seem Red, but of another Colour, which one would guess by her description to be a Dark or Dirty one." When "tufts of Silk that were finely Color'd" were given to her, she could only say that "they seem'd to be a Light-colour, but could not tell which." When asked whether the meadows "did not appear to her Cloathed in Green," she said they did not, but seemed to be "of an odd Darkish colour," adding that when she wished to gather violets, "she was not able to distinguish them by the Colour from the surrounding Grass, but only by the Shape, or by feeling them." Boyle further observed a change in her habits, that she liked now to walk abroad in the evenings, and this "she much delighteth to do."

A number of accounts were published in the nineteenth century — many collected in Mary Collins's *Colour-Blindness* — one of the most vivid (besides that of an achromatopic house painter) being that of a physician who, thrown from his horse, suffered a head injury and concussion. "On recovering sufficiently to notice objects around him," George Wilson recorded in 1853,

As the months went by, he particularly missed the brilliant colors of spring—he had always loved flowers, but now he could only distinguish them by shape or smell. The blue jays were brilliant no longer; their blue, curiously, was now seen as pale grey. He could no longer see the clouds in the sky, their whiteness, or off-whiteness as he saw them, being scarcely distinguishable from the azure, which seemed bleached to a pale grey. Red and green peppers were also indistinguishable, but this was because both appeared black. Yellows and blues, to him, were almost white.[4]

Mr. I. also seemed to experience an excessive tonal contrast, with loss of delicate tonal gradations, especially in direct sunlight or harsh artificial light; he made a comparison here with the effects of sodium lighting, which at once removes color and tonal delicacy, and with certain black-and-white films—"like Tri-X pushed for speed"—which produce a harsh, contrasty effect. Sometimes objects stood out with inordinate contrast and sharpness, like silhouettes. But if the contrast was normal, or low, they might disappear from sight altogether.

Thus, though his brown dog would stand out sharply in silhouette against a light road, it might get lost to sight when it moved into soft, dappled undergrowth. People's figures might be visible and recognizable half a mile off (as he himself said in his original letter, and many times later, his vision had become much sharper, "that of an eagle"), but faces would often be unidentifiable until they were close. This seemed a

---

he found that his perception of colours, which was formerly normal and acute, had become both weakened and perverted. . . . All coloured objects . . . now seem strange to him. Whilst formerly a student in Edinburgh he was known as an excellent anatomist; now he cannot distinguish an artery from a vein by its tint. . . . Flowers have lost more than half their beauty for him, and he recalls the shock which he received on first entering his garden after his recovery, at finding that a favourite damask rose had become in all its parts, petals, leaves, and stem, of one uniform dull colour; and that variegated flowers had lost their characteristic tints.

[4] One sees interesting similarities, but also differences, from the vision of those with congenital achromatopsia. Thus Knut Nordby, a congenitally colorblind vision researcher, writes:

I only see the world in shades that colour-normals describe as black, white and grey. My subjective spectral sensitivity is not unlike that of orthochromatic black and white film. I experience the colour called red as a very dark grey, nearly black, even in very bright light. On a grey-scale the blue and green colours I see as mid-greys, somewhat darker greys if they are saturated, somewhat lighter greys when unsaturated. Yellow typically appears to me as a rather light grey, but is usually not confused with white. Brown usually appears as a dark grey and so does a very saturated orange.

matter of lost color and tonal contrast, rather than a defect in recognition, an agnosia. A major problem occurred when he drove, in that he tended to misinterpret shadows as cracks or ruts in the road and would brake or swerve suddenly to avoid these.

He found color television especially hard to bear: its images always unpleasant, sometimes unintelligible. Black-and-white television, he thought, was much easier to deal with; he felt his perception of black-and-white images to be relatively normal, whereas something bizarre and intolerable occurred whenever he looked at colored images. (When we asked why he did not simply turn off the color, he said he thought that the tonal values of "decolored" color TV seemed different, less "normal," than those of a "pure" black-and-white set.) But, as he now explained, in distinction to his first letter, his world was not really like black-and-white television or film — it would have been much easier to live with had it been so. (He sometimes wished he could wear miniature TV glasses.)

20   His despair of conveying what his world looked like, and the uselessness of the usual black-and-white analogies, finally drove him, some weeks later, to create an entire grey room, a grey universe, in his studio, in which tables, chairs, and an elaborate dinner ready for serving were all painted in a range of greys. The effect of this, in three dimensions and in a different tonal scale from the "black and white" we are all accustomed to, was indeed macabre, and wholly unlike that of a black-and-white photograph. As Mr. I. pointed out, we accept black-and-white photographs or films because they are *representations* of the world — images that we can look at, or away from, when we want. But black and white for him was a *reality*, all around him, 360 degrees, solid and three-dimensional, twenty-four hours a day. The only way he could express it, he felt, was to make a completely grey room for others to experience — but of course, he pointed out, the observer himself would have to be painted grey, so he would be part of the world, not just observing it. More than this: the observer would have to lose, as he himself had, the neural knowledge of color. It was, he said, like living in a world "molded in lead."

Subsequently, he said neither "grey" nor "leaden" could begin to convey what his world was actually like. It was not "grey" that he experienced, he said, but perceptual qualities for which ordinary experience, ordinary language, had no equivalent.

Mr. I. could no longer bear to go to museums and galleries or to see colored reproductions of his favorite pictures. This was not just because they were bereft of color, but because they looked intolerably *wrong*, with washed-out or "unnatural" shades of grey (photographs in black and white, on the other hand, were much more tolerable). This was especially distressing when he knew the artists, and the perceptual debasement of their work interfered with his sense of their identity—this, indeed, was what he now felt was happening with himself.

He was depressed once by a rainbow, which he saw only as a colorless semicircle in the sky. And he even felt his occasional migraines as "dull"—previously they had involved brilliantly colored geometric hallucinations, but now even these were devoid of color. He sometimes tried to evoke color by pressing the globes of his eyes, but the flashes and patterns elicited were equally lacking in color. He had often dreamed in vivid color, especially when he dreamed of landscapes and painting; now his dreams were washed-out and pale, or violent and contrasty, lacking both color and delicate tonal gradations.

Music, curiously, was impaired for him too, because he had previously had an extremely intense synesthesia, so that different tones had immediately been translated into color, and he experienced all music simultaneously as a rich tumult of inner colors. With the loss of his ability to generate colors, he lost this ability as well—his internal "color-organ" was out of action, and now he heard music with no visual accompaniment; this, for him, was music with its essential chromatic counterpart missing, music now radically impoverished.[5]

A certain mild pleasure came from looking at drawings; he had been a fine draftsman in his earlier years. Could he not go back to drawing again? This thought was slow to occur to him, and it only took hold after being suggested repeatedly by others. His own first impulse was to paint in color. He insisted that he still "knew" what colors to use, even though he could no longer see them. He decided, as a first exercise, to paint flowers, taking from his palette what tints

25

---

[5] Only one sense could give him any real pleasure at this time, and this was the sense of smell. Mr. I. had always had a most acute, erotically charged sense of smell—indeed, he ran a small perfume business on the side, compounding his own scents. As the pleasures of seeing were lost, the pleasures of smell were heightened (or so it seemed to him), in the first grim weeks after his accident.

seemed "tonally right." But the pictures were unintelligible, a confusing welter of colors to normal eyes. It was only when one of his artist friends took black-and-white Polaroids of the paintings that they made sense. The contours were accurate, but the colors were all wrong. "No one will get your paintings," one of his friends said, "unless they are as colorblind as you."

"Stop pushing it," said another. "You *can't* use color now." Mr. I. reluctantly allowed all his colored paints to be put away. It's only temporary, he thought. I'll be back to color soon.

These first weeks were a time of agitation, even desperation; he was constantly hoping that he would wake up one fine morning and find the world of color miraculously restored. This was a constant motif in his dreams at the time, but the wish was never fulfilled, even in his dreams. He would dream that he was *about* to see in color, but then he would wake and find that nothing had changed. He constantly feared that whatever had happened would happen again, this time depriving him of all his sight completely. He thought he had probably had a stroke, caused by (or perhaps causing) his accident in the car, and feared that there could be another stroke at any moment. In addition to this medical fear, there was a deeper bewilderment and fear that he found almost impossible to articulate, and it was this that had come to a head in his month of attempted color painting, his month of insisting that he still "knew" color. It had gradually come upon him, during this time, that it was not merely color perception and color imagery that he lacked, but something deeper and difficult to define. He knew all about color, externally, intellectually, but he had lost the remembrance, the inner knowledge, of it that had been part of his very being. He had had a lifetime of experience in color, but now this was only a historical fact, not something he could access and feel directly. It was as if his past, his chromatic past, had been taken away, as if the brain's knowledge of color had been totally excised, leaving no trace, no inner evidence, of its existence behind.[6]

---

[6] The question of "knowing" color is very complex and has paradoxical aspects that are difficult to dissect. Certainly Mr. I. was intensely aware of a profound loss with the change in his vision, so clearly some sort of comparison with past experience was possible for him. Such a comparison is not possible if there is a complete destruction of the primary visual cortex on both sides, say from a stroke, as in Anton's syndrome. Patients with this syndrome become totally blind, but make

By the beginning of February, some of his agitation was calming down; he had started to accept, not merely intellectually, but at a deeper level, too, that he was indeed totally colorblind and might possibly remain so. His initial sense of helplessness started to give way to a sense of resolution — he would paint in black and white, if he could not paint in color; he would try to live in a black-and-white world as fully as he could. This resolution was strengthened by a singular experience, about five weeks after his accident, as he was driving to the studio one morning. He saw the sunrise over the highway, the blazing reds all turned into black: "The sun rose like a bomb, like some enormous nuclear explosion," he said later. "Had anyone ever seen a sunrise in this way before?"

Inspired by the sunrise, he started painting again — he started, indeed, with a black-and-white painting that he called *Nuclear Sunrise*, and then went on to the abstracts he favored, but now painting in black and white only. The fear of blindness continued to haunt him but, creatively transmuted, shaped the first "real" paintings he did after his color experiments. Black-and-white paintings he now found he could do, and do very well. He found his only solace working in the studio, and he worked fifteen, even eighteen, hours a day. This meant for him a kind of artistic survival: "I felt if I couldn't go on painting," he said later, "I wouldn't want to go on at all."

His first black-and-white paintings, done in February and March, 30 gave a feeling of violent forces — rage, fear, despair, excitement — but these were held in control, attesting to the powers of artistry that could disclose, and yet contain, such intensity of feeling. In these two months he produced dozens of paintings, marked by a singular style, a character he had never shown before. In many of these paintings, there was an extraordinary shattered, kaleidoscopic surface, with abstract shapes suggestive of faces — averted, shadowed, sorrowing, raging — and

no complaint or report of their blindness. They do not know they are blind; the whole structure of consciousness is completely reorganized — instantly so — at the moment they are stricken.

Similarly, patients with massive strokes in the right parietal cortex may lose not only the sensation and use but the very knowledge of their left sides, of everything to the left, and indeed of the very concept of leftness. But they are "anosognosic" — they have no knowledge of their loss; *we* may say their world is bisected, but, for them, it is whole and complete.

dismembered body parts, faceted and held in frames and boxes. They had, compared with his previous work, a labyrinthine complexity, and an obsessed, haunted quality — they seemed to exhibit, in symbolic form, the predicament he was in.

Starting in May — it was fascinating to watch — he moved from these powerful but rather terrifying and alien paintings toward themes, living themes, he had not touched in thirty years, back to representational paintings of dancers and racehorses. These paintings, even though still in black and white, were full of movement, vitality, and sensuousness; and they went with a change in his personal life — a lessening of his withdrawal and the beginnings of a renewed social and sexual life, a lessening of his fears and depression, and a turning back to life.

At this time, too, he turned to sculpture, which he had never done before. He seemed to be turning to all the visual modes that still remained to him — form, contour, movement, depth — and exploring them with heightened intensity. He also started painting portraits, although he found that he could not work from life, but only from black-and-white photographs, fortified by his knowledge of and feeling for each subject. Life was tolerable only in the studio, for here he could reconceive the world in powerful, stark forms. But outside, in real life, he found the world alien, empty, dead, and grey.

This was the story Bob Wasserman and I got from Mr. I. — a story of an abrupt and total breakdown of color vision, and his attempts to live in a black-and-white world. I had never been given such a history before, I had never met anyone with total colorblindness before, and I had no idea what had happened to him — nor whether his condition could be reversed or improved.

The first thing was to define his impairments more precisely with various tests, some quite informal, making use of everyday objects or pictures, whatever came to hand. For instance, we first asked Mr. I. about a shelf of notebooks — blue, red, and black — by my desk. He instantly picked out the blue ones (a bright medium blue to normal eyes) — "they're pale." The red and the black were indistinguishable — both, for him, were "dead black."

35   We then gave him a large mass of yarns, containing thirty-three separate colors, and asked him to sort these: he said he could not sort them by color, but only by grey-scale tonal values. He then, rapidly

and easily, separated the yarns into four strange, chromatically random piles, which he characterized as 0–25 percent, 25–50 percent, 50–75 percent, and 75–100 percent on a grey-tone scale (though nothing looked to him purely white, and even white yarn looked slightly "dingy" or "dirty").

We ourselves could not confirm the accuracy of this, because our color vision interfered with our ability to visualize a grey scale, just as normally sighted viewers had been unable to perceive the tonal sense of his confusingly polychromatic flower paintings. But a black-and-white photograph and a black-and-white video camera confirmed that Mr. I. had indeed accurately divided the colored yarns in a grey scale that basically coincided with their own mechanical reading. There was, perhaps, a certain crudeness in his categories, but this went with the sense of sharp contrast, the paucity of tonal gradations, that he had complained of. Indeed, when shown an artist's grey scale of perhaps a dozen gradations from black to white, Mr. I. could distinguish only three or four categories of tone.[7]

We also showed him the classic Ishihara color-dot plates, in which configurations of numerals in subtly differentiated colors may stand out clearly for the normally sighted, but not for those with various types of colorblindness. Mr. I. was unable to see any of these figures (although he was able to see certain plates that are visible to the colorblind but not to normally sighted people, and thus designed to catch pretended or hysterical colorblindness).[8]

---

[7] One anomaly showed itself in the yarn-sorting test; he ranked bright saturated blues as "pale" (as he had complained that the blue sky seemed almost white). But was this an anomaly? Could we be sure that the blue wool was not, under its blueness, rather washed-out or pale? We had to have hues that were otherwise identical — identical in brightness, saturation, reflectivity, so we obtained a set of carefully produced color buttons known as the Farnsworth-Munsell test and gave this to Mr. I. He was unable to put the buttons in any order, but he did separate out the blue ones as "paler" than the rest.

[8] Further testing with the Nagel anomaloscope and the Sloan achromatopsia cards confirmed Mr. I.'s total colorblindness. With Dr. Ralph Siegel, we did tests of depth and motion perception (using Julesz random-dot stereograms and moving random-dot fields) — these were normal, as were tests of his ability to generate structure and depth from motion. There was, however, one interesting anomaly: Mr. I. was unable to "get" red and green stereograms (bicolor anaglyphs), presumably because color vision is needed to segregate the two images. We also obtained electroretinograms, and these were quite normal, indicating that all three cone mechanisms in the retina were intact, and that the colorblindness was indeed of cerebral origin.

We happened to have a postcard that could have been designed for testing achromatopes — a postcard of a coastal scene, with fishermen on a jetty silhouetted against a dark red sunset sky. Mr. I. was totally unable to see the fishermen or the jetty, and saw only the half-engulfed hemisphere of the setting sun.

Though such problems arose when he was shown colored pictures, Mr. I. had no difficulty describing black-and-white photographs or reproductions accurately; he had no difficulty recognizing forms. His imagery and memory of objects and pictures shown to him were indeed exceptionally vivid and accurate, though always colorless. Thus, after being given a classic test picture of a colored boat, he looked intensely, looked away, and then rapidly reproduced it in black and white paint. When asked the colors of familiar objects, he had no difficulties in color association or color naming. (Patients with color anomia, for instance, can match colors perfectly but have lost the *names* of colors, and might speak, uncertainly, of a banana being "blue." A patient with a color agnosia, by contrast, could also match colors, but would evince no surprise if *given* a blue banana. Mr. I., however, had neither of these problems.)[9] Nor did he (now) have any difficulties reading. Testing up to this point, and a general neurological examination, thus confirmed Mr. I.'s total achromatopsia.

40   We could say to him at this point that his problem was real — that he had a true achromatopsia and not a hysteria. He took this, we thought, with mixed feelings: he had half hoped it might be merely a hysteria, and as such potentially reversible. But the notion of something psychological had also distressed him and made him feel that his problem was "not real" (indeed, several doctors had hinted at this). Our testing, in a sense, legitimized his condition, but deepened his fear about brain damage and the prognosis for recovery.

Although it seemed that he had an achromatopsia of cerebral origin, we could not help wondering whether a lifetime of heavy smoking could

---

[9] In 1877, Gladstone, in an article entitled "On the Colour Sense of Homer," spoke of Homer's use of such phrases as "the wine-dark sea." Was this just a poetic convention, or did Homer, the Greeks, actually see the sea differently? There is indeed considerable variation between different cultures in the way they will categorize and name colors — individuals may only "see" a color (or make a perceptual categorization) if there is an existing cultural category or name for it. But it is not clear whether such categorization may actually alter elementary color perception.

have played a part; nicotine can cause a dimming of vision (an amblyopia) and sometimes an achromatopsia — but this is predominantly due to its effects on the cells of the retina. But the major problem was clearly cerebral: Mr. I. could have sustained tiny areas of brain damage as a result of his concussion; he could have had a small stroke either following, or conceivably precipitating, the accident.

The history of our knowledge about the brain's ability to represent color has followed a complex and zigzag course. Newton, in his famous prism experiment in 1666, showed that white light was composite — could be decomposed into, and recomposed by, all the colors of the spectrum. The rays that were bent most ("the most refrangible") were seen as violet, the least refrangible as red, with the rest of the spectrum in between. The colors of objects, Newton thought, were determined by the "copiousness" with which they reflected particular rays to the eye. Thomas Young, in 1802, feeling that there was no need to have an infinity of different receptors in the eye, each tuned to a different wavelength (artists, after all, could create almost any color they wanted by using a very limited palette of paints) postulated that three types of receptors would be enough.[10] Young's brilliant idea, thrown off casually in the course of a lecture, was forgotten, or lay dormant, for fifty years, until Hermann von Helmholtz, in the course of his own investigation of vision, resurrected it and gave it a new precision, so that we now speak of the Young-Helmholtz hypothesis. For Helmholtz, as for Young, color was a direct expression of the wavelengths of light absorbed by each receptor, the nervous system just translating one into the other: "Red light stimulates the

---

[10] "As it is almost impossible to conceive each sensitive point of the retina to contain an infinite number of particles, each capable of vibrating in perfect unison with every possible undulation," Young wrote, "it becomes necessary to suppose the number limited, for instance to the three principal colours, red, yellow, and blue."

The great chemist John Dalton, just five years earlier, had provided a classic description of red-green colorblindness in himself. He thought this was due to a discoloration in the transparent media of the eye — and, indeed, willed an eye to posterity to test this. Young, however, provided the correct interpretation — that one of the three types of color receptor was missing. (Dalton's eye still resides, pickled, on a shelf in Cambridge.)

Lindsay T. Sharpe and Knut Nordby discuss this and many other aspects of the history of colorblindness research in "Total Colorblindness: An Introduction."

red-sensitive fibres strongly, and the other two weakly, giving the *sensation* red."[11]

In 1884, Hermann Wilbrand, seeing in his neurological practice patients with a range of visual losses — in some predominantly the loss of visual field, in others predominantly of color perception, and in still others predominantly of form perception — suggested that there must be separate visual centers in the primary visual cortex for "light impressions," "color impressions," and "form impressions," though he had no anatomical evidence for this. That achromatopsia (and even hemi-achromatopsia) could indeed arise from damage to specific parts of the brain was first confirmed, four years later, by a Swiss ophthalmologist, Louis Verrey. He described a sixty-year-old woman who, in consequence of a stroke affecting the occipital lobe of her left hemisphere, now saw everything in the right half of her visual field in shades of grey (the left half remained normally colored). The opportunity to examine his patient's brain after her death showed damage confined to a small portion (the fusiform and lingual gyri) of the visual cortex — it was here, Verrey concluded, that "the centre for chromatic sense will be found." That such a center might exist, that any part of the cortex might be specialized for the perception or representation of color, was immediately contested and continued to be contested for almost a century. The grounds of this contention go very deep, as deep as the philosophy of neurology itself.

Locke, in the seventeenth century, had held to a "sensationalist" philosophy (which paralleled Newton's physicalist one): our senses are measuring instruments, recording the external world for us in terms of sensation. Hearing, seeing, all sensation, he took to be wholly passive and receptive. Neurologists in the late nineteenth century were quick to accept this philosophy and to embed it in a speculative anatomy of the brain. Visual perception was equated with "sense-data" or "impressions" transmitted from the retina to the primary visual area of the brain, in an exact, point-to-point correspondence — and there experienced, subjec-

---

[11] In 1816, the young Schopenhauer proposed a different theory of color vision, one that envisaged not a passive, mechanical resonance of tuned particles or receptors, as Young had postulated, but their active stimulation, competition, and inhibition — an explicit "opponens" theory such as Ewald Hering was to create seventy years later, in apparent contradiction of the Young-Helmholtz theory. These opponens theories were ignored at the time, and continued to be ignored until the 1950s. We now envisage a combination of Young-Helmholtz and opponens mechanisms: tuned receptors, which converse with one another, are continually linked in an interactional balance. Thus integration and selection, as Schopenhauer divined, start in the retina.

tively, as an image of the visual world. Color, it was presumed, was an integral part of this image. There was no room, anatomically, it was thought, for a separate color center — or indeed, conceptually, for the very idea of one. Thus when Verrey published his findings in 1888, they flew in the face of accepted doctrine. His observations were doubted, his testing criticized, his examination regarded as flawed — but the real objection, behind these, was doctrinal in nature.

If there was no discrete color center, so the thinking went, there could be no isolated achromatopsia either; thus Verrey's case, and two similar ones in the 1890s, were dismissed from neurological consciousness — and cerebral achromatopsia, as a subject, all but disappeared for the next seventy-five years.[12] There was not to be another full case study until 1974.[13]

Mr. I. himself was actively curious about what was going on in his brain. Though he now lived wholly in a world of lightnesses and darknesses, he was very struck by how these changed in different illuminations; red objects, for instance, which normally appeared black to him, became lighter in the long rays of the evening sun, and this allowed him to infer their redness. This phenomenon was very marked if the quality of illumination suddenly changed, as, for example, when a fluorescent light was turned on, which would cause an immediate change in the brightnesses of objects around the room. Mr. I. commented that he now found himself in an inconstant world, a world whose lights and darks fluctuated with the wavelength of illumination, in striking contrast to the relative stability, the constancy, of the color world he had previously known.[14]

---

[12] There is no mention of it in the great 1911 edition of Helmholtz's *Physiological Optics*, though there is a large section on retinal achromatopsia.

[13] There were, however, brief mentions of achromatopsia in these intervening years, which were ignored, or soon forgotten, for the most part. Even Kurt Goldstein, although philosophically opposed to notions of isolated neurological deficits, remarked that he had seen several cases of pure cerebral achromatopsia without visual field losses or other impairments — an observation thrown off casually in the course of his 1948 book, *Language and Language Disturbances*.

[14] A perhaps similar phenomenon is described by Knut Nordby. During his first school year, his teacher presented the class with a printed alphabet, in which the vowels were red and the consonants black.

> I could not see any difference between them and could not understand what the teacher meant, until early one morning late in the autumn when the room-lights had been turned on, and, unexpectedly, I saw that some of the letters, i.e. the AEIOUY Å Ä Ö, were now suddenly a darkish grey, while the others were still solid black. This experience taught me that colours may look different under different light sources, and that the same colour can be matched to different grey-tones in different kinds of illumination.

All of this, of course, is very difficult to explain in terms of classical color theory — Newton's notion of an invariant relationship between wavelength and color, of a cell-to-cell transmission of wavelength information from the retina to the brain, and of a direct conversion of this information into color. Such a simple process — a neurological analogy to the decomposition and recomposition of light through a prism — could hardly account for the complexity of color perception in real life.

This incompatibility between classical color theory and reality struck Goethe in the late eighteenth century. Intensely aware of the phenomenal reality of colored shadows and colored afterimages, of the effects of contiguity and illumination on the appearance of colors, of colored and other visual illusions, he felt that these must be the basis of a color theory and declared as his credo, "Optical illusion is optical truth!" Goethe was centrally concerned with the way we actually see colors and light, the ways in which we *create* worlds, and illusions, in color. This, he felt, was not explicable by Newton's physics, but only by some as-yet unknown rules of the brain. He was saying, in effect, "Visual illusion is neurological truth."

Goethe's color theory, his *Farbenlehre* (which he regarded as the equal of his entire poetic opus), was, by and large, dismissed by all his contemporaries and has remained in a sort of limbo ever since, seen as the whimsy, the pseudoscience, of a very great poet. But science itself was not entirely insensitive to the "anomalies" that Goethe considered central, and Helmholtz, indeed, gave admiring lectures on Goethe and his science, on many occasions — the last in 1892. Helmholtz was very conscious of "color constancy" — the way in which the colors of objects are preserved, so that we can categorize them and always know what we are looking at, despite great fluctuations in the wavelength of the light illuminating them. The actual wavelengths reflected by an apple, for instance, will vary considerably depending on the illumination, but we consistently see it as red, nonetheless. This could not be, clearly, a mere translation of wavelength into color. There had to be some way, Helmholtz thought, of "discounting the illuminant" — and this he saw as an "unconscious inference" or "an act of judgement" (though he did not venture to suggest where such judgement might occur). Color constancy, for him, was a special example of the way in which we achieve perceptual constancy generally, make a stable perceptual world from a chaotic sensory flux — a world that would not be possible if our perceptions were merely passive reflections of the unpredictable and inconstant input that bathes our receptors.

Helmholtz's great contemporary, Clerk Maxwell, had also been   50
fascinated by the mystery of color vision from his student days. He formalized the notions of primary colors and color mixing by the invention of a color top (the colors of which fused, when it was spun, to yield a sensation of grey), and a graphic representation with three axes, a color triangle, which showed how any color could be created by different mixtures of the three primary colors. These prepared the way for his most spectacular demonstration, the demonstration in 1861 that color photography was possible, despite the fact that photographic emulsions were themselves black and white. He did this by photographing a colored bow three times, through red, green, and violet filters. Having obtained three "color-separation" images, as he called them, he now brought these together by superimposing them upon a screen, projecting each image through its corresponding filter (the image taken through the red filter was projected with red light, and so on). Suddenly, the bow burst forth in full color. Maxwell wondered if this was how colors were perceived in the brain, by the addition of color-separation images or their neural correlates, as in his magic-lantern demonstrations.[15]

Maxwell himself was acutely aware of the drawback of this additive process: color photography had no way of "discounting the illuminant," and its colors changed helplessly with changing wavelengths of light.

In 1957, ninety-odd years after Maxwell's famous demonstration, Edwin Land — not merely the inventor of the instant Land camera

---

[15] Maxwell's demonstration of the "decomposition" and "reconstitution" of color in this way made color photography possible. Huge "color cameras" were used at first, which split the incident light into three beams and passed these through filters of the three primary colors (such a camera, reversed, served as a chromoscope, or Maxwellian projector). Though an integral color process was envisaged by Ducos du Hauron in the 1860s, it was not until 1907 that such a process (Autochrome) was actually developed, by the Lumière brothers. They used tiny starch grains dyed red, green, and violet, in contact with the photographic emulsion — these acted as a sort of Maxwellian grid through which the three color-separation images, mosaicked together, could both be taken and viewed. (Color cameras, Lumière-color, Dufaycolor, Finlaycolor, and many other additive color processes were still being used in the 1940s, when I was a boy, and stimulated my own first interest in the nature of color.)

and Polaroid, but an experimenter and theorizer of genius — provided a photographic demonstration of color perception even more startling. Unlike Maxwell, he made only two black-and-white images (using a split-beam camera so they could be taken at the same time from the same viewpoint, through the same lens) and superimposed these on a screen with a double-lens projector. He used two filters to make the images: one passing longer wavelengths (a red filter), the other passing shorter wavelengths (a green filter). The first image was then projected through a red filter, the second with ordinary white light, unfiltered. One might expect that this would produce just an overall pale-pink image, but something "impossible" happened instead. The photograph of a young woman appeared instantly in full color — "blonde hair, pale blue eyes, red coat, bluegreen collar, and strikingly natural flesh tones," as Land later described it. Where did these colors come from, how were they made? They did not seem to be "in" the photographs or the illuminants themselves. These demonstrations, overwhelming in their simplicity and impact, were color "illusions" in Goethe's sense, but illusions that demonstrated a neurological truth — that colors are not "out there" in the world, nor (as classical theory held) an automatic correlate of wavelength, but, rather, are *constructed by the brain*.

These experiments hung, at first, like anomalies, conceptless, in midair; they were inexplicable in terms of existing theory, but did not yet point clearly to a new one. It seemed possible, moreover, that the viewer's knowledge of appropriate colors might influence his perception of such a scene. Land decided, therefore, to replace familiar images of the natural world with entirely abstract, multicolored displays consisting of geometric patches of colored paper, so that expectation could provide no clues as to what colors should be seen. These abstract displays vaguely resembled some of the paintings of Piet Mondrian, and Land therefore terms them "color Mondrians." Using the Mondrians, which were illuminated by three projectors, using long-wave (red), middle-wave (green), and short-wave (blue) filters, Land was able to prove that, if a surface formed part of a complex multicolored scene, there was no simple relationship between the wavelength of light reflected from a surface and its perceived color.

If, moreover, a single patch of color (for example, one ordinarily seen as green) was isolated from its surrounding colors, it would appear only as white or pale grey, whatever illuminating beam was used. Thus the green patch, Land showed, could not be regarded as inherently green, but was, in part, *given* its greenness by its relation to the surrounding areas of the Mondrian.

Whereas color for Newton, for classical theory, was something local and absolute, given by the wavelength of light reflected from each point, Land showed that its determination was neither local nor absolute, but depended upon the surveying of a whole scene and a comparison of the wavelength composition of the light reflected from each point with that of the light reflected from its surround. There had to be a continuous relating, a comparison of every part of the visual field with its own surround, to arrive at that global synthesis — Helmholtz's "act of judgement." Land felt that this computation or correlation followed fixed, formal rules; and he was able to predict which colors would be perceived by an observer under different conditions. He devised a "color cube," an algorithm, for this, in effect a model for the brain's comparison of the brightnesses, at different wavelengths, of all the parts of a complex, multicolored surface. Whereas Maxwell's color theory and color triangle were based on the concept of color addition, Land's model was now one of comparison. He proposed that there were, in fact, two comparisons: first of the reflectance of all the surfaces in a scene within a certain group of wavelengths, or waveband (in Land's term, a "lightness record" for that waveband), and second, a comparison of the three separate lightness records for the three wavebands (corresponding roughly to the red, green, and blue wavelengths). This second comparison generated the color. Land himself was at pains to avoid specifying any particular brain site for these operations and was careful to call his theory of color vision the Retinex theory, implying that there might be multiple sites of interaction between the retina and the cortex.

If Land was approaching the problem of how we see colors at a psychophysical level by asking human subjects to report how they perceived complex, multicolored mosaics in changing illuminations, Semir Zeki, working in London, was approaching the problem at a physiological level, by inserting microelectrodes in the visual cortex of anesthetized monkeys and measuring the neuronal potentials generated when they were given colored stimuli. Early in the 1970s, he was able to make a crucial discovery, to delineate a small area of cells on each side of the brain, in the prestriate cortex of monkeys (areas referred to

55

as V_4), which seemed to be specialized for responding to color (Zeki called these "color-coding cells").[16]

Thus, ninety years after Wilbrand and Verrey had postulated a specific center for color in the brain, Zeki was finally able to prove that such a center existed.

Fifty years earlier, the eminent neurologist Gordon Holmes, reviewing two hundred cases of visual problems caused by gunshot wounds to the visual cortex, had found not a single case of achromatopsia. He went on to deny that an isolated cerebral achromatopsia *could* occur. The vehemence of this denial, coming from such a great authority, played a major part in bringing all clinical interest in the subject to an end.[17] Zeki's brilliant and undeniable demonstration startled the neurological world, reawakening attention to a subject it had for many years dismissed. Following his 1973 paper, new cases of human achromatopsia began appearing in the literature once again, and these could now be examined with new brain-imaging techniques (CAT, MRI, PET, SQUID, etc.) not available to neurologists of an earlier era. Now, for the first time, it was possible to visualize, in life, what areas of the brain might be needed for human color perception. Though many of

---

[16] He was also able to find cells, in an adjacent area, that seemed to respond solely to movement. A remarkable account and analysis of a patient with a pure "motion blindness" was given by Zihl, Von Cramon, and Mai in 1983. The patient's problems are described as follows:

> The visual disorder complained of by the patient was a loss of movement vision in all three dimensions. She had difficulty, for example, in pouring tea or coffee into a cup because the fluid appeared to be frozen, like a glacier. In addition, she could not stop pouring at the right time since she was unable to perceive the movement in the cup (or a pot) when the fluid rose. Furthermore the patient complained of difficulties in following a dialogue because she could not see the movement of the face and, especially, the mouth of the speaker. In a room where more than two other people were walking, she felt very insecure and unwell, and usually left the room immediately, because "people were suddenly here or there but I have not seen them moving." The patient experienced the same problem but to an even more marked extent in crowded streets or places, which she therefore avoided as much as possible. She could not cross the street because of her inability to judge the speed of a car, but she could identify the car itself without difficulty. "When I'm looking at the car first, it seems far away. But then, when I want to cross the road, suddenly the car is very near." She gradually learned to "estimate" the distance of moving vehicles by means of the sound becoming louder.

[17] A vivid account of Holmes's negative influence has been provided by Damasio, who also points out that all of Holmes's cases involved lesions in the dorsal aspect of the occipital lobe, whereas the center for achromatopsia lies on the ventral aspect.

the cases described had other problems, too (cuts in the visual field, visual agnosia, alexia, etc.), the crucial lesions seemed to be in the medial association cortex, in areas homologous to V_4 in the monkey.[18] It had been shown in the 1960s that there were cells in the primary visual cortex of monkeys (in the area termed V_1) that responded specifically to wavelength, but not to color; Zeki now showed, in the early 1970s, that there were other cells in the V_4 areas that responded to color but not to wavelength (these V_4 cells, however, received impulses from the V_1 cells, converging through an intermediate structure, V_2). Thus each V_4 cell received information regarding a large portion of the visual field. It seemed that the two stages postulated by Land in his theory might now have an anatomical and physiological grounding: lightness records for each waveband being extracted by the wavelength-sensitive cells in V_1, but only being compared or correlated to generate color in the color-coding cells of V_4. Every one of these, indeed, seemed to act as a Landian correlator, or a Helmholtzian "judge."

Color vision, it seemed — like the other processes of early vision: motion, depth, and form perception — required no prior knowledge, was not determined by learning or experience, but was, as neurologists say, a "bottom-up" process. Color can indeed be generated, experimentally, by magnetic stimulation of V_4, causing the "seeing" of colored rings and halos — so-called chromatophenes.[19] But color vision, in real life, is part and parcel of our total experience, is linked with our own

---

[18] The work of Antonio and Hanna Damasio and their colleagues at the University of Iowa was particularly important here, both by virtue of the minuteness of the perceptual testing, and the refinement of the neuroimaging they used.

[19] Such chromatophenes may occur spontaneously in visual migraines, and Mr. I. himself had experienced these, on occasion, in migraines occurring before his accident. One wonders what would have been experienced if Mr. I.'s V_4 areas had been stimulated — but magnetic stimulation of circumscribed brain areas was not technically possible at the time. One wonders, too, now that such stimulation is possible, whether it might be tried in individuals with congenital (retinal) achromatopsia (several such achromatopes have expressed their curiosity about such an experiment). It is possible — I am not aware of any studies on this — that V_4 fails to develop in such people, with the absence of any cone input. But if V_4 *is* present as a functional (though never functioning) unit despite the absence of cones, its stimulation might produce an astounding phenomenon — a burst of unprecedented, totally novel sensation, in a brain/mind that had never had a chance to experience or categorize such sensation. Hume wonders if a man could imagine, could even perceive, a color he had never seen before — perhaps this Humean question (propounded in 1738) could find an answer now.

categorizations and values, becomes for each of us a part of our life-world, of us. V_4 may be an ultimate generator of color, but it signals to, it converses with, a hundred other systems in the mind-brain; and perhaps it can also be modulated by these. It is at higher levels that integration occurs, that color fuses with memories, expectations, associations, and desires to make a world with resonance and meaning for each of us. . . .[20]

---

[20] The power of expectation and mental set in the perception of color is clearly shown in those with partial red-green colorblindness. Such people may not, for example, be able to spot scarlet holly berries against the dark green foliage, or the delicate salmon-pink of dawn — until these are pointed out to them. "Our poor impoverished cone cells," says a dyschromatope of my acquaintance, "need the amplification of intellect, knowledge, expectation, and attention in order to 'see' the colors that we are normally 'blind' to."

Oliver Sacks

Housecalls

In his 2001 memoir, *Uncle Tungsten: Memories of a Chemical Boyhood*, Oliver Sacks writes about his "partly war-dominated, partly chemistry-dominated youth." The chapter entitled "House-calls" recounts his early relationship with his father, a physician, in the years just before and after World War II.
For more biographical background on Sacks, see page 199.

M y father was not given to emotion or intimacy, at least in the context, the confines, of the family. But there were certain times, precious times, when I did feel close to him. I have very early memories of seeing him reading in our library, and his concentration was such that nothing could disturb him, for everything outside the circle of his lamp was completely tuned out of his mind. For the most part he read the Bible or the Talmud, though he also had a large collection of books on Hebrew, which he spoke fluently, and Judaism — the library of a grammarian and scholar. Seeing his intense absorption in reading, and the expressions that would appear on his face as he read (an involuntary smile, a grimace, a look of perplexity or delight), perhaps drew me to reading very early myself, so that even before the war I would sometimes join him in the library, reading my book alongside him, in a deep but unspoken companionship.

If there were no housecalls to do in the evening, my father would settle down after dinner with a torpedo-shaped cigar. He would palpate it gently, then hold it to his nose to test its aroma and freshness, and if it was satisfactory he would make a V-shaped incision in its tip with his cutter. He would light it carefully with a long match, rotating it so that it lit evenly. The tip would glow red as he drew, and his first exhalation was a sigh of satisfaction. He would puff away gently as he read, and the air would turn blue and opalescent with smoke, enfolding us both in a fragrant cloud. I loved the smell of the beautiful Havanas he smoked, and loved to watch the grey cylinder of ash grow longer and longer, wondering how long it would get before it dropped on his book.

I felt closest to him, truly his son, when we went swimming together. My father's passion, from an early age, had been swimming (as his father had been a swimmer before him), and he had been a swimming champion when he was younger, having won the fifteen-mile race off the Isle of Wight three years in succession. He had introduced each of us to the water when we were babies, taking us to the Highgate Ponds in Hampstead Heath.

The slow, measured, mile-eating stroke he had was not entirely suited to a little boy. But I could see how my old man, huge and cumbersome on land, became transformed — graceful, like a porpoise — in the water; and I, self-conscious, nervous, and also rather clumsy, found the same delicious transformation in myself, found a new being, a new mode of being, in the water. I have a vivid memory of a summer holiday at the seaside, the month after my fifth birthday, when I ran into my parents' room and tugged at the great whalelike bulk of my father. "Come on, Pop!" I said. "Let's go for a swim." He turned over slowly and opened one eye: "What do you mean, waking an old man of forty-three like this at six in the morning?" Now that my father is dead, and I myself am in my sixties, this memory of so long ago tugs, makes me equally want to laugh and cry.

5   Later we would swim together in the large open-air pool in Hendon, or the Welsh Harp on Edgware Road, a small lake (I was never sure whether it was natural or artificial) where my father had once kept a boat. After the war, as a twelve-year-old, I could begin to match his strokes, and maintain the same rhythm, swimming in unison with him.

I sometimes went along with my father on housecalls on Sunday mornings. He loved doing housecalls more than anything else, for they were social and sociable as well as medical, would allow him to enter a family and home, get to know everybody and their circumstances, see the whole complexion and context of a condition. Medicine, for him, was never just diagnosing a disease, but had to be seen and understood in the context of patients' lives, the particularities of their personalities, their feelings, their reactions.

He would have a typed list of a dozen patients and their addresses, and I would sit next to him in the front seat of the car while he told me, in very human terms, what each patient had. When he arrived, I would get out with him, allowed, usually, to carry his medical bag. Sometimes I would go into the sickroom with him and sit quietly while he questioned and examined a patient — a questioning and examining which seemed swift and light, and yet one that reached depths and exposed for him the origins of each illness. I loved to see him percuss the chest, tapping it delicately but powerfully with his strong stubby fingers, feeling, sensing, the organs and their state beneath. Later, when I became a medical student myself, I realized what a master of percussion he was, and how he could tell more by palpating and percussing and listening to a chest than most doctors could from an X-ray.

At other times, if the patient was very ill, or contagious, I would sit with the family in their kitchen or dining room. After my father had seen the patient upstairs, he would come down, wash his hands carefully, and make for the kitchen. He loved to eat, and he knew the contents of the refrigerators in all his patients' houses — and the families seemed to enjoy giving the good doctor food. Seeing patients, meeting families, enjoying himself, eating, were all inseparable in the medicine he practiced.

Driving through the City, deserted on a Sunday, was a sobering experience in 1946, for the devastation wrought by the bombing was still fresh, and there had been little rebuilding as yet. This was even more evident in the East End, where a fifth of the buildings, perhaps, had been leveled. But there was still a strong Jewish community there, and restaurants and delicatessens like no others in the world. My father had qualified at the London Hospital in White Chapel Road, and as a young man had been the Yiddish-speaking doctor of the Yiddish-speaking community around it for ten years. He looked back on these early days with peculiar affection. We would sometimes visit his old surgery in New Road — it was here that all my brothers had been born, and a physician nephew, Neville, now practiced.

We would walk up and down "the Lane," that section of Petticoat 10 Lane between Middlesex Street and Commercial Street, where all the stallholders hawked their wares. My parents had left the East End in 1930, but my father still knew many of the hawkers by name. Jabbering with them, reverting to the Yiddish of his youth, my old father (what do I mean "old"? I am now fifteen years older than the fifty-year-old he was then) became boyish, rejuvenated, showed an earlier, more alive self that I normally did not see.

We would always go to Marks of the Lane, where one could buy a latke for sixpence, and the best smoked salmon and herrings in London, salmon of an unbelievable melting softness which made it one of the few, genuinely paradisal experiences on this earth.

My father had always had a very robust appetite, and the strudel and herrings at his patients' houses, and the latkes at Marks, were, in his mind, just preludes to the real meal. There were a dozen superb kosher restaurants within a few blocks, each with its own incomparable specialties. Should it be Bloom's on Aldgate, or Ostwind's, where one could enjoy the marvelous smells of the basement bakery wafting upstairs? Or Strongwater's, where there was a particular sort of kreplach, *varenikas*, to which my father was dangerously addicted? Usually, however, we would end up at Silberstein's, where, in addition to the meat restaurant downstairs, there was a dairy restaurant, with wonderful milky soups and fish, upstairs. My father adored carp, in particular, and would suck at the fish heads, noisily, with great gusto.

Pop was a calm, unflappable driver when he went on his housecalls — he had a sedate, rather slow Wolseley at the time, appropriate to the petrol rationing still in force — but before the war there was a very different side to him. His car then was an American one, a Chrysler, with a raw power and a turn of speed unusual in the 1930s. He also had a motorcycle, a Scott Flying Squirrel, with a two-stroke, 600 cc, water cooled engine, and a high-pitched exhaust like a scream. It developed nearly thirty horsepower, and was much more akin, he liked to say, to a flying horse. He loved to take off on this if he had a free Sunday morning, eager to shake off the city and give himself to the wind and the road, his practice, his cares forgotten for a while. Sometimes I had dreams in which I was riding or flying the bike myself, and I determined to get one when I was grown up.

When T. E. Lawrence's *The Mint* came out in 1955, I read my father a piece, "The Road," Lawrence had written about his motorbike (by this time I had a bike, a Norton, myself):

> A skittish motor-bike with a touch of blood in it is better than all the riding animals on earth, because of its logical extension of our faculties, and the hint, the provocation, to excess . . .

My father smiled and nodded in agreement, as he thought back to his own biking days.

My father had originally wondered about an academic career in neurology, and had been a houseman, an intern (along with Jonathan Miller's father), to Sir Henry Head, the famous neurologist, at the London Hospital. At this point, Head himself, still at the height of his powers, had developed Parkinson's disease, and this, my father said, would sometimes cause him to run involuntarily, or festinate, the length of the old neurology ward, so that he would have to be caught by one of his own patients. When I had difficulty imagining what this was like, my father, an excellent mimic, imitated Head's festination, careering down Exeter Road at an ever-accelerating pace, and getting me to catch him. Head's own predicament, my father thought, made him especially sensitive to the predicaments of his patients, and I think my father's imitations — he could imitate asthma, convulsions, paralyses, anything — springing from his vivid imagination of what it was like for others, served the same purpose.

When it was time for my father to open his own practice, he decided, despite this early training in neurology, that general practice would be more real, more "alive." Perhaps he got more than he bargained for, for when he opened his practice in the East End in September 1918, the great influenza epidemic was just getting started. He had seen wounded soldiers when he was a houseman at the London, but this was nothing to the horror of seeing people in paroxysms of coughing and gasping, suffocating from the fluid in their lungs, turning blue and dropping dead in the streets. A strong, healthy young man or woman, it was said, could die from the flu within three hours of getting it. In those three desperate months at the end of 1918, the flu killed more people than the Great War itself had, and my father, like every doctor at the time, found himself overwhelmed, sometimes working forty-eight hours at a stretch.

At this point he engaged his sister Alida — a young widow with two children who had returned to London from South Africa three years before — to work as his assistant in the dispensary. Around the same time, he took on another young doctor, Yitzchak Eban, to help him on his rounds. Yitzchak had been born in Joniški, the same little village in Lithuania where the Sacks family lived. Alida and Yitzchak had been playmates as infants, but then in 1895 his family had gone to Scotland, a few years before the Sackses had come to London. Reunited twenty years later, working together in the febrile and intense atmosphere of the epidemic, Alida and Yitzchak fell in love, and married in 1920.

As children, we had relatively little contact with Auntie Alida (though I thought of her as the quickest and wittiest of my aunts — she had sudden intuitions, sudden swoops of thought and feeling, which I came to think of as characteristic of the "Sacks mind," in contrast to the more methodical, more analytical, mental processes of the Landaus). But Auntie Lina, my father's eldest sister, was a constant presence. She was fifteen years older than Pop, tiny in size — four foot nine in her high heels — but with an iron will, a ruthless determination. She had dyed golden hair, as coarse as a doll's, and gave off a mixed scent of garlic, sweat, and patchouli. It was Lina who had furnished our house, and Lina who would often provide us at 37 with certain special items which she herself cooked — fish cakes (Marcus and David called her Fishcake, or sometimes Fishface, after these), rich crumbly cheesecakes, and, at Passover, matzoh balls of an incredible tellurian density, which would sink like little planetismals below the surface of the soup. Careless of the social graces, she would bend down at the table, when at home, and blow her nose on the tablecloth. Despite this, she was enchanting in company, when she would glitter and coquette, but also listen intently, judging the character and motive of everyone around her. She would draw confidences out of the unwary, and with her diabolical memory, retain all that she had heard.[1]

But her ruthlessness, her unscrupulousness, had a noble purpose, for she used them to raise money for the Hebrew University in Jerusalem. She had dossiers, it seemed, on everyone in England, or so I

---

[1] Many years later, when I read Keynes's wonderful description of Lloyd George (in *The Economic Consequences of the Peace*), I was strangely reminded of Auntie Lina. Keynes speaks of the British prime minister's "unerring, almost medium-like sensibility to everyone immediately around him."

To see [him], watching the company with six or seven senses not available to ordinary men, judging character, motive, and subconscious impulse, perceiving what each was thinking, and even what each was going to say next, compounding with telepathic instinct the argument or appeal best suited to the vanity, weakness, or self-interest of his immediate auditor was to realize that the poor President [Wilson] would be playing blind man's buff in that party.

sometimes imagined, and once she was certain of her information and sources, she would lift the phone. "Lord G.? This is Lina Halper." There would be a pause, a gasp, Lord G. would know what was coming. "Yes," she would continue pleasantly, "yes, you know me. There is that little business — no, we won't go into details — that little affair in Bognor, in March '23. . . . No, of course I won't mention it, it'll be our little secret — what can I put you down for? Fifty thousand, perhaps? I can't tell you what it would mean to the Hebrew University." By this sort of blackmail Lina raised millions of pounds for the university, the most efficient fund-raiser, probably, they had ever known.

Lina, considerably the oldest, had been "a little mother" to her much younger siblings when they came to England from Lithuania in 1899, and after the early death of her husband, she took over my father, in a sense, and vied with my mother for his company and affections. I was always aware of the tension, the unspoken rivalry, between them, and had a sense of my father — soft, passive, indecisive — being pulled this way and that between them.

While Lina was regarded by many in the family as a sort of monster, she had a soft spot for me, as I had for her. She was especially important to me, to all of us perhaps, at the start of the war, for we were in Bournemouth on our summer holiday when war was declared, and our parents, as doctors, had to leave immediately for London, leaving the four of us with the nanny. They came back a couple of weeks later, and my relief, our relief, was prodigious. I remember rushing down the garden path when I heard the hoot of the car, and flinging myself bodily into my mother's arms, so vehemently I almost knocked her over. "I've missed you," I cried, "I've missed you so much." She hugged me, a long hug, holding me tight in her arms, and the sense of loss, of fear, suddenly dissolved.

Our parents promised to come again very soon. They would try to manage the next weekend, they said, but there was a great deal for them to do in London — my mother was occupied with emergency trauma surgery, my father was organizing local G.P.s for casualties in air raids. But this time they did not come at the weekend. Another week passed, and another, and another, and something, I think, broke inside me at this point, for when they did come again, six weeks after their first visit, I did not run up to my mother or embrace her as I had the first time, but treated her coldly, impersonally, like a stranger. She was, I think,

20

shocked and bewildered by this, but did not know how to bridge the gulf that had come between us.

At this point, when the effects of parental absence had become unmistakable, Lina came up, took over the house, did the cooking, organized our lives, and became a little mother to us all, filling in the gap left by our own mother's absence.

This little interlude did not last long — Marcus and David went off to medical school, and Michael and I were packed off to Braefield. But I never forgot Lina's tenderness to me at this time, and after the war I took to visiting her in London, in her high-ceilinged, brocaded room in Elgin Avenue. She would give me cheesecake, sometimes a fish cake, and a little glass of sweet wine, and I would listen to her reminiscences of the old country. My father was only three or four when he left, and had no memories of it; Lina, eighteen or nineteen at the time, had vivid and fascinating memories of Joniški, the shtetl near Vilna where they had all been born, and of her parents, my grandparents, as they were in comparative youth. It may be that she had a special feeling for me as the youngest, or because I had the same name as her father, Elivelva, Oliver Wolf. I had the sense, too, that she was lonely and enjoyed the visits of her young nephew.

25 Then there was my father's brother, Bennie. Bennie had been excommunicated, left the family fold, at nineteen, when he had gone to Portugal and married a gentile, a shiksa. This was a crime so scandalous, so heinous in the eyes of the family that his name was never mentioned thereafter. But I knew there was something hidden, a family secret of sorts; I surprised certain silences, certain awkwardness, sometimes, when my parents whispered together, and I once saw a photo of Bennie on one of Lina's embossed cabinets (she said it was someone else, but I picked up the hesitation in her voice).

My father, always powerfully built, started to put on weight after the war and decided to go at regular intervals to a fat farm in Wales. These visits never seemed to do him much good, weight-wise, but he would come back from them looking happy and well, his London pallor replaced by a healthy tan. It was only after his death, many years later, that, looking through his papers, I found a sheaf of plane tickets that told the true story — he had never been to the fat farm at all, but loyally, secretly, had been going to visit Bennie in Portugal all these years.

David Sedaris

Genetic Engineering

David Sedaris was born in Johnson City, New York, in 1956 and grew up in Raleigh, North Carolina. He attended Kent State University but dropped out in 1977. Sedaris characterizes his early adult years as aimless: he hitchhiked around the country, then settled in Chicago, making a living by doing odd jobs. He also read voraciously and kept a diary, which became a rich source of material for his later writing. In 1987, Sedaris graduated from the School of the Art Institute of Chicago.

Sedaris transformed experiences recorded in his diary into humorous sketches. While reading one of his sketches at a Chicago nightclub, he was "discovered" by Ira Glass, who invited him to appear on his local radio program. Sedaris first read for a national radio audience in December of 1992, reading a story about his experience as a Christmas elf at Macy's in New York. He quickly became a regular contributor to the National Public Radio series "This American Life." His stories—about his family, his work, the odd characters he met—were enormously popular, and he soon contracted with Little, Brown to publish a collection.

His first book, *Barrel Fever: Stories and Essays,* was published in 1994. In the years since its publication, Sedaris has written stories for magazines, published four more book-length collections, collaborated with his sister Amy Sedaris on plays, and traveled across the United States and Europe on lecture tours. He likes the opportunity to do public readings, not only because it's important to hear the sound of the prose but because the responses of the audience guide his revisions.

Sedaris's writing is autobiographical, often featuring the eccentricities of his family. "Genetic Engineering" focuses on his father, who worked for IBM as an engineer, and mentions his brother, four sisters, and his mother, all of whom play key roles in other stories. Given the broad exaggeration of Sedaris's humor, it is difficult to know where autobiography ends and fiction begins. Asked about the accuracy of events in his stories, Sedaris has said, "I think autobiography is the last place you would look for truth." "Genetic Engineering," first published in *The New Yorker* in 1998, appears in *Me Talk Pretty One Day* (2000).

In 2001, Sedaris won the Thurber Prize for American Humor. He has been nominated for Grammy Awards for his recordings of *Dress Your Family in Corduroy and Denim* and *David Sedaris: Live at Carnegie Hall.* He lives in Paris with his partner, Hugh Hamrick.

My father always struck me as the sort of man who, under the right circumstances, might have invented the microwave oven or the transistor radio. You wouldn't seek him out for advice on a personal problem, but he'd be the first one you'd call when the dishwasher broke or someone flushed a hairpiece down your toilet. As children, we placed a great deal of faith in his ability but learned to steer clear while he was working. The experience of watching was ruined, time and time again, by an interminable explanation of how things were put together. Faced with an exciting question, science tended to provide the dullest possible answer. Ions might charge the air, but they fell flat when it came to charging the imagination — my imagination, anyway. To this day I prefer to believe that inside every television there lives a community of versatile, thumb-size actors trained to portray everything from a thoughtful newscaster to the wife of a millionaire stranded on a desert island. Fickle gnomes control the weather, and an air conditioner is powered by a team of squirrels, their cheeks packed with ice cubes.

Once, while rifling through the tool shed, I came across a poster advertising an IBM computer the size of a refrigerator. Sitting at the control board was my dad the engineer, years younger, examining a printout no larger than a grocery receipt. When I asked about it, he explained that he had worked with a team devising a memory chip capable of storing up to fifteen pages' worth of information. Out came the notepad and pencil, and I was trapped for hours as he answered every question except the one I had asked: "Were you allowed to wear makeup and run through a variety of different poses, or did they get the picture on the first take?"

To me, the greatest mystery of science continues to be that a man could father six children who shared absolutely none of his interests. We certainly expressed enthusiasm for our mother's hobbies, from smoking and napping to the writings of Sidney Sheldon. (Ask my mother how the radio worked and her answer was simple: "Turn it on and pull out the goddamn antenna.") I once visited my father's office, and walked away comforted to find that at least there he had a few people he could talk to. We'd gone, my sister Amy and I, to settle a bet. She thought that my father's secretary had a sharp, protruding chin and long blond hair, while I imagined that the woman might more closely resemble a tortoise — chinless, with a beaky nose and a loose, sagging neck. The correct answer was somewhere in between. I was right about the nose and the neck, but Amy won on the chin and the hair color. The bet had been the sole reason for our visit, and the resulting insufferable tour of Buildings A through D taught us never again to express an interest in our father's workplace.

My own scientific curiosity eventually blossomed, but I knew enough to keep my freakish experiments to myself. When my father discovered my colony of frozen slugs in the basement freezer, I chose not to explain my complex theories of suspended animation. Why was I filling the hamster's water beaker with vodka? "Oh, no reason." If my experiment failed, and the drunken hamster passed out, I'd just put her in the deep freeze, alongside the slugs. She'd rest on ice for a few months and, once thawed and fully revived, would remember nothing of her previous life as an alcoholic. I also took to repairing my own record-player and was astonished by my ingenuity for up to ten minutes at a time — until the rubber band snapped or the handful of change came unglued from the arm, and the damned thing broke all over again.

During the first week of September, it was my family's habit to 5
rent a beach house on Ocean Isle, a thin strip of land off the coast of North Carolina. As youngsters, we participated in all the usual seaside activities — which were fun, until my father got involved and systematically chipped away at our pleasure. Miniature golf was ruined with a lengthy dissertation on impact, trajectory, and wind velocity, and our sand castles were critiqued with stifling lectures on the dynamics of the vaulted ceiling. We enjoyed swimming, until the mystery of tides was explained in such a way that the ocean seemed nothing more than

an enormous saltwater toilet, flushing itself on a sad and predictable basis.

By the time we reached our teens, we were exhausted. No longer interested in the water, we joined our mother on the beach blanket and dedicated ourselves to the higher art of tanning. Under her guidance, we learned which lotions to start off with, and what worked best for various weather conditions and times of day. She taught us that the combination of false confidence and Hawaiian Tropic could result in a painful and unsightly burn, certain to subtract valuable points when, on the final night of vacation, contestants gathered for the annual Miss Emollient Pageant. This was a contest judged by our mother, in which the holder of the darkest tan was awarded a crown, a sash, and a scepter.

Technically, the prize could go to either a male or a female, but the sash read MISS EMOLLIENT because it was always assumed that my sister Gretchen would once again sweep the title. For her, tanning had moved from an intense hobby to something more closely resembling a psychological dysfunction. She was what we called a tanorexic: someone who simply could not get enough. Year after year she arrived at the beach with a base coat that the rest of us could only dream of achieving as our final product. With a mixture of awe and envy, we watched her broiling away on her aluminum blanket. The spaces between her toes were tanned, as were her palms and even the backs of her ears. Her method involved baby oil and a series of poses that tended to draw crowds, the mothers shielding their children's eyes with sand-covered fingers.

It is difficult for me to sit still for more than twenty minutes at a stretch, so I used to interrupt my tanning sessions with walks to the pier. On one of those walks, I came across my father standing not far from a group of fishermen who were untangling knots in a net the size of a circus tent. A lifetime of work beneath the coastal sun had left them with what my sisters and I referred to as the Samsonite Syndrome, meaning that their enviable color was negated by a hard, leathery texture reminiscent of the suitcase my mother stored all our baby pictures in. The men drank from quart bottles of Mountain Dew as they paused from their work to regard my father, who stood at the water's edge, staring at the shoreline with a stick in his hand.

I tried to creep by unnoticed, but he stopped me, claiming that I was just the fellow he'd been looking for. "Do you have any idea how many grains of sand there are in the world?" he asked. It was a question that had never occurred to me. Unlike guessing the number of pickled eggs in a jar or the amount of human brains it might take to equal the weight of a portable television set, this equation was bound to involve the hateful word *googolplex*, a term I'd heard him use once or twice before. It was an *idea* of a number and was, therefore, of no use whatsoever.

I'd heard once in school that if a single bird were to transport all the sand, grain by grain, from the eastern seaboard to the west coast of Africa, it would take . . . I didn't catch the number of years, preferring to concentrate on the single bird chosen to perform this thankless task. It hardly seemed fair, because, unlike a horse or a Seeing Eye dog, the whole glory of being a bird is that nobody would ever put you to work. Birds search for grubs and build their nests, but their leisure time is theirs to spend as they see fit. I pictured this bird looking down from the branches to say, "You want me to do what?" before flying off, laughing at the foolish story he now had to tell his friends. How many grains of sand are there in the world? A lot. Case closed.

My father took his stick and began writing an equation in the sand. Like all the rest of them, this one was busy with x's and y's resting on top of one another on dash-shaped bunks. Letters were multiplied by symbols, crowded into parentheses, and set upon by dwarfish numbers drawn at odd angles. The equation grew from six to twelve feet long before assuming a second line, at which point the fishermen took an interest. I watched them turn from their net, and admired the way they could smoke entire cigarettes without ever taking them from their mouths — a skill my mother had mastered and one that continues to elude me. It involves a symbiotic relationship with the wind: you have to know exactly how and when to turn your head in order to keep the smoke out of your eyes.

One of the men asked my father if he was a tax accountant, and he answered, "No, an engineer." These were poor men, who could no longer afford to live by the ocean, who had long ago sold their one-story homes for the valuable sand beneath them. Their houses had been torn down to make room for high-priced hotels and the A-frame cottages that now rented in season for a thousand dollars a week.

"Let me ask a little something," one of the men said, spitting his spent cigarette butt into the surf. "If I got paid twelve thousand dollars in 1962 for a half-acre beachfront lot, how much would that be worth per grain of sand by today's standard?"

"That, my friend, is a very interesting question," my father said.

15   He moved several yards down the beach and began a new equation, captivating his audience with a lengthy explanation of each new and complex symbol. "When you say *pie*," one man asked, "do you mean a real live pie, or one of those pie shapes they put on the news sometimes to show how much of your money goes to taxes?"

My father answered their questions in detail, and they listened intently — this group of men with nets, blowing their smoke into the wind. Stooped and toothless, they hung upon his every word while I stood in the lazy surf, thinking of the upcoming pageant and wondering if the light reflecting off the water might tan the underside of my nose and chin.

Jane Smiley

Say It Ain't So, Huck

Jane Smiley was born in Los Angeles, California, in 1949. Her parents had met in France four years earlier when her father, James Smiley, was stationed there and her mother, Frances Graves, was working as a journalist for the U.S. Army. After the war, the couple reunited and settled in Los Angeles, where James Smiley found work as an aeronautical engineer. However, he suffered from mental problems associated with his wartime service, and the marriage faltered. When Jane was four years old, the couple divorced, and she moved with her mother to Missouri, where she grew up surrounded by her extended family. Explaining that "an affinity for language" is essential for novelists, Smiley writes, "Possibly it runs in families—my relatives were always telling stories, making jokes, coming up with expressions and sayings. They were talkative, and they took pleasure in talk the way musical families take pleasure in music."

Smiley's youthful passions were books and horses. After graduating from a private preparatory school in Saint Louis, she took a summer job as a horse groomer before entering her freshman year at Vassar College. She married John Whitson and, upon graduating in 1971, traveled with him first to England and then to Iowa where Whitson pursued graduate study in history. She studied creative writing at the Iowa Writer's Workshop and linguistics and literature in the University of Iowa's English Department, where she earned her Ph.D.

Though the marriage to Whitson was short-lived, Smiley remained in Iowa, teaching at Iowa State University from 1981 until 1996. This was a prolific period: she wrote literary criticism, short stories, and magazine articles on topics ranging from motherhood to horse training to women's friendships to natural food. And she wrote nine novels including *A Thousand Acres* (1991), a feminist reinterpretation of *King Lear* that won the Pulitzer Prize for fiction, and the comic masterpiece *Moo* (1995), a satire of life and politics at a Midwestern university.

Smiley married twice more and gave birth to two daughters and a son. In 1996, she divorced her husband, gave up her position at Iowa State, and moved to Carmel, California, in order to devote more time to her writing and her horses. She lives in California "with her three children, three dogs, and her sixteen (and counting) horses." Recent books include the novels *Horse Heaven* (2000), *Good Faith* (2003), and *Ten Days in the Hills* (2007); a book about the life and writing of Charles Dickens (to whom Smiley is sometimes compared); and *Thirteen Ways of Looking at the Novel* (2005).

"Say It Ain't So, Huck" contrasts *Huckleberry Finn* to *Uncle Tom's Cabin*, arguing that Twain's novel is both artistically and politically flawed while Stowe's is underappreciated. Although the article, published in *Harper's* in 1996, was criticized by Twain scholars, Smiley can take some credit for a resurgence of interest in Stowe's work in this century.

So I broke my leg. Doesn't matter how — since the accident I've heard plenty of broken-leg tales, and, I'm telling you, I didn't realize that walking down the stairs, walking down hills, dancing in high heels, or stamping your foot on the brake pedal could be so dangerous. At any rate, like numerous broken-legged intellectuals before me, I found the prospect of three months in bed in the dining room rather seductive from a book-reading point of view, and I eagerly got started. Great novels piled up on my table, and right at the top was *The Adventures of Huckleberry Finn*, which, I'm embarrassed to admit, I hadn't read since junior high school. The novel took me a couple of days (it was longer than I had remembered), and I closed the cover stunned. Yes, stunned. Not, by any means, by the artistry of the book but by the notion that this is the novel all American literature grows out of, that this is a great novel, that this is even a serious novel.

Although Huck had his fans at publication, his real elevation into the pantheon was worked out early in the Propaganda Era, between 1948 and 1955, by Lionel Trilling, Leslie Fiedler, T. S. Eliot, Joseph Wood Krutch, and some lesser lights, in the introductions to American and British editions of the novel and in such journals as *Partisan Review* and *The New York Times Book Review*. The requirements of Huck's installation rapidly revealed themselves: the failure of the last twelve chapters (in which Huck finds Jim imprisoned on the Phelps plantation and Tom Sawyer is reintroduced and elaborates a cruel and unnecessary scheme for Jim's liberation) had to be diminished, accounted for, or forgiven; after that, the novel's special qualities had to be placed in the context first of other American novels (to their detriment) and then of world literature. The best bets here seemed to be Twain's style and the river setting, and the critics invested accordingly: Eliot, who had never read the novel as a boy, traded on his own childhood beside the big river, elevating Huck to the Boy, and the Mississippi to the River God, therein finding the sort of mythic resonance that he admired. Trilling liked the river god idea, too, though he didn't bother to capitalize it. He also thought that Twain, through Huck's lying, told truths, one of them being (I kid you not) that "something . . . had gone out of American life after the [Civil War], some simplicity, some innocence, some peace." What Twain himself was proudest of in the novel — his style — Trilling was glad to dub "not less than definitive in American literature. The prose of *Huckleberry Finn* established for written prose the virtues of American colloquial speech. . . . He is the master of the style that escapes the fixity of the printed page, that sounds in our ears with the immediacy of the heard voice, the very voice of unpretentious truth." The last requirement was some quality that would link Huck to other, though "lesser," American novels such as Herman Melville's *Moby-Dick*, that would possess some profound insight into the American character. Leslie Fiedler obligingly provided it when he read homoerotic attraction into the relationship between Huck and Jim, pointing out the similarity of this to such other white man–dark man friendships as those between Ishmael and Queequeg in *Moby-Dick* and Natty Bumppo and Chingachgook in James Fenimore Cooper's *Last of the Mohicans*.

The canonization proceeded apace: great novel (Trilling, 1950), greatest novel (Eliot, 1950), world-class novel (Lauriat Lane Jr., 1955). Sensible naysayers, such as Leo Marx, were lost in the shuffle of propaganda. But, in fact, *The Adventures of Huckleberry Finn* has little to offer in the way of greatness. There is more to be learned about the American character *from* its canonization than *through* its canonization.

Let me hasten to point out that, like most others, I don't hold any grudges against Huck himself. He's just a boy trying to survive. The villain here is Mark Twain, who knew how to give Huck a voice but didn't know how to give him a novel. Twain was clearly aware of the story's difficulties. Not finished with having revisited his boyhood in *Tom Sawyer*, Twain conceived of a sequel and began composition while still working on *Tom Sawyer*'s page proofs. Four hundred pages into it, having just passed Cairo and exhausted most of his memories of Hannibal and the upper Mississippi, Twain put the manuscript aside for three years. He was facing a problem every novelist is familiar with: his original conception was beginning to conflict with the implications of the actual story. It is at this point in the story that Huck and Jim realize two things: they have become close friends, and they have missed the Ohio River and drifted into what for Jim must be the most frightening territory of all — down the river, the very place Miss Watson was going to sell him to begin with. Jim's putative savior, Huck, has led him as far astray as a slave can go, and the farther they go, the worse it is going to be for him. Because the Ohio was not Twain's territory, the fulfillment of Jim's wish would necessarily lead the novel away from the artistic integrity that Twain certainly sensed his first four hundred pages possessed. He found himself writing not a boy's novel, like *Tom Sawyer*, but a man's novel, about real moral dilemmas and growth. The patina of nostalgia for a time and place, Missouri in the 1840s (not unlike former President Ronald Reagan's nostalgia for his own boyhood, when "Americans got along"), had been transformed into actual longing for a timeless place of friendship and freedom, safe and hidden, on the big river. But the raft had floated Huck and Jim, and their author with them, into the truly dark heart of the American soul and of American history: slave country.

5   Twain came back to the novel and worked on it twice again, once to rewrite the chapters containing the feud between the Grangerfords and the Shepherdsons, and later to introduce the Duke and the Dauphin. It is with the feud that the novel begins to fail, because from here on the episodes are mere distractions from the true subject of the work: Huck's affection for and responsibility to Jim. The signs of this failure are everywhere, as Jim is pushed to the side of the narrative, hiding on the raft and confined to it, while Huck follows the Duke and the Dauphin onshore to the scenes of much simpler and much less philosophically taxing moral dilemmas, such as fraud. Twain was by nature an improviser, and he was pleased enough with these improvisations to

continue. When the Duke and the Dauphin finally betray Jim by selling him for forty dollars, Huck is shocked, but the fact is neither he nor Twain has come up with a plan that would have saved Jim in the end. Tom Sawyer does that.

Considerable critical ink has flowed over the years in an attempt to integrate the Tom Sawyer chapters with the rest of the book, but it has flowed in vain. As Leo Marx points out, and as most readers sense intuitively, once Tom reappears, "[m]ost of those traits which made [Huck] so appealing a hero now disappear.... It should be added at once that Jim doesn't mind too much. The fact is that he has undergone a similar transformation. On the raft he was an individual, man enough to denounce Huck when Huck made him the victim of a practical joke. In the closing episode, however, we lose sight of Jim in the maze of farcical invention." And the last twelve chapters are boring, a sure sign that an author has lost the battle between plot and theme and is just filling in the blanks.

As with all bad endings, the problem really lies at the beginning, and at the beginning of *The Adventures of Huckleberry Finn* neither Huck nor Twain takes Jim's desire for freedom at all seriously; that is, they do not accord it the respect that a man's passion deserves. The sign of this is that not only do the two never cross the Mississippi to Illinois, a free state, but they hardly even consider it. In both *Tom Sawyer* and *Huckleberry Finn*, the Jackson's Island scenes show that such a crossing, even in secret, is both possible and routine, and even though it would present legal difficulties for an escaped slave, these would certainly pose no more hardship than locating the mouth of the Ohio and then finding passage up it. It is true that there could have been slave catchers in pursuit (though the novel ostensibly takes place in the 1840s and the Fugitive Slave Act was not passed until 1850), but Twain's moral failure, once Huck and Jim link up, is never even to account for their choice to go down the river rather than across it. What this reveals is that for all his lip service to real attachment between white boy and black man, Twain really saw Jim as no more than Huck's sidekick, homoerotic or otherwise. All the claims that are routinely made for the book's humanitarian power are, in the end, simply absurd. Jim is never autonomous, never has a vote, always finds his purposes subordinate to Huck's, and, like every good sidekick, he never minds. He grows ever more passive and also more affectionate as Huck and the Duke and the Dauphin and

Tom (and Twain) make ever more use of him for their own purposes. But this use they make of him is not supplementary; it is integral to Twain's whole conception of the novel. Twain thinks that Huck's affection is a good enough reward for Jim.

The sort of meretricious critical reasoning that has raised Huck's paltry good intentions to a "strategy of subversion" (David L. Smith) and a "convincing indictment of slavery" (Eliot) precisely mirrors the same sort of meretricious reasoning that white people use to convince themselves that they are not "racist." If Huck *feels* positive toward Jim, and *loves* him, and *thinks* of him as a man, then that's enough. He doesn't actually have to act in accordance with his feelings. White Americans always think racism is a feeling, and they reject it or they embrace it. To most Americans, it seems more honorable and nicer to reject it, so they do, but they almost invariably fail to understand that how they *feel* means very little to black Americans, who understand racism as a way of structuring American culture, American politics, and the American economy. To invest *The Adventures of Huckleberry Finn* with "greatness" is to underwrite a very simplistic and evasive theory of what racism is and to promulgate it, philosophically, in schools and the media as well as in academic journals. Surely the discomfort of many readers, black and white, and the censorship battles that have dogged *Huck Finn* in the last twenty years are understandable in this context. No matter how often the critics "place in context" Huck's use of the word "nigger," they can never excuse or fully hide the deeper racism of the novel — the way Twain and Huck use Jim because they really don't care enough about his desire for freedom to let that desire change their plans. And to give credit to Huck suggests that the only racial insight Americans of the nineteenth or twentieth century are capable of is a recognition of the obvious — that blacks, slave and free, are human.

Ernest Hemingway, thinking of himself, as always, once said that all American literature grew out of *Huck Finn*. It undoubtedly would have been better for American literature, and American culture, if our literature had grown out of one of the best-selling novels of all time, another American work of the nineteenth century, *Uncle Tom's Cabin*, which for its portrayal of an array of thoughtful, autonomous, and passionate black characters leaves *Huck Finn* far behind. *Uncle Tom's Cabin* was published in 1852, when Twain was seventeen, still living in Hannibal and contributing to his brother's newspapers, still sympathizing with the South, nine years before his abortive career in the Confederate Army. *Uncle Tom's Cabin* was the most popular novel of its era, universally controversial. In 1863, when Harriet Beecher Stowe visited the White House, Abraham Lincoln condescended to remark to her, "So this is the little lady who made this great war."

The story, familiar to most nineteenth-century Americans, either through the novel or through the many stage adaptations that sentimentalized Stowe's work, may be sketched briefly: A Kentucky slave, Tom, is sold to pay off a debt to a slave trader, who takes him to New Orleans. On the boat trip downriver, Tom is purchased by the wealthy Augustine St. Clare at the behest of his daughter, Eva. After Eva's death, and then St. Clare's, Tom is sold again, this time to Simon Legree, whose remote plantation is the site of every form of cruelty and degradation. The novel was immediately read and acclaimed by any number of excellent judges: Charles Dickens, George Eliot, Leo Tolstoy, George Sand — the whole roster of nineteenth-century liberals whose work we read today and try to persuade ourselves that *Huck Finn* is equal to. English novelist and critic Charles Kingsley thought *Uncle Tom's Cabin* the best novel ever written. These writers honored Stowe's book for all its myriad virtues. One of these was her adept characterization of a whole world of whites and blacks who find themselves gripped by slavery, many of whose names have entered the American language as expressions — not only Uncle Tom himself but Simon Legree and, to a lesser extent, little Eva and the black child Topsy. The characters appear, one after another, vivified by their attitudes, desires, and opinions as much as by their histories and their fates. Surely Augustine St. Clare, Tom's owner in New Orleans, is an exquisite portrayal of a humane but indecisive man, who knows what he is doing but not how to stop it. Surely Cassy, a fellow slave whom Tom meets on the Legree plantation, is one of the great angry women in all of literature — not only bitter, murderous, and nihilistic but also intelligent and enterprising. Surely the midlife spiritual journey of Ophelia St. Clare, Augustine's Yankee cousin, from self-confident ignorance to affectionate understanding is most convincing, as is Topsy's parallel journey from ignorance and self-hatred to humanity. The ineffectual Mr. Shelby and his submissive, and subversive, wife; the slave trader Haley; Tom's wife, Chloe; Augustine's wife, Marie; Legree's overseers, Sambo and Quimbo — good or evil, they all live.

As for Tom himself, we all know what an "Uncle Tom" is, except we don't. The popular Uncle Tom sucks up to the master and exhibits bovine patience. The real Uncle Tom is both a realist and a man of deep principle. When he is sold by Mr. Shelby in Kentucky, he knows enough of Shelby's affairs to know that what his master asserts is true: it's Tom who must go or the whole estate will be sold off for debt, including Tom's wife and three children. Later, on the Legree estate, his religious faith tells him that the greatest danger he finds there is not to his life but to his soul. His logic is impeccable. He holds fast to his soul, in the face of suffering, in a way that even nonbelievers like myself must respect. In fact, Tom's story eerily prefigures stories of spiritual solace through deep religious belief that have come out of both the Soviet Gulag and the Nazi concentration camp in the same way that the structure of power on Legree's plantation, and the suffering endured there, forecasts and duplicates many stories of recent genocides.

The power of *Uncle Tom's Cabin* is the power of brilliant analysis married to great wisdom of feeling. Stowe never forgets the logical end of any relationship in which one person is the subject and the other is the object. No matter how the two people feel, or what their intentions are, the logic of the relationship is inherently tragic and traps both parties until the false subject/object relationship is ended. Stowe's most oft-repeated and potent representation of this inexorable logic is the forcible separation of family members, especially of mothers from children. Eliza, faced with the sale of her child, Harry, escapes across the breaking ice of the Ohio River. Lucy, whose ten-month-old is sold behind her back, kills herself. Prue, who has been used for breeding, must listen to her last child cry itself to death because her mistress won't let her save it; she falls into alcoholism and thievery and is finally whipped to death. Cassy, prefiguring a choice made by one of the characters in Toni Morrison's *Beloved*, kills her last child so that it won't grow up in slavery. All of these women have been promised something by their owners — love, education, the privilege and joy of raising their children — but, owing to slavery, all of these promises have been broken. The grief and despair these women display is no doubt what T. S. Eliot was thinking of when he superciliously labeled *Uncle Tom's Cabin* "sensationalist propaganda," but, in fact, few critics in the nineteenth century ever accused Stowe of making up or even exaggerating such stories. One group of former slaves who were asked to comment on Stowe's depiction of slave life said that she had failed to portray the very worst, and Stowe herself was afraid that if she told some of what she had heard from escaped slaves and other informants during her eighteen years in Cincinnati, the book would be too dark to find any readership at all.

Stowe's analysis does not stop with the slave owners and traders, or with the slaves themselves. She understands perfectly that slavery is an economic system embedded in America as a whole, and she comments ironically on Christian bankers in New York whose financial dealings result in the sale of slaves, on Northern politicians who promote the capture of escaped slaves for the sake of the public good, on ministers of churches who give the system a Christian stamp of approval. One of Stowe's most skillful techniques is her method of weaving a discussion of slavery into the dialogue of her characters. Especially interesting is a conversation Mark Twain could have paid attention to. Augustine St. Clare and his abolitionist cousin, Ophelia, are discussing his failure to act in accordance with his feelings of revulsion against slavery. After entertaining Ophelia's criticisms for a period, Augustine points out that Ophelia herself is personally disgusted by black people and doesn't like to come into contact with them. He says, "You would think no harm in a child's caressing a large dog, even if he was black . . . custom with us does what Christianity ought to do, — obliterates the feeling of personal prejudice." When Ophelia takes over the education of Topsy, a child who has suffered a most brutal previous upbringing, she discovers that she can do nothing with her until she takes her, literally, to her bosom. But personal relationships do not mitigate the evils of slavery; Ophelia makes sure to give Topsy her freedom.

Stowe also understands that the real root of slavery is that it is profitable as well as customary. Augustine and his brother live with slavery because it is the system they know and because they haven't the imagination to live without it. Simon Legree embraces slavery because he can make money from it and because it gives him even more absolute power over his workers than he could find in the North or in England.

The very heart of nineteenth-century American experience and litera- 15 ture, the nature and meaning of slavery, is finally what Twain cannot face in *The Adventures of Huckleberry Finn*. As Jim and Huck drift down Twain's beloved river, the author finds himself nearing what must have been a crucial personal nexus: how to reconcile the felt memory of boyhood with the cruel implications of the social system within which that boyhood was lived. He had avoided this problem for the most part in *Tom Sawyer*: slaves hardly impinge on the lives of Tom and the other boys. But once Twain allows Jim a voice, this voice must speak in counterpoint to Huck's voice and must raise issues that cannot easily be resolved, either personally or culturally. Harriet Beecher Stowe, New Englander, daughter of Puritans and thinkers, active in the abolitionist movement and in the effort to aid and educate escaped slaves, had no such personal conflict when she sat down to write *Uncle Tom's Cabin*. Nothing about slavery was attractive to her either as a New Englander or as a resident of Cincinnati for almost twenty years. Her lack of conflict is apparent in the clarity of both the style and substance of the novel.

Why, then, we may ask, did *Uncle Tom's Cabin*, for all its power and popularity, fail to spawn American literature? Fail, even, to work as a model for how to draw passionate, autonomous, and interesting black literary characters? Fail to keep the focus of the American literary imagination on the central dilemma of the American experience: race? Part of the reason is certainly that the public conversation about race and slavery that had been a feature of antebellum American life fell silent after the Civil War. Perhaps the answer is to be found in *The Adventures of Huckleberry Finn*: everyone opted for the ultimate distraction, lighting out for the territory. And the reason is to be found in *Uncle Tom's Cabin*: that's where the money was.

But so what? These are only authors, after all, and once a book is published the author can't be held accountable for its role in the culture. For that we have to blame the citizens themselves, or their teachers, or *their* teachers, the arbiters of critical taste. In "Melodramas of Beset Manhood: How Theories of American Fiction Exclude Women Authors," the scholar Nina Baym has already detailed how the canonization of a very narrow range of white, Protestant, middle-class male authors (Twain, Hawthorne, Melville, Emerson, etc.) has misrepresented our literary life — first by defining the only worthy American literary subject as "the struggle of the individual against society [in which] the essential quality of America comes to reside in its unsettled wilderness and the opportunities that such a wilderness offers to the individual as the medium on which he may inscribe, unhindered, his own destiny and his own nature," and then by casting women, and especially women writers (specialists in the "flagrantly bad best-seller," according to Leslie Fiedler), as the enemy. In such critical readings, all other themes and modes of literary expression fall out of consideration as "un-American." There goes *Uncle Tom's Cabin*, there goes Edith Wharton, there goes domestic life as a subject, there go almost all the best-selling novelists of the nineteenth century and their readers, who were mostly women. The real loss, though, is not to our literature but to our culture and ourselves, because we have lost the subject of how the various social groups who may not escape to the wilderness are to get along in society; and, in the case of *Uncle Tom's Cabin*, the hard-nosed, unsentimental dialogue about race that we should have been having since before the Civil War. Obviously, *Uncle Tom's Cabin* is no more the last word on race relations than *The Brothers Karamazov* or *David Copperfield* is on any number of characteristically Russian or English themes and social questions. Some of Stowe's ideas about inherent racial characteristics (whites: cold, heartless; blacks: naturally religious and warm) are bad and have been exploded. One of her solutions to the American racial conflicts that she foresaw, a colony in Africa, she later repudiated. Nevertheless, her views about many issues were brilliant, and her heart was wise. She gained the respect and friendship of many men and women of goodwill, black and white, such as Frederick Douglass, the civil-rights activist Mary Church Terrill, the writer and social activist James Weldon Johnson, and W. E. B. Du Bois. What she did was find a way to talk about slavery and family, power and law, life and death, good and evil, North and South. She truly believed that all Americans together had to find a solution to the problem of slavery in which all were implicated. When her voice, a courageously public voice — as demonstrated by the public arguments about slavery that rage throughout *Uncle Tom's Cabin* — fell silent in our culture and was replaced by the secretive voice of Huck Finn, who acknowledges Jim only when they are alone on the raft together out in the middle of the big river, racism fell out of the public world and into the private one, where whites think it really is but blacks know it really isn't.

Should *Huckleberry Finn* be taught in the schools? The critics of the Propaganda Era laid the groundwork for the universal inclusion of the book in school curriculums by declaring it great. Although they predated the current generation of politicized English professors, this was clearly a political act, because the entry of *Huck Finn* into classrooms sets the terms of the discussion of racism and American history, and sets them very low: all you have to do to be a hero is acknowledge that your poor sidekick is human; you don't actually have to act in the interests of his humanity. Arguments about censorship have been regularly turned into nonsense by appeals to Huck's "greatness." Moreover, so much critical thinking has gone into defending Huck so that he *can* be great, so that American literature can be found different from and maybe better than Russian or English or French literature, that the very integrity of the critical enterprise has been called into question. That most readers intuitively reject the last twelve chapters of the novel on the grounds of tedium or triviality is clear from the fact that so many critics have turned themselves inside out to defend them. Is it so mysterious that criticism has failed in our time after being so robust only a generation ago? Those who cannot be persuaded that *The Adventures of Huckleberry Finn* is a great novel have to draw *some* conclusion.

I would rather my children read *Uncle Tom's Cabin*, even though it is far more vivid in its depiction of cruelty than *Huck Finn*, and this is because Stowe's novel is clearly and unmistakably a tragedy. No whitewash, no secrets, but evil, suffering, imagination, endurance, and redemption — just like life. Like little Eva, who eagerly but fearfully listens to the stories of the slaves that her family tries to keep from her, our children want to know what is going on, what has gone on, and what we intend to do about it. If "great" literature has any purpose, it is to help us face up to our responsibilities instead of enabling us to avoid them once again by lighting out for the territory.

Andrew Sullivan

Marriage or Bust

Andrew Sullivan was born in 1963, and he grew up in southern England, not far from London. At age eighteen, he entered Magdalen College in Oxford, where he studied modern history and languages. He was elected president of the Oxford Union, a center for debating and politics. After receiving a Harkness Fellowship to study in the United States, Sullivan earned his master's degree in public administration and doctorate in political science from Harvard's John F. Kennedy School of Government.

Sullivan's career as a journalist began with summer internships— at the *Daily Telegraph* in London and, in the summer of 1986, at *The New Republic*, a magazine about news and politics. In 1991, at the age of twenty-seven, he was appointed acting editor, and at the end of that year he took over as editor. During his five-year tenure as editor of *The New Republic*, Sullivan reshaped the magazine, expanding its scope to include such social issues as affirmative action, health care, and gay rights. Sullivan's choices as editor were sometimes controversial; for example, when he opted to print chapters from the 1995 book *The Bell Curve*, which was widely regarded as racist, seasoned staff writers threatened to resign. But the magazine's circulation and revenues grew under his leadership. In 1996, *Adweek* awarded Sullivan the Editor of the Year award.

Sullivan identifies himself as a conservative, favoring low taxes and limited government, and he is a practicing Catholic. However, he breaks from the political right and from his church on the issue of gay rights. His 1993 essay, "The Politics of Homosexuality" is a landmark in gay rights literature. His 1995 book *Virtually Normal* argues for an end to state-sponsored discrimination against homosexuals, particularly the prohibition on military careers and the denial of civil marriage. In *Love Undetectable: Notes on Friendship, Sex, and Survival* (1998), Sullivan draws on his experiences as an HIV-positive gay man trying to make sense of the AIDS epidemic.

Since leaving *The New Republic* in 1996, Sullivan has written for many publications including *Esquire*, the *New York Times*, the *Sunday Times of London*, *The Atlantic*, and *Time*. In 2000, Sullivan began his own blog, the *Daily Dish*, which he moved to *The Atlantic Online* in 2007. "Marriage or Bust," published by *The New Republic* in May 2000, features the clear, carefully reasoned argumentation that characterizes Sullivan's work.

Sullivan was married in 2007. He lives in Washington, D.C., with his husband, Aaron Tone.

Perhaps the current moment was inevitable. Around one-third of Americans support civil marriage for gay men and lesbians; another third are strongly opposed; the final third are sympathetic to the difficulties gay couples face but do not approve of gay marriage as such. In the last ten years or so, there has been some movement in these numbers, but not much. The conditions, in short, were ripe for a compromise: a pseudomarital institution, designed specifically for gay couples, that would include most, even all, of the rights and responsibilities of civil marriage but avoid the word itself. And last week, in a historic decision, Vermont gave it to us: a new institution called "civil union."

Understandably, many gay rights groups seem ready to declare victory. They have long been uncomfortable with the marriage battle. The platform of this weekend's Millennium March on Washington for gay rights merely refers to security for all kinds of "families." The Human Rights Campaign, the largest homosexual lobbying group, avoids the m-word in almost all its literature. They have probably listened to focus groups that included people like my mother. "That's all very well," she told me in my first discussion with her on the subject, "but can't you call it something other than 'marriage'?"

The answer to that question is no. Marriage, under any interpretation of American constitutional law, is among the most basic civil rights. "Separate but equal" was a failed and pernicious policy with regard to race; it will be a failed and pernicious policy with regard to sexual orientation. The many advances of recent years — the "domestic partnership" laws passed in many cities and states, the generous package of benefits finally granted in Hawaii, the breakthrough last week in Vermont — should not be thrown out. But neither can they be accepted as a solution, as some straight liberals and gay pragmatists seem to want. In fact, these half-measures, far from undermining the case for complete equality, only sharpen it. For there are no arguments for civil union that do not apply equally to marriage. To endorse one but not the other, to concede the substance of the matter while withholding the name and form of the relationship, is to engage in an act of pure stigmatization. It risks not only perpetuating public discrimination against a group of citizens but adding to the cultural balkanization that already plagues American public life.

This essay is not intended for those who believe that homosexual love is sinful or immoral, or who hold that homosexuality is a sickness that can be cured, or who claim that homosexual relationships are inherently dysfunctional; these are not the people pushing the civil-union compromise. With at least a veneer of consistency, these groups want no recognition for gay couples at all. No, the people heralding civil unions are generally sympathetic to homosexual rights. They are the allies that the marriage cause cannot afford to lose. They acknowledge the equal humanity of their gay friends and fellow citizens. But they need to see that supporting civil union while opposing marriage is an incoherent position — based more on sentiment than on reason, more on prejudice than principle. Liberals, of all people, should resist it.

The most common liberal argument for civil union but against   5
marriage was summed up by First Lady Hillary Rodham Clinton in January. "Marriage," she said, when pressed to take a position, "has got historic, religious, and moral content that goes back to the beginning of time, and I think a marriage is as a marriage has always been: between a man and a woman." This statement, which is more elaborate than anything said by Vice President Al Gore or Texas Governor George W. Bush on the topic, is worth examining.

It has two aspects. The first is an appeal to the moral, historical, and religious content of an institution unchanged since "the beginning of time." But even a cursory historical review reveals this to be fragile. The institution of civil marriage, like most human institutions, has undergone vast changes over the last two millennia. If marriage were the same today as it has been for 2,000 years, it would be possible to marry a twelve-year-old you had never met, to own a wife as property and dispose of her at will, or to imprison a person who married someone of a different race. And it would be impossible to get a divorce. One might equally say that New York's senators are men and have always been men. Does that mean a woman should never be a senator from New York?

Equally, an appeal to the religious content of marriage is irrelevant in this case. No one is proposing that faith communities be required to change their definitions of marriage, unless such a community, like Reform Jewry, decides to do so of its own free will. The question at hand is civil marriage and only civil marriage. In a country where church and state are separate, this is no small distinction. Many churches, for example, forbid divorce. But civil divorce is still legal. Many citizens adhere to no church at all. Should they be required to adhere to a religious teaching in order to be legally married?

So, if we accept that religion doesn't govern civil marriage and that civil marriage changes over time, we are left with a more nebulous worry. Why is this change to marriage more drastic than previous ones? This, I think, is what Clinton is getting at in her second point: "I think a marriage is as a marriage has always been: between a man and a woman." On the face of it, this is a statement of the obvious, which is why formulations of this kind have been favorites of those behind "defense of marriage" acts and initiatives across the country. But what, on further reflection, can it possibly mean? There are, I think, several possibilities.

The first is that marriage is primarily about procreation. It is an institution fundamentally designed to provide a stable environment for the rearing of children — and only a man and a woman, as a biological fact, can have their own children within such a marriage. So civil marriage is reserved for heterosexuals for a good, demonstrative reason. The only trouble with this argument is that it ignores the fact that civil marriage is granted automatically to childless couples, sterile couples, couples who marry too late in life to have children, couples who adopt other people's children, and so on. The proportion of marriages that conform to the "ideal" — two people with biological children in the home — has been declining for some time. The picture is further complicated by the fact that an increasing number of gay couples, especially women, also have children. Is there some reason a heterosexual couple without children should have the rights and responsibilities of civil marriage but a lesbian couple with biological children from both mothers should not? Not if procreation is your guide.

Indeed, if it is, shouldn't we exclude *all* childless couples from marriage?   10
That, at least, would be coherent. But how would childless heterosexual couples feel about it? They would feel, perhaps, what gay couples now feel, which is that society is diminishing the importance of their relationships by consigning them to a category that seems inferior to the desired social standard. They would resist and protest. They would hardly be satisfied with a new legal relationship called civil union.

Another interpretation of Hillary Clinton's comment is that real marriage must involve the unique experience of a man attempting to relate to a woman and vice versa. Some theologians have even argued that a heterosexual relationship is a unique opportunity for personal growth, because understanding a person of the opposite sex is more daunting and enriching than understanding a person of the same sex. So opposite-sex marriage builds character and empathy in a way same-sex marriage does not and therefore deserves greater social encouragement. Opposite-sex marriage fosters the virtues — communication, empathy, tolerance — necessary in a liberal democracy.

Leave aside the odd idea that heterosexual relationships are more difficult than gay ones. The problem with the character-building argument is that today's marriage law is utterly uninterested in character. There are no legal requirements that a married couple learn from each other, grow together spiritually, or even live together. A random woman can marry a multimillionaire on a Fox TV special and the law will accord that marriage no less validity than a lifelong commitment between Billy Graham and his wife. The courts have upheld an absolutely unrestricted right to marry for deadbeat dads, men with countless divorces behind them, prisoners on death row, even the insane. In all this, we make a distinction between what religious and moral tradition expect of marriage and what civil authorities require to sanction it under law. It may well be that some religious traditions want to preserve marriage for heterosexuals in order to encourage uniquely heterosexual virtues. And they may have good reason to do so. But civil law asks only four questions before handing out a marriage license: Are you an adult; are you already married; are you related to the person you intend to marry; and are you straight? It's that last question that rankles. When civil law already permits the delinquent, the divorced, the imprisoned, the sterile, and the insane to marry, it seems — how should I put this? — revealing that it draws the line at homosexuals.

Indeed, there is no moral reason to support civil unions and not same-sex marriage unless you believe that admitting homosexuals would weaken a vital civil institution. This was the underlying argument for the Defense of Marriage Act (DOMA), which implied that allowing homosexuals to marry constituted an "attack" on the existing institution. Both Gore and Bush take this position. Both Bill and Hillary Clinton have endorsed it. In fact, it is by far the most popular line of argument in the debate. But how, exactly, does the freedom of a gay couple to marry weaken a straight couple's commitment to the same institution? The obvious answer is that since homosexuals are inherently depraved and immoral, allowing them to marry would inevitably spoil, even defame, the institution of marriage. It would wreck the marital neighborhood, so to speak, and fewer people would want to live there. Part of the attraction of marriage for some heterosexual males, the argument goes, is that it confers status. One of the ways it does this is by distinguishing such males from despised homosexuals. If you remove that social status, you further weaken an already beleaguered institution.

This argument is rarely made explicitly, but I think it exists in the minds of many who supported the DOMA. One wonders, for example, what Bill Clinton or Newt Gingrich, both conducting or about to conduct extramarital affairs at the time, thought they were achieving by passing the DOMA. But, whatever its rationalization, this particular argument can only be described as an expression of pure animus. To base the prestige of marriage not on its virtues, responsibilities, and joys but on the fact that it keeps gays out is to engage in the crudest demagoguery. As a political matter, to secure the rights of a majority by eviscerating the rights of a minority is the opposite of what a liberal democracy is supposed to be about. It certainly should be inimical to anyone with even a vaguely liberal temperament.

15   Others argue that they base their opposition to gay marriage not on mere prejudice but on reality. Gay men, they argue, are simply incapable of the commitment, monogamy, and responsibility of heterosexuals. They should therefore be excluded as a group from an institution that rests on those virtues. They suspect that if gay marriage were legal, homosexuals would create a new standard of adultery, philandery, and infidelity that would lower the standards for the population as a whole. But, again, this is to set a bar for homosexual marriage that doesn't exist

for any other group. The law as it now stands makes no judgments about the capacity of those seeking a marriage license to fulfill its obligations. Perhaps if it did the divorce rate would be lower. But it doesn't, and in a free society it shouldn't. The law understands that different people will have different levels of achievement in marriage. Many will experience divorce; some marriages may not last a week, while others may last a lifetime; still other couples might construct all sorts of personal arrangements to keep their marriages going. But the right to marry does not take any of this into account, and failing marriages and successful marriages are identical in the eyes of the law. Why should this sensible and humane approach work for everyone but homosexuals?

Or look at it this way. Even if you concede that gay men — being men — are, in the aggregate, less likely to live up to the standards of monogamy and commitment that marriage demands, this still suggests a further question: Are they less likely than, say, an insane person? A straight man with multiple divorces behind him? A murderer on death row? A president of the United States? The truth is, these judgments simply cannot be fairly made against a whole group of people. We do not look at, say, the higher divorce and illegitimacy rates among African Americans and conclude that they should have the right to marry taken away from them. In fact, we conclude the opposite: It's precisely *because* of the high divorce and illegitimacy rates that the institution of marriage is so critical for black America. So why is that argument not applied to homosexuals?

This, however, is to concede for the sake of argument something I do not in fact concede. The truth is that there is little evidence that same-sex marriages will be less successful than straight marriages. Because marriage will be a new experience for most gay people, one they have struggled for decades to achieve, its privileges will not be taken for granted. My own bet is that gay marriages may well turn out to be more responsible, serious, and committed than straight ones. Many gay men may not, in practice, want to marry. But those who do will be making a statement in a way no heterosexual couple now can. They will be pioneers. And pioneers are rarely disrespectful of the land they newly occupy. In Denmark, in the decade since Vermont-style partnerships have been legal, gays have had a lower divorce rate than straights. And that does not even take into account the fact that a significant proportion of same-sex marriages in America will likely be between women.

If gay men, being men, are less likely to live up to the monogamy of marriage, then gay women, being women, are more likely to be faithful than heterosexual couples. Far from wrecking the neighborhood, gay men and women may help fix it up.

There remains the more genuine worry that marriage is such a critical institution that we should tamper with it in any way only with extreme reluctance. This admirable concern seems to me easily the strongest argument against equal marriage rights. But it is a canard that gay men and women are unconcerned about the stability of heterosexual marriage. Most homosexuals were born into such relationships; we know and cherish them. It's precisely because these marriages are the context of most gay lives that homosexuals seek to be a part of them. But the inclusion of gay people is, in fact, a comparatively small change. It will affect no existing heterosexual marriage. It will mean no necessary change in religious teaching. If you calculate that gay men and women amount to about three percent of the population, it's likely they will make up perhaps one or two percent of all future civil marriages. The actual impact will be tiny. Compare it to, say, the establishment in this century of legal divorce. That change potentially affected not one percent but 100 percent of marriages and today transforms one marriage out of two. If any legal change truly represented the "end of marriage," it was forged in Nevada, not Vermont.

But if civil union gives homosexuals everything marriage grants heterosexuals, why the fuss? First, because such an arrangement once again legally divides Americans with regard to our central social institution. Like the miscegenation laws, civil union essentially creates a two-tiered system, with one marriage model clearly superior to the other. The benefits may be the same, as they were for black couples, but the segregation is just as profound. One of the greatest merits of contemporary civil marriage as an institution is its civic simplicity. Whatever race you are, whatever religion, whatever your politics or class or profession, marriage is marriage is marriage. It affirms a civil equality that emanates outward into the rest of our society. To carve within it a new, segregated partition is to make the same mistake we made with miscegenation. It is to balkanize one of the most important unifying institutions we still have. It is an illiberal impulse in theory and in practice, and liberals should oppose it.

And, second, because marriage is not merely an accumulation of 20
benefits. It is a fundamental mark of citizenship. In its rulings, the
Supreme Court has found that the right to marry is vested not merely
in the Bill of Rights but in the Declaration of Independence itself. In
the Court's view, expressed by Chief Justice Earl Warren in *Loving v.
Virginia* in 1967, "the freedom to marry has long been recognized as
one of the vital personal rights essential to the orderly pursuit of happiness by free men." It is one of the most fundamental rights accorded
under the Constitution. Hannah Arendt put it best in her evisceration
of miscegenation laws in 1959: "The right to marry whoever one wishes
is an elementary human right compared to which 'the right to attend an
integrated school, the right to sit where one pleases on a bus, the right
to go into any hotel or recreation area or place of amusement, regardless
of one's skin or color or race' are minor indeed. Even political rights, like
the right to vote, and nearly all other rights enumerated in the Constitution, are secondary to the inalienable human rights to 'life, liberty and
the pursuit of happiness' . . . and to this category the right to home and
marriage unquestionably belongs."

Prior even to the right to vote! You can see Arendt's point. Would
any heterosexual in America believe he had a right to pursue happiness if he could not marry the person he loved? What would be more
objectionable to most people — to be denied a vote in next November's
presidential election or to no longer have legal custody over their child
or legal attachment to their wife or husband? Not a close call.

In some ways, I think it's because this right is so taken for granted
that it still does not compute for some heterosexuals that gay people
don't have it. I have been invited to my fair share of weddings. At no
point, I think, has it dawned on any of the participants that I was being
invited to a ceremony from which I was legally excluded. I have heard no
apologies, no excuses, no reassurances that the couple marrying would
support my own marriage or my legal right to it. Friends mention their
marriages with ease and pleasure without it even occurring to them
that they are flaunting a privilege constructed specifically to stigmatize
the person they are talking to. They are not bad people; they are not
homophobes. Like whites inviting token black guests to functions at
all-white country clubs, they think they are extending you an invitation
when they are actually demonstrating your exclusion. They just don't
get it. And some, of course, never will.

There's one more thing. When an extremely basic civil right is involved, it seems to me the burden of proof should lie with those who seek to deny it to a small minority of citizens, not with those who seek to extend it. So far, the opposite has been the case. Those of us who have argued for this basic equality have been asked to prove a million negatives: that the world will not end, that marriage will not collapse, that this reform will not lead to polygamy and incest and bestiality and the fall of Rome. Those who wish to deny it, on the other hand, have been required to utter nothing more substantive than Hillary Clinton's terse, incoherent dismissal. Gore, for example, has still not articulated a persuasive reason for his opposition to gay marriage, beyond a one-sentence affirmation of his own privilege. But surely if civil marriage involves no substantive requirement that adult gay men and women cannot fulfill, if gay love truly is as valid as straight love, and if civil marriage is a deeper constitutional right than the right to vote, then the continued exclusion of gay citizens from civil marriage is a constitutional and political enormity. It is those who defend the status quo who should be required to prove their case beyond even the slightest doubt.

They won't have to, of course. The media will congratulate George W. Bush merely for conceding that the gay people supporting his campaign are human beings. Gore will be told by his pollsters that supporting the most basic civil right for homosexuals would be political suicide, and he will surely defer to them. That is politics, and I have learned to expect nothing more from either candidate. But the principle of the matter is another issue. To concede that gay adults are responsible citizens, to concede that there will be no tangible damage to the institution of marriage by their inclusion within it, and then to offer gay men and women a second-class institution called civil union makes no sense. It's a well-meaning surrender to unfounded fear. Liberals of any stripe should see this. The matter is ultimately simple enough. Gay men and women are citizens of this country. After two centuries of invisibility and persecution, they deserve to be recognized as such.

Amy Tan

Mother Tongue

Amy Tan's first publication was a brief essay called "What the Library Means to Me." The essay, printed in the Santa Rosa *Press Democrat* in 1960, begins,

> My name is Amy Tan, 8 years old, a third grader in Matanzas School. It is a brand new school and everything is so nice and pretty. I love school because the many things I learn seem to turn on a light in the little room in my mind. . . . My father takes me to the library every two weeks, and I check five or six books each time. These books seem to open many windows in my little room.

Tan's father, John Tan, was trained as an electrical engineer, but shortly after moving from China to the United States in 1947, he settled in California and entered the Baptist ministry. He nurtured his daughter's love of language not only through biweekly trips to the library but by reading bedtime stories, drafts of his sermons, even his homework for graduate courses in engineering. When Amy was fifteen, she lost both her father and her older brother to brain tumors; they died within eight months of each other. Her mother, Daisy Tan, moved with her surviving children to the Netherlands and then to Switzerland. After Amy's graduation from a high school in Switzerland, her family returned to California where she studied English and linguistics at San Jose State University.

Tan's relationship with her mother was strained, the unavoidable tensions of family life having been heightened by Mrs. Tan's expectations that her daughter have both "American circumstances and Chinese character." Tan and her mother were estranged during her college years but later reconciled and, in 1987, traveled together to China where Tan came to appreciate the hardships her mother had endured as a young woman.

Much of Tan's fiction explores mother-daughter relationships in Chinese American families. Her first book, *The Joy Luck Club* (1989), was an extraordinary success. A finalist for the National

Book Award and the National Book Critics Circle award, it was on the *New York Times* bestseller list for eight months. Tan's second novel, *The Kitchen God's Wife* (1991), is based on her mother's life. More recent novels include *The Hundred Secret Senses* (1995), *The Bonesetter's Daughter* (2001), and *Saving Fish from Drowning* (2005).

The intellectual curiosity evident in "What the Library Means to Me" motivates Tan's work as a writer. "I write for very much the same reason that I read: to startle my mind, to churn my heart, to tingle my spine, to knock the blinders off my eyes and allow me to see beyond the pale." Writers who have influenced Tan's work include Jamaica Kincaid, Vladimir Nabokov, and Louise Erdrich (she identifies Erdrich's *Love Medicine* as "the book that made me want to find my own voice").

"Mother Tongue" was written as a speech in 1989 and later revised for publication in *The Threepenny Review*. It was selected for *Best American Essays 1991*, and Tan included it in her 2003 collection, *The Opposite of Fate: A Book of Musings*.

Amy Tan lives in San Francisco with her husband, Lou DeMattei.

I am not a scholar of English or literature. I cannot give you much more than personal opinions on the English language and its variations in this country or others.

I am a writer. And by that definition, I am someone who has always loved language. I am fascinated by language in daily life. I spend a great deal of my time thinking about the power of language — the way it can evoke an emotion, a visual image, a complex idea, or a simple truth. Language is the tool of my trade. And I use them all — all the Englishes I grew up with.

Recently, I was made keenly aware of the different Englishes I do use. I was giving a talk to a large group of people, the same talk I had already given to half a dozen other groups. The nature of the talk was about my writing, my life, and my book, *The Joy Luck Club*. The talk was going along well enough, until I remembered one major difference that made the whole talk sound wrong. My mother was in the room. And it was perhaps the first time she had heard me give a lengthy speech, using the kind of English I have never used with her. I was saying things like, "The intersection of memory upon imagination" and "There is an aspect of my fiction that relates to thus-and-thus" — a speech filled with carefully wrought grammatical phrases, burdened, it suddenly seemed to me, with nominalized forms, past perfect tenses, conditional phrases, all the forms of standard English that I had learned in school and through books, the forms of English I did not use at home with my mother.

Just last week, I was walking down the street with my mother, and I again found myself conscious of the English I was using, the English I do use with her. We were talking about the price of new and used furniture and I heard myself saying this: "Not waste money that way." My husband was with us as well, and he didn't notice any switch in my English. And then I realized why. It's because over the twenty years we've been together I've often used that same kind of English with him, and sometimes he even uses it with me. It has become our language of intimacy, a different sort of English that relates to family talk, the language I grew up with.

So you'll have some idea of what this family talk I heard sounds like, I'll quote what my mother said during a recent conversation which I videotaped and then transcribed. During this conversation, my mother was talking about a political gangster in Shanghai who had the same last name as her family's, Du, and how the gangster in his early years wanted to be adopted by her family, which was rich by comparison. Later, the gangster became more powerful, far richer than my mother's family, and one day showed up at my mother's wedding to pay his respects. Here's what she said in part:

"Du Yusong having business like fruit stand. Like off the street kind. He is Du like Du Zong — but not Tsung-ming Island people. The local people call putong, the river east side, he belong to that side local people. That man want to ask Du Zong father take him in like become own family. Du Zong father wasn't look down on him, but didn't take seriously, until that man big like become a mafia. Now important person, very hard to inviting him. Chinese way, came only to show respect, don't stay for dinner. Respect for making big celebration, he shows up. Mean gives lots of respect. Chinese custom. Chinese social life that way. If too important won't have to stay too long. He come to my wedding. I didn't see, I heard it. I gone to boy's side, they have YMCA dinner. Chinese age I was nineteen."

5

You should know that my mother's expressive command of English belies how much she actually understands. She reads the *Forbes* report, listens to *Wall Street Week*, converses daily with her stockbroker, reads all of Shirley MacLaine's books with ease — all kinds of things I can't begin to understand. Yet some of my friends tell me they understand 50 percent of what my mother says. Some say they understand 80 to 90 percent. Some say they understand none of it, as if she were speaking pure Chinese. But to me, my mother's English is perfectly clear, perfectly natural. It's my mother tongue. Her language, as I hear it, is vivid, direct, full of observation and imagery. That was the language that helped shape the way I saw things, expressed things, made sense of the world.

Lately, I've been giving more thought to the kind of English my mother speaks. Like others, I have described it to people as "broken" or "fractured" English. But I wince when I say that. It has always bothered me that I can think of no way to describe it other than "broken," as if it were damaged and needed to be fixed, as if it lacked a certain wholeness and soundness. I've heard other terms used, "limited English," for example. But they seem just as bad, as if everything is limited, including people's perceptions of the limited English speaker.

I know this for a fact, because when I was growing up, my mother's "limited" English limited *my* perception of her. I was ashamed of her English. I believed that her English reflected the quality of what she had to say. That is, because she expressed them imperfectly her thoughts were imperfect. And I had plenty of empirical evidence to support me: the fact that people in department stores, at banks, and at restaurants did not take her seriously, did not give her good service, pretended not to understand her, or even acted as if they did not hear her.

10   My mother has long realized the limitations of her English as well. When I was fifteen, she used to have me call people on the phone to pretend I was she. In this guise, I was forced to ask for information or even to complain and yell at people who had been rude to her. One time it was a call to her stockbroker in New York. She had cashed out her small portfolio and it just so happened we were going to go to New York the next week, our very first trip outside California. I had to get on the phone and say in an adolescent voice that was not very convincing, "This is Mrs. Tan."

And my mother was standing in the back whispering loudly, "Why he don't send me check, already two weeks late. So mad he lie to me, losing me money." And then I said in perfect English, "Yes, I'm getting rather concerned. You had agreed to send the check two weeks ago, but it hasn't arrived." Then she began to talk more loudly. "What he want, I come to New York tell him front of his boss, you cheating me?" And I was trying to calm her down, make her be quiet, while telling the stockbroker, "I can't tolerate any more excuses. If I don't receive the check immediately, I am going to have to speak to your manager when I'm in New York next week." And sure enough, the following week there we were in front of this astonished stockbroker, and I was sitting there red-faced and quiet, and my mother, the real Mrs. Tan, was shouting at his boss in her impeccable broken English.

We used a similar routine just five days ago, for a situation that was far less humorous. My mother had gone to the hospital for an appointment, to find out about a benign brain tumor a CAT scan had revealed a month ago. She said she had spoken very good English, her best English, no mistakes. Still, she said, the hospital did not apologize when they said they had lost the CAT scan and she had come for nothing. She said they did not seem to have any sympathy when she told them she was anxious to know the exact diagnosis, since her husband and son had both died of brain tumors. She said they would not give her any more information until the next time and she would have to make another appointment for that. So she said she would not leave until the doctor called her daughter. She wouldn't budge. And when the doctor finally called her daughter, me, who spoke in perfect English — lo and behold — we had assurances the CAT scan would be found, promises that a conference call on Monday would be held, and apologies for any suffering my mother had gone through for a most regrettable mistake.

I think my mother's English almost had an effect on limiting my 15 possibilities in life as well. Sociologists and linguists probably will tell you that a person's developing language skills are more influenced by peers. But I do think that the language spoken in the family, especially in immigrant families which are more insular, plays a large role in shaping the language of the child. And I believe that it affected my results on achievement tests, IQ tests, and the SAT. While my English skills were never judged as poor, compared to math, English could not be considered my strong suit. In grade school I did moderately well, getting perhaps B's, sometimes B-pluses, in English and scoring perhaps in the sixtieth or seventieth percentile on achievement tests. But those scores were not good enough to override the opinion that my true abilities lay in math and science, because in those areas I achieved A's and scored in the ninetieth percentile or higher.

This was understandable. Math is precise; there is only one correct answer. Whereas, for me at least, the answers on English tests were always a judgment call, a matter of opinion and personal experience. Those tests were constructed around items like fill-in-the-blank sentence completion, such as "Even though Tom was _____, Mary thought he was _____." And the correct answer always seemed to be the most bland combinations of thoughts, for example, "Even though Tom was shy, Mary thought he was charming," with the grammatical structure "even though " limiting the correct answer to some sort of semantic opposites, so you wouldn't get answers like, "Even though Tom was foolish, Mary thought he was ridiculous." Well, according to my mother, there were very few limitations as to what Tom could have been and what Mary might have thought of him. So I never did well on tests like that.

The same was true with word analogies, pairs of words in which you were supposed to find some sort of logical, semantic relationship — for example, "Sunset is to nightfall as _____ is to _____." And here you would be presented with a list of four possible pairs, one of which showed the same kind of relationship: red is to stoplight, bus is to arrival, chills is to fever, yawn is to boring. Well, I could never think that way. I knew what the tests were asking, but I could not block out of my mind the images already created by the first pair, "sunset is to nightfall" — and I would see a burst of colors against a darkening sky, the moon rising, the lowering of a curtain of stars. And all the other pairs of words — red, bus, stoplight, boring — just threw up a mass of confusing images, making it impossible for me to sort out something as logical as saying: "A sunset precedes nightfall" is the same as "a chill precedes a fever." The only way I would have gotten that answer right would have been to imagine an associative situation, for example, my being disobedient and staying out past sunset, catching a chill at night, which turns into feverish pneumonia as punishment, which indeed did happen to me.

I have been thinking about all this lately, about my mother's English, about achievement tests. Because lately I've been asked, as a writer, why there are not more Asian Americans represented in American literature. Why are there few Asian Americans enrolled in creative writing programs? Why do so many Chinese students go into engineering? Well, these are broad sociological questions I can't begin to answer. But I have noticed in surveys — in fact, just last week — that Asian students, as a whole, always do significantly better on math achievement tests than in English. And this makes me think that there are other Asian-American students whose English spoken in the home might also be described as "broken" or "limited." And perhaps they also have teachers who are steering them away from writing and into math and science, which is what happened to me.

Fortunately, I happen to be rebellious in nature and enjoy the challenge of disproving assumptions made about me. I became an English major my first year in college, after being enrolled as pre-med. I started writing nonfiction as a freelancer the week after I was told by my former boss that writing was my worst skill and I should hone my talents toward account management.

But it wasn't until 1985 that I finally began to write fiction. And at first I wrote using what I thought to be wittily crafted sentences, sentences that would finally prove I had mastery over the English language. Here's an example from the first draft of a story that later made its way into *The Joy Luck Club*, but without this line: "That was my mental quandary in its nascent state." A terrible line, which I can barely pronounce.

Fortunately, for reasons I won't get into today, I later decided I should envision a reader for the stories I would write. And the reader I decided upon was my mother, because these were stories about mothers. So with this reader in mind — and in fact she did read my early drafts — I began to write stories using all the Englishes I grew up with: the English I spoke to my mother, which for lack of a better term might be described as "simple"; the English she used with me, which for lack of a better term might be described as "broken"; my translation of her Chinese, which could certainly be described as "watered down"; and what I imagined to be her translation of her Chinese if she could speak in perfect English, her internal language, and for that I sought to preserve the essence, but neither an English nor a Chinese structure. I wanted to capture what language ability tests can never reveal: her intent, her passion, her imagery, the rhythms of her speech and the nature of her thoughts.

Apart from what any critic had to say about my writing, I knew I had succeeded where it counted when my mother finished reading my book and gave me her verdict: "So easy to read."

Amy Tan

My Grandmother's Choice

"My Grandmother's Choice" appears in Amy Tan's 2003 publication, *The Opposite of Fate: A Book of Musings.* In this piece, Tan tells the stories behind an old family photograph (see p. 268), revisiting the "secrets and tragedies" of the past.
For more biographical background on Amy Tan, see page 259.

In my writing room, on my desk, sits an old family photo in a plain black frame, depicting five women and a girl at a temple pavilion by a lake. When I first saw this photo as a child, I thought it was exotic and remote, of a faraway time and place, with people who had no connection to my American life. Look at their bound feet! Look at that funny lady with the plucked forehead!

The solemn little girl is, in fact, my mother. She looks to be around eight. And behind her, leaning against the rock, is my grandmother Jingmei. "She called me Baobei," my mother told me. "It means 'treasure.'"

The picture was taken in Hangzhou, in 1924 or so, my mother said, possibly spring or fall, to judge by the clothes. At first glance, it appears the women are on a pleasure outing.

But see the white bands on their skirts? The white shoes? They are in mourning for my mother's grandmother Divong, known as the "replacement wife." The women have come to this place, a Buddhist retreat, to perform yet another ceremony for her. Monks hired for the occasion have chanted the proper words. And the women and little girl have walked in circles clutching smoky sticks of incense. They have knelt and prayed, then burned a huge pile of spirit money so that Divong might ascend to a higher position in her new world.

5   This is also a picture of secrets and tragedies, the reasons that warnings have been passed along in our family like heirlooms. Each of these
women suffered a terrible fate, my mother said. And they were not peas-
ant women but big-city people, very modern. They went to dance halls
and wore stylish clothes. They were supposed to be the lucky ones.

Look at the pretty woman with her finger on her cheek. She is my
mother's second cousin Nunu Aiyi, "Precious Auntie." You cannot see
this, but Nunu Aiyi's entire face was scarred from smallpox. Fortunately for her, a year or so after this picture was taken, she received
marriage proposals from two families. She turned down a lawyer and
married another man. Later she divorced her husband — a daring thing
for a woman to do. But then, finding no means to support herself or
her young daughter, Nunu Aiyi eventually accepted the lawyer's second
proposal — this time, to become his number-two concubine. "Where
else could she go?" my mother said. "Some people said she was lucky the
lawyer still wanted her."

Now look at the small woman with the sour face. There's a reason
that Uncle's Wife, Jyou Ma, has this expression. Her husband, my
great-uncle, often complained aloud that his family had chosen an ugly

woman for his wife. To show his displeasure, he insulted Jyou Ma's cooking. During one of their raucous dinner arguments, the table was shoved and a pot of boiling soup tipped and spilled all over his niece's neck, causing a burn that nearly killed her. My mother was the little niece, and for the rest of her life she bore that scar on her neck. Great-Uncle's family eventually arranged for a prettier woman to become his second wife. But the complaints about his first wife's cooking did not stop. When she became ill with an easily treatable disease, she refused to take any medication. She swore she would rather die than live another unnecessary day. And soon after, she died.

Dooma, "Big Mother," is the regal-looking woman with the plucked forehead who sits on a rock. The dark-jacketed woman next to her is a servant, remembered by my mother only as someone who cleaned but did not cook. Dooma was my mother's aunt, the daughter of her grandfather and his "original wife," Nu-pei. But Divong, the replacement wife, my mother's grandmother, shunned Dooma, her stepdaughter, for being "too strong," while her own daughter, my grandmother, loved Dooma. She did not care that Dooma's first daughter was born with a hunchback — a sign, some said, of Dooma's own crooked nature. She did not stop seeing Dooma after Dooma remarried, disobeying her family's orders to remain a widow forever. Later Dooma killed herself, using some mysterious means that made her die slowly over three days. "Dooma died the same way she lived," my mother said, "strong, suffering lots."

Jingmei, my own grandmother, lived only a year or two after this picture was taken. She was the widow of a poor scholar, a man who had the misfortune of dying from influenza shortly after he was appointed vice-magistrate in a small county. I only assume it was influenza, since his death in 1918 was sudden, as were the millions of other deaths during the great pandemic. Family lore, however, reports that the ghost of a man on whom he had passed a judgment for execution returned from hell and killed him.

Around the time this photo was taken, during another lakeside   10 outing, a rich man who liked to collect pretty women spotted my widowed grandmother and had one of his wives invite her to the house for a few days to play mah jong. One night he raped her, making her an outcast. My grandmother became a concubine to the rich man, and took her young daughter to live on an island near Shanghai. She left her son behind, to save his face. After she gave birth to a baby boy, the rich man's first son, she killed herself by swallowing raw opium buried in the New Year's rice cakes. "Don't follow my footsteps," she told her young daughter, who wept at her deathbed.

At my grandmother's funeral, monks tied chains to my mother's ankles so she would not fly away with her mother's ghost. "I tried to take them off," my mother told me. "I was her treasure. I was her life." She also tried to follow her mother's footsteps. Since that time she was a small girl, she often talked of killing herself. She never stopped feeling the urge.

My mother could never talk about the shame of being a concubine's daughter, even with her closest friends. "Don't tell anyone," she said once to me. "People don't understand. A concubine was like some kind of prostitute. My mother was a good woman, high-class. She had no choice."

I told her I understood.

"How can you understand?" she blurted. "You did not live in China then. You do not know what it's like to have no position in life. I was her daughter. We had no face! We belonged to nobody! This is a shame I can never push off my back." By the end of this outburst, she was crying.

15   On a trip with my mother to Beijing, I learned that my uncle had found a way to push the shame off his back. He was the son my grandmother had left behind. In 1936 he joined the Communist Party — in large part, he told me, to overthrow the society that had forced his mother into concubinage. He published a story about his mother. I told him I was writing about my grandmother in a book of fiction. We agreed that my grandmother was the source of strength running through our family. My mother cried to hear this.

I look at that photo often, and it's safe to guess that my grandmother never envisioned that she would one day have a granddaughter who lives in a house she co-owns with a husband she loves, and a dog and a cat she spoils (no children by choice, not bad luck), and that this granddaughter would have her own money, be able to shop — fifty percent off, full price, doesn't matter, she never has to ask anyone's permission — because she makes her own living, doing what is important to her, which is to tell stories, many of them about her grandmother, a woman who believed death was the only way to change her life.

A relative once scolded my mother, "Why do you tell your daughter these useless stories? She can't change the past." And my mother replied, "It *can* be changed. I tell her, so she can tell everyone, tell the whole world so they know what my mother suffered. That's how it *can* be changed."

I think about what my mother said. Isn't the past what people remember — who did what, how and why? And what people remember, isn't that mostly what they've already chosen to believe? For so many years, my family believed my grandmother was a victim of society, who, sadly, took her own life, no more, no less.

In my writing room, I go back into the past, to that moment when my grandmother told my mother not to follow her footsteps. My grandmother and I are walking side by side, imagining the past differently, remembering it another way. Together we come upon a tomb of memories. We open it and release what has been buried for too long — the terrible despair, the destructive rage. We hurt, we grieve, we cry. And then we see what remains: the hopes, broken to bits but still there.

I look at the photograph of my grandmother. Together we write   20
stories of things that were and shouldn't have been, or could have been, or might still be. We know the past can be changed. We can choose what we should believe. We can choose what we should remember. That is what frees us, this choice, frees us to hope that we can redeem these same memories for the little girl who became my mother.

Glossary of Grammatical Terms

Many of the terms listed in this glossary are introduced in Chapter 1, "The Sentence's Working Parts." Terms in boldface within a definition have their own glossary entries.

Absolute phrase A **modifier** that is headed by a **noun** and modifies the whole sentence to which it is attached. The noun in an absolute phrase works like a **subject**, beginning an assertion, but there is no complete **verb**; the verb either appears as a **verbal** or is absent altogether.

> She spent most of her time at the church, <u>her ivory-and-silver rosary draped over her right fist</u>, <u>her left hand wearing the beads smoother, smaller</u>.

> It was the middle of September on the reservation, <u>the mornings chill</u>, <u>the afternoons warm</u>, <u>the leaves still green and thick in their final sweetness</u>.

Active voice In an active voice construction, the **subject** performs the action described by the **verb**. (*Compare to* **passive voice**.) In the sentences below, the subjects and verbs have been underlined.

| ACTIVE VOICE | <u>Corwin</u> <u>shut</u> the door. |
| PASSIVE VOICE | The <u>door</u> <u>was shut</u> by Corwin. |

| ACTIVE VOICE | <u>Stowe</u> <u>exposes</u> the abuses of slavery to a wide audience. |
| PASSIVE VOICE | The <u>abuses of slavery</u> <u>are exposed</u> to a wide audience by Stowe. |

Adjectival A word, **phrase**, or **clause** that modifies a **noun**. (*See also* **adjective**, **adjective clause**, and **adjective phrase**.)

Adjective A word that modifies a **noun**, typically by naming a quality or characteristic.

> Anyone could see that he had been <u>handsome</u>, and he still cut a <u>graceful</u> figure, <u>slim</u> and of <u>medium</u> height.

> In our loss, we were cut off from the <u>true</u>, <u>bright</u>, <u>normal</u> routines of living.

Adjective clause   A **dependent clause** that modifies a **noun**. Most adjective clauses are introduced by the words *who, whom, whose, which, that, when,* or *where.*

He was depressed by a rainbow, which he saw only as a colorless semicircle in the sky.

Doubly intriguing is the occurrence of colorblindness in an artist, a painter for whom color has been of primary importance, and who can directly paint as well as describe what has befallen him.

Adjective phrase   A **phrase** that is headed by an **adjective** and that stands outside the **noun phrase** it modifies.

Anyone could see that he had been handsome, and he still cut a graceful figure, slim and of medium height.

I could see how my old man, huge and cumbersome on land, became transformed in the water.

Adverb   A word that modifies a **verb**, an **adjective**, or another adverb. When modifying verbs, adverbs describe when, where, why, how, or under what conditions an action takes place. When modifying adjectives or other adverbs, they typically specify degree or extent, as in *very cold* or *somewhat cold.*

All the claims that are routinely made for the book's humanitarian power are, in the end, simply absurd.

Any pretense that black admissions would be anything but staunchly and firmly middle class had ended during my absence.

Adverb clause   A **dependent clause** that does the work of an adverb, telling where, when, why, how, or under what conditions an action takes place. An adverb clause is introduced by a **subordinating conjunction** and contains a **subject-verb pair**.

Even though I want a piece of cherry pie, I'm committed to my diet.

I went off to Cambridge, England, and when I returned a few years later to teach at Yale, so very much had changed.

Appositive   A **noun phrase** that appears in a sentence next to another noun phrase with the same referent.

I'd like you to meet Jerry Allen, my brother-in-law from Texas.

I saw no unity of purpose, <u>no consensus on matters of philosophy or history or law.</u>

Auxiliary A word that combines with a main **verb** to establish the time, duration, or certainty of its action. Auxiliaries include forms of *be, have,* and *do* as well as modals such as *can, will, shall, should, could, would, may, might,* and *must.*

Because he <u>had</u> been an artist, he <u>could</u> speak of colors with special insight.

Most of this I<u>'ve</u> told before, or at least hinted at, but what I <u>have</u> never told is the full truth.

Clause A group of words containing a **subject** and a **predicate.** (*See also specific types of clauses:* **adjective clause, adverb clause, dependent clause, independent clause,** and **noun clause.**)

Complement In a clause with a **linking verb,** the complement is an **adjective** or **noun phrase** that follows the **verb.**

The sharpness of focus is <u>incredible.</u>

Her novel became <u>a bestseller.</u>

Conjunction A word such as *and, or,* and *but* used to join words or larger grammatical units. (*See also* **coordinating conjunction, correlative conjunction,** and **subordinating conjunction.**)

My father always struck me as the sort of man who, under the right circumstances, might have invented the microwave oven <u>or</u> the transistor radio. You wouldn't seek him out for advice on a personal problem, <u>but</u> he'd be the first one you'd call <u>when</u> the dishwasher broke <u>or</u> someone flushed a hairpiece down your toilet.

Coordinating conjunction A word used to join similar syntactic units within a sentence. The seven coordinating conjunctions are *and, or, nor, but, for, yet, so.*

Correlative conjunction A two-part conjunction used to join similar syntactic units within a sentence. The correlative conjunctions are *both/and, either/or, neither/nor, not/but,* and *not only/but* (*also*).

Cumulative sentence   A sentence that begins with the **independent clause**, then continues with a series of **modifiers**. In the sentences below, the modifiers have been underlined.

Sitting at the control board was my dad the engineer, years younger, examining a printout no larger than a grocery receipt.

The men drank from quart bottles of Mountain Dew as they paused from their work to regard my father, who stood at the water's edge, staring at the shoreline with a stick in hand.

Dangling modifier   A **modifier** that is not attached carefully to a **clause**, leading to ambiguity about what is being modified.

DANGLING MODIFIER	After reading Gates's essay, our understanding of ethnic identity changed.
REVISED	After reading Gates's essay, we had a new understanding of ethnic identity.
DANGLING MODIFIER	Once, while rifling through the toolshed, an old poster caught my eye.
REVISED	Once, while rifling through the toolshed, I noticed an old poster.

Dependent clause   A **clause** (a group of words with a **subject** and **predicate**) that cannot stand on its own as a sentence. (*See also* **adjective clause, adverb clause,** and **noun clause.**) Dependent clauses are sometimes referred to as **subordinate clauses.**

As soon as he entered, he found his entire studio, which was hung with brilliantly colored paintings, now utterly grey and void of color.

The weeks that followed were very difficult.

Determiner   A function word that precedes a **noun.** Determiners include articles (*a, an, the*), demonstratives (*this, that, these, those*), possessives (such as *David's, Amy's, my, our, your, his, her, its, their*), and quantifiers (such as *some, many, a few, one, a dozen, most, all*).

He could identify the green of van Gogh's billiard table in this way unhesitatingly.

He knew the colors in his favorite paintings, but he could no longer see them, either when he looked or in his mind's eye.

Early modifier   A **modifier** that appears early in the sentence; initial modifiers open their sentences and medial modifiers are embedded within the **independent clause**.

As <u>children</u>, we placed a great deal of faith in his ability but learned to steer clear while he was working.

The experience of watching was ruined, <u>time and time again</u>, by an interminable explanation of how things were put together.

End modifier   A **modifier** that appears at the end of a sentence, following the **independent clause**.

Sitting at the control board was my dad the engineer, <u>years younger</u>, <u>examining a printout no larger than a grocery receipt</u>.

The men drank from quart bottles of Mountain Dew <u>as they paused</u> <u>from their work</u> to regard my father, <u>who stood at the water's edge</u>, <u>staring at the shoreline with a stick in hand</u>.

Fragment   A grammatical unit punctuated as a sentence but lacking an **independent clause**.

<u>Because marriage is not merely an accumulation of benefits</u>.

Some thought he had no redeeming value whatsoever. <u>A sociopath</u>.

Headword   The key word in any phrase—the **noun** in a **noun phrase**, the **verb** in a **verb phrase**, the **adjective** in an **adjective phrase**.

NOUN PHRASE	a <u>man</u> of great compassion
VERB PHRASE	<u>introduced</u> herself to the neighbors
ADJECTIVE PHRASE	always <u>ready</u> to help a friend

Human subject   A **noun phrase** in the subject position that refers to a person or people rather than to objects or abstract ideas.

<u>My mother</u> was in the room.

And it was perhaps the first time <u>she</u> had heard me give a lengthy speech using the kind of English <u>I</u> have never used with her.

Independent clause   A **clause** (a group of words with a **subject** and **predicate**) that can stand on its own as a complete sentence.

<u>My grandmother and I are walking side by side</u>, imagining the past differently, remembering it another way.

<u>Together we come upon a tomb of memories</u>.

Intransitive verb   A **verb** that does not take an **object**.

My grandmother and I <u>are walking</u> side by side.

We <u>hurt</u>, we <u>grieve</u>, we <u>cry</u>.

Linking verb   A verb that links the **subject** to a word or **phrase** that appears after the **verb**, called the **complement**. The most common linking verb is *be*.

The desolate landscape of Afghanistan <u>was</u> the burial ground of Soviet communism.

I <u>became</u> an English major my first year in college.

Main clause   Another term for **independent clause.**

Modifier   A word, **phrase**, or **clause** that elaborates upon some other element in the sentence, describing it, limiting it, or providing extra information about it.

My father kissed her, spoke <u>gently</u> <u>into her ear</u>, combed her hair <u>into a</u>

<u>shawl</u> <u>around her shoulders.</u>

Noun   A word that names a person, place, thing, or idea.

My <u>father</u> kissed her, spoke gently into her <u>ear</u>, combed her <u>hair</u> into a <u>shawl</u> around her <u>shoulders.</u>

<u>Marriage</u> is not merely an <u>accumulation</u> of <u>benefits</u>.

Noun clause   A **dependent clause** that performs the function of a **noun**, serving as a **subject, object,** or **complement.**

We learned <u>that his accident had been accompanied by a transient amnesia.</u>

<u>What he feared</u> was <u>that he had suffered some sort of stroke.</u>

Noun phrase   A **noun** and its **modifiers.** A noun phrase can serve as a **subject, object, complement,** or a **modifier.** (*See also* **appositive** and **absolute phrase.**)

Although <u>his arm</u> was so twisted and disfigured that <u>his shirts</u> had to be carefully altered and pinned to accommodate <u>the gnarled shape</u>, he had <u>agility</u> in <u>that arm</u>, even <u>strength</u>.

My father kissed her, spoke gently into her ear, combed her hair into a shawl around her shoulders.

Object   In a clause with a **transitive verb**, the object is a **noun phrase** that follows the **verb**, naming the person or thing that receives the action.

I have visited ophthalmologists.

Stowe exposed the abuses of slavery to a wide audience.

Parallel structure   When items in a pair or series are the same kind of grammatical unit and fit into the same "slot" in the sentence, they are said to be parallel in structure.

My speech was about Vietnam, abortion, and civil rights, about the sense of community our class shared, since so many of us had been together for twelve years, about the individual's rights and responsibilities in his or her community, and about the necessity to defy norms out of love.

I pretended to sleep, not because I wanted to keep up the appearance of being sick but because I could not bear to return to the way things had been.

Passive voice   In a passive voice construction, the **subject** names the person or thing that receives the action of the **verb**. (*Compare to* **active voice**.) In the sentences below, the subjects and verbs have been underlined.

ACTIVE VOICE   From that rock, I could see all that happened on the water.

PASSIVE VOICE   From that rock, all that happened on the water could be seen (by me).

ACTIVE VOICE   In the Ojibwa language that we speak on our reservation, . . .

PASSIVE VOICE   In the Ojibwa language that is spoken on our reservation, . . .

Periodic sentence   A sentence in which the **modifiers** come at the beginning, building toward the **independent clause**. In the sentence below, the modifiers have been underlined.

In Denmark, in the decade since Vermont-style partnerships have been legal, gays have had a lower divorce rate than straights.

Somehow, in the late sixties, in the aftermath of the King assassination, what was held to be "authentically" black began to change.

Phrase   A group of words that serves a grammatical function. Unlike **clauses**, phrases do not contain a **subject-verb pair**. (*See also* **absolute phrase, adjective phrase, appositive, noun phrase, prepositional phrase,** and **verbal phrase.**)

Predicate   The **verb** in a clause and any elements (**modifiers, objects, complements**) that accompany it. Typically, the predicate states what the **subject** is or does.

He described a very active and productive life as an artist.

The young Spinoza wrote his first treatise on the rainbow; the young Newton's most joyous discovery was the composition of white light.

Preposition   A word that indicates the relationship between a **noun phrase** and the rest of the sentence. English has a large but finite set of prepositions; examples are *about, above, across, after, against, as, at, before, behind, below, beside, between, by, down, during, for, from, in, into, like, of, off, on, out, over, past, since, through, toward, under, until, up, upon, with, without.* Some prepositions are more complex: *according to, apart from, because of, by means of, except for, instead of, such as.*

There, lashed to a crosspiece in the bow, was a black case of womanly shape that fastened on the side with two brass locks.

Prepositional phrase   A phrase made up of a **preposition** and its object, a **noun phrase.**

There, lashed to a crosspiece in the bow, was a black case of womanly shape that fastened on the side with two brass locks.

Pronoun   A function word that takes the place of a **noun.** (*See also* **relative pronoun.**)

As children, we placed a great deal of faith in his ability but learned to steer clear while he was working.

I felt closest to him, truly his son, when we went swimming together.

Relative clause   Another term for **adjective clause.**

Relative pronoun   A word used to introduce an **adjective clause.** The relative pronouns are *who, whom, whose, which,* and *that.*

She was the widow of a poor scholar, who died of influenza.

We write stories of things that were and shouldn't have been, or could have been, or might still be.

Subject   A **noun phrase** that appears before the **verb**, typically naming the actor or topic of the clause.

My own scientific curiosity eventually blossomed, but I knew enough to keep my freakish experiments to myself.

When my father discovered my colony of frozen slugs in the basement freezer, I chose not to explain my complex theories of suspended animation.

Subject-verb pair   The core of a **clause**: the **headword** of the **noun phrase** that serves as **subject,** and the **verb** itself (with **auxiliaries**) within the **predicate**. Stripping away **modifiers** to isolate the subject-verb pair highlights the key elements of the clause.

My own scientific curiosity eventually blossomed, but I knew enough to keep my freakish experiments to myself.

When my father discovered my colony of frozen slugs in the basement freezer, I chose not to explain my complex theories of suspended animation.

Subordinate clause   Another term for **dependent clause**.

Subordinating conjunction   A word used to introduce an **adverb clause**. English has a large but finite set of subordinating conjunctions; examples are *although, as, as if, as soon as, because, before, if, since, though, unless, until, when, where, whereas, while.*

Because marriage will be a new experience for most gay people, its privileges will not be taken for granted.

When an extremely basic civil right is involved, it seems to me the burden of proof should lie with those who seek to deny it to a small minority of citizens, not with those who seek to extend it.

Subordinator   Another term for **subordinating conjunction.**

Transitive verb   A **verb** that takes an **object.**

I can see a worm wriggling a block away.

The young Spinoza wrote his first treatise on the rainbow.

Verb   A word that identifies an action or state of being.

My father always struck me as the sort of man who, under the right circumstances, might have invented the microwave oven or the transistor radio.

We dragged Fisher to the car, ducking the bottles and cans as we sped away.

Verbal   A **verb** form that is not paired with a **subject**, functioning instead as a **noun** or a **modifier**. Verbals appear in three forms: the present participle (*-ing*), past participle (*-ed* or irregular form), and infinitive (*to*).

On two or three afternoons, to pass the time, I helped Elroy get the place ready for winter, sweeping down the cabins and hauling in the boats.

I saw a sixteen-year-old kid decked out for his first prom, looking spiffy in a white tux and a black bow tie.

Verbal phrase   A group of words headed by a **verbal**.

On two or three afternoons, to pass the time, I helped Elroy get the place ready for winter, sweeping down the cabins and hauling in the boats.

I saw a sixteen-year-old kid decked out for his first prom, looking spiffy in a white tux and a black bow tie.

Verb phrase   A group of words headed by a **verb**.

My father was an engineer.

We dragged Fisher to the car, ducking the bottles and cans as we sped away.

Sample Responses to Selected Exercises

EXERCISE 1A *(pp. 13–14)*

1. Oliver Sacks — <u>is</u> a neurologist.
2. Sacks — <u>studies</u> patients with unusual neurological disorders.
3. He — sometimes <u>publishes</u> his case studies in *The New Yorker.*
4. His <u>description</u> of Mr. I. — also <u>appears</u> in the book *An Anthropologist on Mars.*
5. Mr. I.'s <u>world</u> — <u>changed</u> profoundly.
6. As an artist, <u>he</u> — <u>could speak</u> of his colorblindness with special insight.
7. <u>Sacks</u> — <u>conveys</u> Mr. I.'s dismay at the loss of color vision.
8. As a clinician, <u>Sacks</u> — <u>has developed</u> empathy for his patients.
9. His <u>compassion</u> — <u>enriches</u> his work as a doctor and as a writer.
10. Sacks's <u>readers</u> — <u>glimpse</u> the complexity of the human mind.

EXERCISE 1B *(p. 14)*

1. Linking
2. Transitive (patients)
3. Transitive (case studies)
4. Intransitive
5. Intransitive
6. Intransitive
7. Transitive (dismay)
8. Transitive (empathy)
9. Transitive (work)
10. Transitive (complexity)

EXERCISE 1C *(pp. 20–21)*

1. (if)he could bring himself to use the blackish stuff
2. (although)his brown dog would stand out sharply in silhouette against a light road

Why "would stand out" rather than "would stand"? "Stand out" is what's called a phrasal verb: the word "out" is an essential part of it. When a dog "stands out," he's doing something different from a dog who "stands."

3. (when) it moved into soft, dappled undergrowth
4. (whereas) something bizarre and intolerable occurred
5. (whenever) he looked at colored images

EXERCISE 1D *(pp. 22–23)*

1. I sometimes went along with my father on housecalls on Sunday mornings.
   independent clause

2. He loved doing housecalls more than anything else,
   independent clause

3. for they were social and sociable as well as medical.
   independent clause

Why is this clause, with "for" at the beginning, independent? Because "for" is a coordinator (one of the seven coordinating conjunctions—for, and, nor, but, or, yet, so) rather than a subordinator. This clause could be punctuated as a separate sentence. I wouldn't choose to punctuate it that way—but if I did, I'd be guilty of having a tin ear, not of violating a punctuation rule.

4. He would have a typed list of a dozen patients and their addresses,
   independent clause

5. and I would sit next to him in the front seat of the car
   independent clause

6. while he told me, in very human terms,
   dependent (adverb) clause

7. what each patient had.
   dependent (noun) clause

This can be identified as a noun clause not only by the presence of "what," which often introduces noun clauses, but also by its function. This clause is the object of the verb "told." What did Sacks's father tell him? What each patient had.

8. When he arrived,

dependent (adverb) clause

9. I would get out with him, allowed, usually, to carry his medical bag.

independent clause

10. He also had a motorcycle, a Scott Flying Squirrel, with a two-stroke, 600 cc, watercooled engine, and a high-pitched exhaust like a scream.

independent clause

11. He loved to take off on this

independent clause

12. if he had a free Sunday morning.

dependent (adverb) clause

13. Sometimes I had dreams

independent clause

14. in which I was riding or flying the bike myself,

dependent (adjective) clause

15. and I determined to get one

independent clause

16. when I was grown up.

dependent (adverb) clause

EXERCISE 2A *(p. 28)*

1. Even after two decades I can close my eyes and return to that porch at the Tip Top Lodge. I can see the old guy staring at me. Elroy Berdahl: eighty-one years old, skinny and shrunken and mostly bald. He wore a flannel shirt and brown work pants. In one hand, I remember, he carried a green apple, a small paring knife in the other.

2. He continued fishing. He worked his line with the tips of his fingers, patiently, his eyes squinting out at his red and white bobber on the Rainy River. His eyes were flat and impassive. He didn't speak. He was simply there, like the river and the late-summer sun.

This is O'Brien's language. As you worked on the passages, you probably made some different choices in wording. The point is not to reproduce O'Brien's language exactly but to bring the passages into focus, beginning most of the sentences with human subjects, I and he.

EXERCISE 2B *(p. 29)*

1. *Before:*

Even after two decades it is possible for me to close my eyes and return to that porch at the Tip Top Lodge. There is an image in my mind of the old guy staring at me. Elroy Berdahl: eighty-one years old, skinny and shrunken and mostly bald. His outfit was a flannel shirt and brown work pants. In one hand, if memory serves, was a green apple, a small paring knife in the other.

His fishing continued. His line was worked with the tips of his fingers, patiently, his eyes squinting out at his red and white bobber on the Rainy River. His eyes were flat and impassive. There was no speech. There was simply his presence, like the river and the late-summer sun.

After:

Even after two decades I can close my eyes and return to that porch at the Tip Top Lodge. I can see the old guy staring at me. Elroy Berdahl: eighty-one years old, skinny and shrunken and mostly bald. He wore a flannel shirt and brown work pants. In one hand, I remember, he carried a green apple, a small paring knife in the other.

He kept fishing. He worked his line with the tips of his fingers, patiently, his eyes squinting out at his red and white bobber on the Rainy River. His eyes were flat and impassive. He didn't speak. He was simply there, like the river and the late-summer sun.

In the revised passages with human subjects, the verbs have shifted as well. The revised passages rely less heavily on forms of *be*.

2. Yes. Before revising, the passages had 75 and 50 words; after revising, the passages have 65 and 48 words.

3. passage from paragraph 19: two words used as subject *(I, he)*
   passage from paragraph 75: two words used as subject *(he, eyes)*

EXERCISE 2C *(p. 32)*

Communication is the key to employer-employee relationships. This point seems obvious, but both bosses and employees can have difficulty being explicit about what they expect of each other. For example, when I started working as a secretary at the university, I expected my assignments to come from the department chair, and I was puzzled when other faculty gave me tasks. Should I set aside the project I was working on for the chair in order to make photocopies for another professor? The department chair was so accustomed to the collective authority structure that she never explained to me that I actually had eighteen "bosses"! And like many new employees, I hesitated to ask out of fear that I would appear ignorant or uncooperative. My career as a secretary would have had a smoother beginning if the chair had been more informative about the department's culture or if I had been more assertive about raising questions.

EXERCISE 2D *(pp. 35–36)*

1. The government had ended most graduate school deferments.
2. A marching band played fight songs.
3. A squad of cheerleaders did cartwheels along the banks of the Rainy River.
4. You can't fix your mistakes.
5. . . . you have to put your own precious fluids on the line.

EXERCISE 2E *(p. 36)*

The story, familiar to most nineteenth-century Americans, . . . may be sketched briefly. A Kentucky slave, Tom, is sold to pay off a debt to a slave trader, who takes him to New Orleans. On the boat trip downriver, Tom is purchased by the wealthy Augustine St. Clare at the behest of his daughter, Eva. After Eva's death, and then St. Clare's, Tom is sold again, this time to Simon Legree, whose remote plantation is the site of every form of cruelty and degradation. The novel was immediately read and acclaimed by any number of excellent judges: Charles Dickens, George Eliot, Leo Tolstoy, George Sand— the whole roster of nineteenth-century liberals. . . .

EXERCISE 2F *(pp. 37–38)*

Text #1

Mike O'Connell caught me just as I was punching in. He was cordial, but I could tell that something was eating him, so I followed him to the smoking tent and commented on the rainclouds as he lit his cigarette. Mike is an easygoing guy, the sort who never knocks on the door of the stewards' office.

He did have a complaint, though. "I think I was passed over for overtime," he said. "When I came in last Monday, Ray Tomoko was already taking a break. He'd been here since 12:30. Why did Ray get two hours of OT? I thought they were supposed to go through the rotation, and I'm sure my name is ahead of Ray's."

At some level, I think the overtime grievances are nuts. Mike and Ray run mail processing machines—loud, dusty machines that read 800 addresses per minute, shoot letters down a belt, and sort them into metal drawers. Eight hours of that is enough for me. But with Mike's seniority, the overtime pay runs to about $30 per hour, so a clerk who works a couple extra hours can earn several days' groceries or a nice birthday present for one of his kids. The clerks on swing shift especially like hours at the beginning of the tour; they're happier to come in at 12:30 than to work past the shift's 11:00 closing time.

"Let me check on it," I told Mike. "If it was a simple mistake, Denny will probably fix it without a grievance."

"Ray won't get into trouble, will he?"

"No, it wasn't Ray's mistake. He isn't responsible for keeping track of the OT list; that's Denny's job."

As I headed to my machine, I jotted down some notes. As soon as I got some steward time, I'd write up a Request For Information to get the OT rotation and last Monday's clock rings for both Mike and Ray. Denny was back in town after three days at a training meeting in Denver. I sent up a prayer that the trip had improved his mood.

Text #2

My job as a shop steward is to enforce the contract between the United States Postal Service and the American Postal Workers Union. The contract is negotiated nationally, but a contract is only as strong as the local stewards who show up at work every day, keep their eyes open, and make sure the provisions of the contract are observed.

The most important mechanism for enforcing the contract is the grievance. We file grievances of three kinds. First, if an employee has a complaint—say, if he or she is being badgered by a supervisor, or if requests for days off or overtime aren't being treated fairly—the steward represents the employee at Step One, an informal conversation with the supervisor, and if necessary, at Step Two, a more formal meeting with the plant manager or his representative. The steward needs to know the contract well so that he or she can point to the specific language that applies to the case and can suggest an appropriate remedy. If the grievance is denied at these steps, the local union president takes it to the next stages, up to binding arbitration.

Second, the union files grievances for employees who have been disciplined. In these cases, the shop steward acts like a defense attorney, making the case for the employee's innocence or for the least damaging disciplinary measure. Discipline must be corrective rather than punitive, and it should be progressive so that people don't suffer dire consequences for first-time offenses. On this basis, a shop steward might argue for a verbal reprimand rather than a letter of warning, or for a few days' suspension rather than termination.

Finally, the union files class action grievances for groups. Postal managers frequently make mistakes when setting up holiday schedules or assigning overtime. In addition, they sometimes overlook safety concerns. The APWU initiates grievances to correct these problems on behalf of all the affected workers.

EXERCISE 2G (p. 40)

1. The incidence of moonlighting among schoolteachers is high.

   Many schoolteachers moonlight.

2. The reason for Maybelle's desire to leave Minneapolis was her desire to avoid the harsh winter weather.

   Maybelle wanted to leave Minneapolis to avoid the harsh winter weather.

3. Similarities exist in the strategies Jackson and Le Guin use to portray the conflict between individual conscience and the influence of the social group.

   Jackson and Le Guin use similar strategies to portray the conflict between individual conscience and the influence of the social group.

4. The reason the characters in the stories are willing to victimize their neighbors is because they think their own comfort depends on somebody's sacrifice.

   The characters in the stories are willing to victimize their neighbors because they think their own comfort depends on somebody's sacrifice.

5. With the growing use of PowerPoint in academic and business settings, the advantages and disadvantages of the technology should be considered by speakers.

   With the growing use of PowerPoint in academic and business settings, speakers should consider the advantages and disadvantages of the technology.

EXERCISE 2H (p. 41)

1. Far too many children are spending their days in underfunded daycare centers.

2. To comply with the new laws, a family daycare provider must contend with too many extra expenses.

3. Outside, an ice cream truck was ringing its bell, but the children were all indoors watching television.

4. In the story "The Ones Who Walk Away from Omelas," a single boy is chosen to suffer in order for the rest of the town to prosper.

5. At three points in the story, the author uses foreshadowing.

EXERCISE 2I *(p. 42)*

1. Commitment to ethical behavior, respect for the rules of confidentiality, courtesy to co-workers and customers, and fully professional behavior on all occasions should be demonstrated by every employee.

   Every employee should demonstrate commitment to ethical behavior, respect. . . .

2. Disorderly conduct, horseplay in the work area, fighting, threatening behavior, and profane or insulting remarks are strictly prohibited by company policy.

   Company policy strictly prohibits disorderly conduct, horseplay. . . .

3. An unprecedented number of layoffs, a reduction of earnings, profits, and stock values, and a steadily worsening competitive position vis-à-vis the other high-tech companies in the area were among the factors being responded to by the CEO's decision to resign.

   The CEO resigned because of an unprecedented number of layoffs, a reduction. . . .

4. Accounting irregularities in both the purchasing office and the president's operating accounts were discovered by the auditors.

   The auditors discovered accounting irregularities. . . .

5. Planning your whole trip, from searching for the lowest airfare to finding an affordable rental car to locating a convenient hotel and even making restaurant reservations, can now be done using the Internet.

   You can now plan your whole trip using the Internet, from searching. . . .

EXERCISE 2J *(p. 43)*

1. The health food store features good bargains every weekend.
2. The store manager said he would be happy to stock more locally produced produce if he saw evidence of customer demand.
3. The desk clerk at the hotel did not know whether the rooms would be available both nights.
4. San Francisco's beaches are beautiful but too cold for sunning or swimming.
5. A visit to Chinatown made her nostalgic for her childhood in Shanghai.

EXERCISE 2K *(p. 44)*

1. The candidate decided to drop out of the race when she fell to sixth place in the polls.

2. The main character tends to damage relationships with everyone she meets.
3. Every Saturday morning, local truck farmers distribute fresh, organic produce at the farmer's market.
4. The city council won't establish a more equitable tax policy until council members have to answer to voters in district elections.
5. The project will succeed only if every team member contributes a 100% effort.

EXERCISE 3A (p. 48)

1. Once we were at college, Maura (and) I started having long talks on the phone, first about nothing at all (and) then about everything.
2. In his own redneck way, 'Bama Gibson was a perfectly nice man, (but) he was not exactly mayoral material.
3. My grandfather was colored, my father was Negro, (and) I am black.
4. Geraldine, a dedicated, headstrong woman who six years back had borne a baby, dumped its father, (and) earned a degree in education, sometimes drove Shamengwa to fiddling contests.
5. He treated this instrument with the reverence we accord our drums, which are considered living beings (and) require from us food, water, shelter, (and) love.
6. I am a tribal judge, (and) things come to me through the grapevine of the court system (or) the tribal police.
7. I took my bedroll, a scrap of jerky, (and) a loaf of bannock, (and) sat myself down on the crackling lichen of the southern rock.
8. There were rivers flowing in (and) flowing out, secret currents, six kinds of weather working on its surface (and) a hidden terrain beneath.
9. Each wave washed in from somewhere unseen (and) washed out again to somewhere unknown.
10. He had taken the old man's fiddle because he needed money, (but) he hadn't thought much about where he would sell it (or) who would buy it.

EXERCISE 3B (p. 49)

1. I wrote to Harvard, Yale, and Princeton.
2. Horse Lowe put his big red face into Maura's window, beat on the windshield with his fist, and told me to get the hell off his property.
3. Geraldine was not surprised to see the lock of the cupboard smashed and the violin gone.

4. As the days passed, Corwin lay low and picked up his job at the deep fryer.

5. He straightened out, stayed sober, used his best manners, and when questioned was convincingly hopeful about his prospects and affable about his failures.

6. A surge of unfamiliar zeal filled him, and he took up the instrument again, threw back his hair, and began to play a swift, silent passage of music.

7. I remember my father playing chansons, reels, and jigs on his fiddle.

8. He smiled, shook his fine head, and spoke softly.

EXERCISE 3C *(pp. 51–52)*

1. He was always looking for money—scamming, betting, shooting pool, even now and then working a job.

2. My mother out of grief became strict with my father, my older sister, and me.

3. The U.S. government has, in a rush of publicity and embarrassing rhetoric, cobbled together an "international coalition against terror," mobilized its army, its air force, its navy and its media, and committed them to battle.

4. In fact, the problem for an invading army is that Afghanistan has no conventional coordinates or signposts to plot on a military map—no big cities, no highways, no industrial complexes, no water treatment plants.

5. Dropping more bombs on Afghanistan will only shuffle the rubble, scramble some old graves, and disturb the dead.

6. During her first two years, Lucienne declared four majors: French, history, philosophy, and her favorite subject, computer science.

In this sentence, you can make the units match closely if you drop off some detail: French, history, philosophy, and computer science. *But just as Gates, in the sentence about his valedictory speech, lets one of the phrases spread out a bit, it would be perfectly permissible to keep the words identifying computer science as Lucienne's favorite subject. As long as the fourth item is a noun phrase, the series is parallel.*

7. The function of a university is to develop students' analytical skills and to teach them to express themselves.

8. He argued for financial aid for the children of immigrants in order to ensure equal rights to study the liberal arts, to get a chance at higher paying jobs, and to prepare for full participation in a democracy.

EXERCISE 3D *(pp. 54–55)*

1. Both Shamengwa and his father loved the fiddle.

2. Both his mother and, ultimately, his father lost their capacity for joy.

3. The narrator gives Corwin a break not because he believes he is innocent but because he hopes he can be redeemed.

4. Either he would learn to play the violin or he would do time.

The sample response above is parallel, with an independent clause following either *and another independent clause following* or. *Interestingly, Erdrich's sentence in the story is a bit different: "He would either learn to play the violin or he would do time." Either is followed by a verb phrase, or by an independent clause. Can the rule requiring parallel structure with correlative conjunctions be broken? No. Never? Well, hardly ever.*

5. Neither Billy Peace nor his brother Edwin played fair in the race for the violin.

6. Both Shamengwa and Billy Peace, who owned the violin before him, can face the past without blinking.

7. The violin brings both great heartache and great joy.

8. The violin brings not only great heartache but also great joy.
   The violin brings not only great joy but also great heartache.

EXERCISE 3E *(pp. 56–57)*

For discussion.

EXERCISE 3F *(pp. 59–60)*

For discussion.

EXERCISE 3G *(p. 60)*

1. All of them—I held them personally and individually responsible—the uniformed baseball team, the prom king and prom queen, the ornamented Goths, the boho fashionistas, the kinda-friend and the lockermate and the counselor and all the teachers in the lounge.

2. They didn't know conversation from gossip.

3. They didn't understand depression.

4. They didn't know a real detail about Matthew's death, or the nature of loneliness, or the many, many chances each of them had to prevent it.

(by Evan Freemyer)

EXERCISE 4A *(p. 66)*

1. Because he has no interest in smoking or tanning, preferring to spend his time on intellectual pursuits, the engineer is isolated from his family.

2. Poor men, unable to afford living on the beach, the fishermen have sold their homes near the ocean.

3. Because they're hoping to avoid controversy and because they don't understand the importance of absolute equality in this area, many gay rights groups have avoided a discussion of marriage.

4. In the United States, where our legal tradition insists on a separation of church from state, social policy is not driven by religious doctrine.

EXERCISE 4B *(pp. 66–67)*

1. The engineer is isolated from his family because he has no interest in smoking or tanning, preferring to spend his time on intellectual pursuits.

2. The fishermen have sold their homes near the ocean because, as poor men, they are unable to afford living on the beach.

3. Many gay rights groups have avoided a discussion of marriage because they're hoping to avoid controversy and because they don't understand the importance of absolute equality in this area.

4. Social policy is not driven by religious doctrine in the United States, where our legal tradition insists on a separation of church and state.

EXERCISE 4C *(pp. 68–69)*

1.　　As youngsters
　　　modifies "we"

　　we participated in all the usual seaside activities
　　independent clause

　　　which were fun
　　　modifies "activities"

　　　　　until my father got involved and systematically chipped away at our pleasure.
　　　　　modifies the clause above, telling when the activities were fun

2. We enjoyed swimming
　　independent clause

　　　　until the mystery of the tides was explained in such a way that the ocean seemed nothing more than an enormous saltwater toilet
　　　　modifies the independent clause, telling when we enjoyed swimming

　　　　　flushing itself on a sad and predictable basis
　　　　　modifies "toilet"

3. He had *become* colorblind
   independent clause

   after sixty-five years of seeing colors normally
   modifies the independent clause, telling when he'd become colorblind

   totally colorblind
   modifies "colorblind," restating it more emphatically

   as if "viewing a black and white television screen."
   modifies "totally colorblind"

4. Black and white for him was a *reality*
   independent clause

   all around him
   modifies "reality"

   360 degrees
   modifies "all around him," restating it more emphatically

   solid and three-dimensional
   modifies "reality"

   twenty-four hours a day
   modifies the independent clause, telling when black and white was a reality

5. Helmholtz was very conscious of "color constancy"
   independent clause

   the way in which the colors of objects are preserved
   modifies "color constancy," defining the term

   so that we can categorize them and always know what we are looking at
   modifies the clause above, telling the consequence of preserving colors

   despite great fluctuations in the wavelength of the light illuminating them
   modifies the clause above, explaining the conditions under which we can know what we are looking at

EXERCISE 4D *(pp. 71–73)*

1. During one of those trips,
   I saw my brother,
   gazing longingly at some jet skis
   that had caught his eye a few days earlier.

2. The jet skis glistened in the sun
   as they called out to my brother,
   who stood restlessly on the dock
   waiting to catch the vendor's attention.

3. He finally requested to rent the skis,
   and the vendor was more than happy to oblige,
   this bronzed man with wild hair,
   making a meager living in a beachside town.

4. Smiling and helpful,
   the ski vendor explained the precautions to my brother
   while I began to want some skis for myself
   envisioning great fun to be had on the water
   and ignoring the warnings about the dangerous swells on the lake.

(by Bob Vacanti)

EXERCISE 5A *(pp. 77–78)*

reader I decided on
Englishes I grew up with
English I spoke to my mother
English which for lack of a better term might be described as "simple"
English she used with me
English which for lack of a better term might be described as "broken"
translation which could certainly be described as "watered down"

questions I can't begin to answer
students whose English spoken in the home might also be described as "broken" or "limited"
teachers who are steering them away from writing and into math and science

EXERCISE 5B *(pp. 78–79)*

1. The young Oliver liked to swim with his father who, as a young man, had been a champion swimmer.
2. The young Oliver liked to swim with his father, whose strokes were slow and smooth.
3. The young Oliver liked to swim with his father, who became graceful in the water though he was huge and cumbersome on land.

4. They swam in the Welsh Harp pond, which was a small lake not far from their house.

5. They swam in the Welsh Harp pond, where they also enjoyed fishing.

6. They swam in the Welsh Harp pond, where Sacks's father once kept a boat.

7. Sacks went with his father to visit his patients, who knew that Dr. Sacks loved to eat.

8. Sacks went with his father to visit his patients, whose refrigerators were stocked with Dr. Sacks's favorite foods.

9. Sacks went with his father to visit his patients, whom Dr. Sacks examined in their own living rooms.

10. Sacks went with his father to visit his patients, whom Dr. Sacks expertly diagnosed by means of chest percussion.

How about "who Dr. Sacks examined" or "who Dr. Sacks diagnosed"? The who/whom *rule requires* whom *because the relative pronoun replaces an object (Dr. Sacks examined* them, *Dr. Sacks diagnosed* them*). Is it okay to ignore the rule? That's a judgment call; it depends on the formality of the context. (For more on the* who/whom *question, see pp. 80–81.)*

EXERCISE 5C (p. 79)

The streets of Nagoya were lined with a variety of restaurants, each with a sign announcing its specialty. Should it be Yakinobu on Nishidori, or Kaiten-zushi, where one could enjoy low-quality raw fish served on a conveyor belt like a miniature, edible train set? Or Ono's, where there was a particular sort of pastry that looked innocent enough from the outside, but in which was hidden a strange sweet bean paste that seemed not to belong in a breakfast roll? Usually, however, we would end up at Outback, where, in addition to the familiar Bloomin' Onion, there were a variety of steaks, all of which came in acceptably Westernized sizes.

(by Kim Schwab)

EXERCISE 5D (pp. 85–86)

See model texts.

EXERCISE 5E (pp. 87–88)

1. The overworked, preoccupied nurse could not locate the CAT scan.

The nurse, overworked and preoccupied, could not locate the CAT scan.

Overworked and preoccupied, the nurse could not locate the CAT scan.

2. My aging, frail, but determined mother asked me to call her stockbroker.

   My mother, aging and frail but determined, asked me to call her stockbroker.

   Aging and frail but determined, my mother asked me to call her stockbroker.

3. The stockbroker's spacious, well-appointed office was in a brick building on Wall Street.

   The stockbroker's office, spacious and well-appointed, was in a brick building on Wall Street.

   Spacious and well-appointed, the stockbroker's office was in a brick building on Wall Street.

4. The noisy, cluttered, aromatic streets of Chinatown still feel like home to me.

   The streets of Chinatown, noisy, cluttered, and aromatic, still feel like home to me.

   Noisy, cluttered, and aromatic, the streets of Chinatown still feel like home to me.

5. The cool, grey fog hovers over the Golden Gate Bridge.

   The fog, cool and grey, hovers over the Golden Gate Bridge.

   Cool and grey, the fog hovers over the Golden Gate Bridge.

EXERCISE 6A (pp. 93–94)

On weekends during the summer of 1969, I'd drive over to Rehoboth Beach, in Delaware, to see Maura, who was working as a waitress at the Crab Pot. I'd leave work on Friday at about four o'clock, then drive all the way to Delaware, arriving at Rehoboth before midnight, with as much energy as if I had just awakened. We'd get a motel room after her shift ended, and she'd bring a bushel of crabs, steamed in hot spice. We'd get lots of ice-cold Budweiser and we'd have a feast, listening to Junior Walker play "What Does It Take" over and over and over again.

It was because of 'Bama's new office that I learned that the West Virginia State Police had opened a file on me in Mineral County, identifying me for possible custodial detention if and when race riots started. Maura gave me the news late one night, whispering it over the phone. Old 'Bama, feeling magnanimous after his victory, had wanted me to know and to be warned.

EXERCISE 6B (pp. 94–95)

See model texts.

EXERCISE 6C *(p. 95)*

Forcing myself to put the liver in my mouth, I gagged down the meal.

The dog, forced to defend himself, bit the child on the arm.

I pushed on the door with my shoulder to force it open.

While writing a short story, I discovered that I have a talent for storytelling.

The letter, written in Greek, had to be translated.

I went back home early yesterday to write a quick letter to my sister.

(by Kim Schwab and Danny Kang)

EXERCISE 6D *(p. 97)*

1. Hiding behind a tree, her father had watched her climb into my car.

   Her father had hidden behind a tree, watching her climb into my car.

2. Following us around town, the police dared us to go even one mile over the speed limit.

   The police followed us around town, daring us to go even one mile over the speed limit.

3. Eugene would make up words as he went along, using sounds similar to those he could not remember but making no sense.

   Making up words as he went along, using sounds similar to those he could not remember, Eugene made no sense.

4. We spruced up the Soul Mobile for the occasion, replacing the old masking tape over the holes in the roof.

   Sprucing up the Soul Mobile for the occasion, we replaced the old masking tape over the holes in the roof.

5. Having lived in Keyser all his life, Maura's father worked for the post office, visiting with just about everyone in town.

   Maura's father had lived in Keyser all his life, working for the post office and visiting with just about everyone in town.

EXERCISE 6E *(p. 98)*

For discussion.

EXERCISE 6F *(pp. 99–100)*

1. These students were not so much a new black middle-class bourgeoisie ~~that had been~~ recruited to scale the ladder of class as the scions of an old and colored middle class ~~that had been~~ recruited to integrate a white

male elite. We clung to a soft black nationalist politics ~~because we wanted~~ to keep ourselves on the straight and narrow.

2. For me one crucial scene of instruction on the path of nationalist politics came while I was watching a black program ~~that had been~~ produced by students at Howard. In the film, a student, ~~who was~~ happily dating a white co-ed, comes to see the error of his ways after ~~he meets~~ meeting the activist Maulana Ron Karenga.

3. Our community and our families prepared us to be successful, ~~as they told~~ telling us over and over, "Get all the education you can."

4. ~~Because he wished~~ To show his displeasure, he insulted Jyou Ma's cooking. During one of their raucous dinner arguments, the table was shoved and a pot of boiling soup tipped and spilled all over his niece's neck, ~~which caused~~ causing a burn that almost killed her.

5. One night he raped her, ~~which made~~ making her an outcast. ~~Because she realized~~ Realizing that she had no other choice, my grandmother became a concubine to a rich man, and took her young daughter to live on an island near Shanghai. She left her son behind ~~because she wanted~~ to save his face.

EXERCISE 6G *(pp. 101–02)*

1. Discovering the frozen slugs, my parents thought it best not to ask too many questions.

   When my parents discovered the frozen slugs, it seemed best not to ask too many questions.

2. Soon after repairing my record player, I was dismayed when the rubber band snapped and the damned thing broke all over again.

   Soon after I repaired my record player, the rubber band snapped and the damned thing broke all over again.

3. Choosing between their mother's interest in tanning and their father's interest in science, the children did not hesitate.

   When they chose between their mother's interest in tanning and their father's interest in science, it was no contest.

4. After visiting my father's office, we took comfort in knowing he had some colleagues who shared his interests.

   After we visited my father's office, there was comfort in knowing he had some colleagues who shared his interests.

5. Once completed, the experiment seemed, to the young scientist, to require a completely different design.

   Once he had completed it, the young scientist wished he could redesign his experiment.

6. Having sold their homes on the beach, the fishermen were interested in the engineer's comments about the value of sand.

Because they had sold their homes on the beach, the engineer's comments about the value of sand were interesting to the fishermen.

7. After selling their homes to retirees from out of state, the fishermen saw the property value go up.

After the fishermen sold their homes to retirees from out of state, the property value went up.

EXERCISE 6H *(pp. 102–04)*

1. I got my first real job in 1988,
   when I was seventeen,
       just starting high school,
       still thinking $3.50 an hour was a lot of money.

2. I began smoking cigarettes in 1988,
   when I was seventeen,
       feeling cool and in control of my life,
       mimicking the older kids I had begun spending time with.

3. The next morning,
   opening my eyes reluctantly,
   shaking from the previous evening's bender,
   I understood that the decisions I was making were not good for me at all.

4. The next morning,
   waking in my grandmother's guest bedroom,
   running to see that my dad had returned and was resting in the adjacent room,
   I understood that I had a new baby brother.

(by Kim Schwab)

EXERCISE 7A *(p. 107)*

1. The characters appear, one after another, vivified by their attitudes, desires, and opinions as much as by their histories and their fates. Surely Augustine St. Clare, <u>Tom's owner in New Orleans</u>, is an exquisite portrayal of a humane but indecisive man, who knows what he is doing but not how to stop it. Surely Cassy, <u>a fellow slave whom Tom meets on the Legree plantation</u>, is one of the great angry women in all of literature—not only bitter, murderous, and nihilistic but also intelligent and enterprising. Surely the midlife spiritual journey of Ophelia St. Clare, <u>Augustine's</u>

Yankee <u>cousin</u>, from self-confident ignorance to affectionate understanding is most convincing, as is Topsy's parallel journey from ignorance and self-hatred to humanity. . . . The slave trader, <u>Haley</u>; Tom's wife, <u>Chloe</u>; Augustine's wife, <u>Marie</u>; Legree's overseers, <u>Sambo and Quimbo</u>—good or evil, they all live.

2. Each member of the USS Enterprise from *Star Trek: The Next Generation* is not only unique but complementary to the rest of the crew. The captain, Jean-Luc Picard, and his first-in-command, William T. Riker, take the Federation ship where no one has gone before. Other important members of the crew include Lieutenant Commander Data, the only android sophisticated enough to achieve such a rank in the Federation; Lieutenant Worf, a temperamental yet skillful Klingon in charge of security operations; Wesley Crusher, a young ensign with great potential; and Dr. Beverly Crusher, head of the Enterprise's medical team. Though each character is different from the others, together they comprise the best crew ever to traverse space on television.

(by Bob Vacanti)

EXERCISE 7B *(pp. 110–11)*

See model texts.

EXERCISE 7C *(pp. 111–12)*

1. I'll never forget the day I met my piano teacher, a warm-hearted woman with miniature, ivory-colored Beethoven busts scattered throughout her house.
2. She gave lessons in her living room, a cozy room full of books, sheet music, metronomes, and busts of Beethoven.
3. She had a large, grey cat, a Tabby she affectionately called Middle C.
4. I'll never forget the day I met my piano teacher, a cross, uncompromising woman who struck fear into the hearts of all the neighborhood children.
5. She gave lessons in her living room, a room that reeked of cat urine.
6. She had a large, grey cat, a mangy creature with a hostile attitude and a bladder disorder.

(by Kim Schwab)

EXERCISE 7D *(pp. 114–15)*

1. Shamengwa's arm was injured in a childhood accident, an encounter with a startled cow.

2. Corwin drove a 1991 Impala with all the signs of old age and hard use, with some parts missing and others rusted through.

3. The narrator is surprised to discover how deeply he misses Shamengwa's music, how completely he relies on the music to awaken emotions that he needs to experience.

4. At Geraldine's urging, Shamengwa tells the story of how his fiddle came to him, how it found him by traveling across the lake.

5. After the death of her youngest child, Shamengwa's mother fell into a state of numb despair, slipped further and further from her family.

6. Corwin's sentence was to study with Shamengwa, to learn from the man he had robbed.

7. Shamengwa was proud of Corwin, pleased with his slow progress toward musicianship.

8. When the moon slipped behind the clouds, when the night was illuminated only by the dim light of the stars, Billy applied pitch to Edwin's canoe.

(by Kim Schwab)

EXERCISE 7E *(pp. 117–18)*

1. He saw the sunrise over the highway, the blazing reds all turned into black.

2. It was not just that colors were missing, but that what he did see had a distasteful, "dirty" look, the whites glaring, the blacks cavernous, everything wrong, unnatural, stained, and impure.

3. For Helmholtz, color was a direct expression of the wavelengths of light absorbed by each receptor, the nervous system just translating one into the other.

4. Edwin Land used two filters to make the images, one passing longer wavelengths (a red filter), the other passing shorter wavelengths (a green filter).

5. Fickle gnomes control the weather, and an air conditioner is powered by a team of squirrels, their cheeks packed with ice cubes.

6. Gretchen's method of tanning involved baby oil and a series of poses that tended to draw crowds, the mothers shielding their children's eyes with sand-covered fingers.

7. All around me the options seemed to be narrowing, as if I were hurtling down a huge black funnel, the whole world squeezing in tight.

8. Down in my chest there was still that leaking sensation, something very warm and precious spilling out.

EXERCISE 7F *(pp. 118–19)*

1. I was prepared for my new job, my pin-striped suit tailored to fit, my hair pulled smartly back in a perfect ponytail, my new leather briefcase sleek but empty.
2. The vampire entered the bedroom, silk cape casually draped around her shoulders, blonde curls streaming down her back, a childlike grin playing at the corners of her mouth to reveal needle-sharp teeth.
3. The cottage appeared to be uninhabited, the path almost completely obscured by weeds, the windows broken, the door hanging loosely from one hinge.
4. The waiter brought us a hamburger, the thick beef patty slightly pink in the middle, cheese oozing from beneath the bun, a generous dollop of ketchup topping it off—a sandwich meant for royalty.
5. The waiter brought us a hamburger, the patty dripping with grease, the stale bun smelling of the refrigerator, a gooey mess of limp lettuce and mushy tomato creating a wet spot in the bread.

(by Kim Schwab and Bob Vacanti)

EXERCISE 8A *(pp. 124–25)*

1. It was about that time that I received a terrible kick from the cow.
2. It was the cow's kick that injured Shamengwa's arm.
3. What injured Shamengwa's arm was the cow's kick.
4. It was on the first hot afternoon in early May that I opened my window.
5. It was the sound of Corwin's music that I heard.
6. What I heard was the sound of Corwin's music.
7. It was the narrator who finally learned the story of the violin's past.
8. What stuck in my mind, woke me in the middle of the night, was the date on the letter, 1897.

EXERCISE 8B *(pp. 125–26)*

For discussion.

EXERCISE 8C *(p. 129)*

1. Corwin was one of those I see again and again. <u>A bad thing waiting for a worse thing to happen.</u> <u>A mistake, but one that we kept trying to salvage, because he was so young.</u> Some thought he had no redeeming value what-

soever. A sociopath. A clever manipulator, who drugged himself dangerous each weekend. Others pitied him and blamed his behavior on his mother's drinking. F.A.E. F.A.S. A.D.D. He wore those initials after his name the way educated people append their degrees. Still others thought they saw something in him that could be saved—perhaps the most dangerous idea of all. . . . He was, unfortunately, good-looking, with the features of an Edward Curtis subject, though the crack and vodka were beginning to make him puffy.

2. Corwin was one of those I see again and again, a bad thing waiting for a worse thing to happen. He was a mistake, but one that we kept trying to salvage, because he was so young. Some thought he had no redeeming value whatsoever—a sociopath, a clever manipulator who drugged himself dangerous each weekend. Others pitied him and blamed his behavior on his mother's drinking. He wore the initials F.A.E., F.A.S., and A.D.D. after his name the way educated people append their degrees. Still others thought they saw something in him that could be saved; perhaps this was the most dangerous idea of all. . . . He was, unfortunately, good-looking, with the features of an Edward Curtis subject, though the crack and the vodka were beginning to make him puffy.

EXERCISE 8D *(p. 129)*

1. I was a *liberal*, for Christ sake: If they needed fresh bodies, why not draft some back-to-the-stone-age hawk? Some dumb jingo in his hard hat and Bomb Hanoi button. Or one of LBJ's pretty daughters. Or Westmoreland's whole handsome family—nephews and nieces and baby grandson. There should be a law, I thought. If you support a war, if you think it's worth the price, that's fine, but you have to put your own precious fluids on the line. You have to head for the front and hook up with an infantry unit and help spill the blood. And you have to bring along your wife, or your kids, or your lover. A law, I thought.
2. For discussion.

EXERCISE 8E *(pp. 132–33)*

1. one word *("Owehzhee.")* The shortest complete sentence, "He played the fiddle," is four words.
2. 66 words ("In the Ojibwa language . . .")
3. five short sentences
4. three long sentences
5. no sequences of very short sentences

6. no sequences of long sentences

7. one exclamation ("How he played the fiddle!") and one fragment
   ("*Owehzhee.*")

EXERCISE 8F *(pp. 133–34)*

1. three words

2. 52 words

3. five short sentences

4. four long sentences

5. Yes, she ends the paragraph with a series of four short sentences.

6. no sequences of long sentences

7. two questions ("Why not the Statue of Liberty?" "Could it be . . . outside
   America?") and three fragments ("Why not the Statue of Liberty?" "An absence of surprise." "The tired wisdom of knowing that what goes around
   eventually comes around.")

EXERCISE 8G *(p. 136)*

1. Except for round pools of light below each streetlamp, the alley was dark.
   I knew that he had entered that alley but suspected that he hadn't come
   out. The cabbie didn't want to stop, but I insisted. I took my flashlight
   and stepped cautiously into the darkness. When I tripped over the body, I
   wasn't really surprised. I called for the cabbie, but he didn't even answer.
   Instead, I heard his engine start up and he drove away. Suddenly fearful,
   I ran back to the street looking for somebody to help me. I was relieved
   to see a bus heading my way. I hadn't been on a city bus for years, so I
   didn't know the fare. It was just lucky that I had enough money, eight
   quarters. I told the bus driver to get me to the police station right away.
   The other passengers protested that they had places to go, too. But the
   bus driver drove me right to the station. Again, there was no light because
   the station was totally empty. The bus pulled away, leaving me on the
   sidewalk outside the abandoned building.

2. Except for round pools of light at the base of each streetlamp, the alley
   was dark. Knowing somehow that he had entered that alley hours ago,
   suspecting that he had never come out, I insisted that the cabbie stop so
   I could get out and have a look. I took my flashlight and stepped cautiously into the darkness, creeping slowly, steadily, until . . . What's that?
   Just as I feared. A soft mound on the street. Perfectly cold, perfectly still.
   I called for the cabbie, but instead of an answer, I heard the growl of his

engine starting up and of the car pulling away from the curb, the sound gradually fading as he disappeared into the night. Alone, I was suddenly fearful, and I ran back to the street to look for help. A bus! What a relief! Since I hadn't been on a city bus for years, I didn't even know the fare but fortunately found eight quarters in my pocket. "The police station! Right away!" The other passengers protested that they had places to go, too, but the bus driver took me right to the station. Again, no light. No people. The bus pulled away, leaving me on the sidewalk outside the abandoned building.

Index